Contents

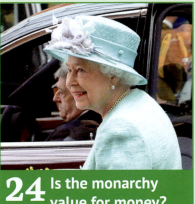

Hello

Thank you for purchasing Essential Articles and Facts, the user-friendly resource for effective research and learning

Did you know that the 294 pages of colourful articles and statistics in this book are also available online as PDF files for easy printing and sharing around school?

Your purchase of this book covers single-user access to this service. You can find your login details on your covering letter or by contacting us. There is space to record your login details on page 1 of this volume.

In addition, **Complete Issues** subscribers can access all of these pages, plus 1000s more online at completeissues.co.uk. The web service includes a **fully searchable library of over 1700 specially selected articles**, with **accessible statistics** presented using **interactive graphs**. **Focus Guides** help students get right to the heart of an issue and understand all sides of an argument. **Complete Issues** also provides **1000s of live weblinks** for further research.

We have been able to extend a number of articles in this book online to provide even more relevant information and to include extra articles that wouldn't fit in the book.

A **Complete Issues** subscription includes an **unlimited site licence** and allows students to use the service at home.

Complete Issues is the best place to discover and understand the challenges of the world around us.

If you don't already subscribe, why not sample the service on a month's free trial? completeissues.co.uk/trial

Any Questions? We're happy to chat!

+44 (0)1228 538928
office@carelpress.co.uk

Disability

50 Autism
A hidden disability

Education

Environment

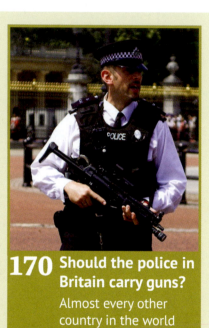

Wider world

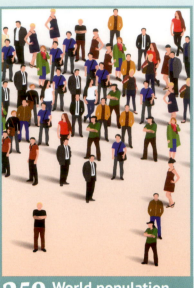

Work

How we see Britain

We get some things very wrong – but some things right

Around 1,000 GB adults were asked a series of questions to see how accurate their perceptions were compared to reality.

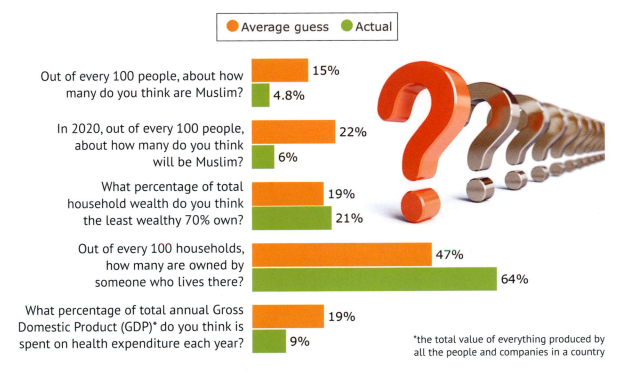

● Average guess ● Actual

Out of every 100 people, about how many do you think are Muslim?
- 15%
- 4.8%

In 2020, out of every 100 people, about how many do you think will be Muslim?
- 22%
- 6%

What percentage of total household wealth do you think the least wealthy 70% own?
- 19%
- 21%

Out of every 100 households, how many are owned by someone who lives there?
- 47%
- 64%

What percentage of total annual Gross Domestic Product (GDP)* do you think is spent on health expenditure each year?
- 19%
- 9%

*the total value of everything produced by all the people and companies in a country

What percentage of people do you think say...

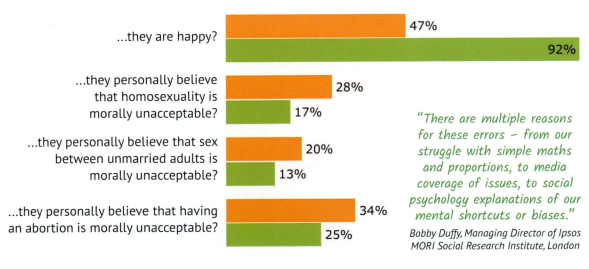

...they are happy?
- 47%
- 92%

...they personally believe that homosexuality is morally unacceptable?
- 28%
- 17%

...they personally believe that sex between unmarried adults is morally unacceptable?
- 20%
- 13%

...they personally believe that having an abortion is morally unacceptable?
- 34%
- 25%

"There are multiple reasons for these errors – from our struggle with simple maths and proportions, to media coverage of issues, to social psychology explanations of our mental shortcuts or biases."

Bobby Duffy, Managing Director of Ipsos MORI Social Research Institute, London

Source: Ipsos MORI Perils of Perception survey 2016   www.ipsos-mori.com

WHAT DO YOU THINK?

- **Where do most people get their facts and opinions?**
- **How helpful is social media as a place to obtain information?**
- **There is a big gap in the perception of how happy people are. Why would this be?**

Issues facing Britain

A snapshot of opinion

1,020 GB adults aged 18+ were asked:

What would you say is the MOST important issue facing Britain today?

What do you see as OTHER important issues facing Britain today?

The top mentions were:

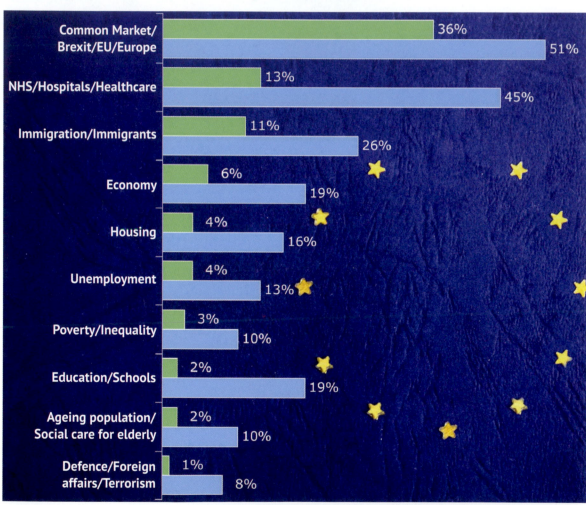

Issue	MOST important	OTHER important
Common Market/Brexit/EU/Europe	36%	51%
NHS/Hospitals/Healthcare	13%	45%
Immigration/Immigrants	11%	26%
Economy	6%	19%
Housing	4%	16%
Unemployment	4%	13%
Poverty/Inequality	3%	10%
Education/Schools	2%	19%
Ageing population/Social care for elderly	2%	10%
Defence/Foreign affairs/Terrorism	1%	8%

Source: Ipsos MORI Issues Index, March 2017 www.ipsos-mori.com

WHAT DO YOU THINK?

- What is the most important issue for you at the moment?

- What do you think will be the most important issue in ten years' time?

- Other issues did not get mentioned as many times. These included prices, low pay, benefits, crime and the environment. Why are these seen as less important?

The struggle to be British: my life as a second-class citizen

After arriving in Britain as a child, I fought hard to feel like I belonged. Now it feels that the status of migrants like me is permanently up for review

Ismail Einashe

I used my British passport for the first time on a January morning in 2002, to board a Eurostar train to Paris.

I was taking a paper on the French Revolution for my history A-level and was on a trip to explore the key sites of the period. I had become a naturalised British citizen only the year before. As I got closer to border control my palms became sweaty, clutching my new passport. A voice inside told me the severe-looking French officers would not accept that I really was British and would not allow me to enter France. To my great surprise, they did.

Back then, becoming a British citizen was a dull bureaucratic procedure. When my family arrived as refugees from Somalia's civil war, a few days after Christmas 1994, we were processed at the airport, and then largely forgotten. A few years after I got my passport all that changed. From 2004, adults who applied for British citizenship were required to attend a ceremony; to take an oath of allegiance to the monarch and make a pledge to the UK.

These ceremonies marked a shift in how the British state viewed citizenship. Before, it was a result of how long you had stayed in Britain – now it was supposed to be earned through active participation in society. In 2002, the government had also introduced a "life in the UK" test for prospective citizens. The tests point to something important: being a citizen on paper is not the same as truly belonging.

There were no warm welcomes from the locals.

But in the last 15 years, citizenship, participation and "shared values" have been given ever more emphasis. They have also been accompanied by a deepening atmosphere of suspicion around people of Muslim background, particularly those who were born overseas or hold dual nationality. This is making people like me, who have struggled to become British, feel like second-class citizens.

When I arrived in Britain aged nine, I spoke no English and knew virtually nothing about this island. My family was moved into a run-down hostel on London's Camden Road, which housed refugees – Kurds, Bosnians, Kosovans. Spending my first few months in Britain among other new arrivals was an interesting experience. Although, like my family, they were Muslim, their habits were different to ours. The Balkan refugees liked to drink vodka. After some months we had to move, this time to Colindale in north London.

Colindale was home to a large white working-class community, and our arrival was met with hostility. There were no warm welcomes from the locals, just a cold thud. None of my family spoke English, but I had soon mastered a few phrases in my new tongue: "Excuse me", "How

much is this?", "Can I have …?", "Thank you". It was enough to allow us to navigate our way through the maze of shops in Grahame Park, the largest council estate in Barnet.

As with other refugee communities before us, Britain had been generous in giving Somalis sanctuary, but was too indifferent to help us truly join in. Families like mine were plunged into unfamiliar cities, alienated and unable to make sense of our new homes. For us, there were no guidebooks on how to fit into British society or a map of how to become a citizen.

My family – the only black family on our street – stuck out like a sore thumb. Some neighbours would throw rubbish into our garden. That first winter in Britain was brutal for us. We had never experienced anything like it and my lips cracked. But whenever it snowed I would run out to the street, stand in the cold, chest out and palms ready to meet the sky, and for the first time feel the sensation of snowflakes on my hands. The following summer I spent my days blasting Shaggy's Boombastic on my cherished cassette player. But I also realised just how different I was from the children around me. Though most of them were polite, others called me names I did not understand. At the playground they would not let me join in their games – instead they would stare at me. I knew then, aged 11, that there was a distance between them and me, which even childhood curiosity could not overcome.

Although it was hard for me to fit in and make new friends, at least my English was improving. This was not the case for the rest

Being a citizen on paper is not the same as truly belonging.

of my family, so they held on to each other, afraid of what was outside our four walls. It was mundane growing up in working-class suburbia: we rarely left our street, except for occasional visits to the Indian cash-and-carry in Kingsbury to buy lamb, cumin and basmati rice. Sometimes one of our neighbours would swerve his van close to the pavement edge if it rained and he happened to spot my mother walking past, so he could splash her long dirac and hijab with dirty water. My mother's response was always the same. She would walk back to the house, grab a towel and dry herself.

> **I grew up minutes from the centre of Europe's biggest city but I rarely ventured far beyond my own community.**

When I was in my early teens, we were rehoused and I had to move to the south Camden Community school in Somers Town. There, a dozen languages were spoken and you could count the number of white students in my year on two hands. Though I grew up minutes from the centre of Europe's biggest city, I rarely ventured far beyond my own community. For us, there were no trips to museums, seaside excursions or cinema visits. MTV Base, the chicken shop and McDonald's marked my teen years. I had little connection to other parts of Britain, beyond the snippets of middle-class life I observed via my white teachers. And I was still living with refugee documents, given "indefinite leave to remain" that could still be revoked at some future point.

I realised then that no amount of identification with my new-found culture could make up for the reality that, without naturalisation, I was not considered British.

At 16, I took my GCSEs and got the grades to leave behind one of the worst state schools in London for one of the best: the mixed sixth form at Camden School for Girls. Most of the teens at my new school had previously attended some of Britain's best private schools – City of London, Westminster, Highgate – and were in the majority white and middle-class.

It was strange to go from a Muslim-majority school to a sixth form where the children of London's liberal set attended: only a mile apart, but worlds removed. A few days after starting there, I got my naturalisation certificate, which opened the way for me to apply for my British passport.

Around the time I became a British citizen, the political mood had started to shift. In the summer of 2001, Britain experienced its worst race riots in a generation, involving white and Asian communities in towns in the north-west of England. They provoked a fraught public conversation on Muslims' perceived lack of integration, and how we could live together in a multi-ethnic society. This conversation was intensified by the 9/11 attacks in the US. President George W Bush's declaration of a "war on terror" created a binary between the good and the bad immigrant, and the moderate and the radical Muslim. The London bombings of 7 July 2005 added yet more intensity to the conversation in Britain.

Politicians from across the spectrum agreed that a shared British identity was important, but they couldn't agree on what that might be. Many commentators questioned whether being a Muslim and British were consistent identities; indeed whether Islam itself was compatible with liberal democracy.

I went in one direction, but other people chose different paths.

For me, at least, becoming a British citizen was a major milestone. It not only signalled that I felt increasingly British but that I now had the legal right to feel this way. But my new identity was less secure than I realised. Only a few months after my trip to Paris, the Blair government decided to use a little-known law – the 1914 British Nationality and Status of Aliens Act – to revoke the citizenship of naturalised British persons, largely in terrorism cases.

In 2006, the home secretary was given further powers to revoke British citizenship, to strip people of their citizenship without giving a clear reason. No court approval is required, and the person concerned does not need to have committed a crime.

People have largely accepted these new powers because they are presented as a way to keep the country safe from terrorism. After 9/11, the public became more aware of the Islamist preachers who had made London their home. Abu Hamza, who was then the imam of Finsbury Park mosque, and became a notorious figure in the media, was, like me, a naturalised British citizen. For several years as a teenager, I attended the Finsbury Park mosque. I remember Abu Hamza as a larger-than-life character, whose presence dominated mosque life, especially at Friday prayers when he would go into very long sermons – usually about the dangers of becoming too British. For much of my teens, this mosque held a kind of control over me, based on fear. That changed when I moved to my new sixth form and felt able to start exploring the world for myself, and began to realise that I could be secular, liberal and humanist.

I went in one direction, but other people I knew chose different paths. Before 2001, I don't recall many women wearing the niqab, but as the years wore on it became a more common sight on the streets of London. The way that young Muslims practised Islam in Britain changed. They began a journey to a distinct British Islam – something that connected the Somali refugee and the second-generation Bangladeshi, the Irish and Jamaican converts.

I felt increasingly British and I now had the legal right to feel this way.

Some of the white working-class kids I grew up with converted to Islam. Daniel became Yusef and Emma became Khadija. Before I knew it, they were giving me advice about how Muslims should behave. I also saw the young men I had grown up with move away from a life sat on bikes wearing hoods under bridges in Camden listening to grime, to practising their Islam more visibly. Out went the sneaky pints, spliffs and casual sex. Now it was beards, sermons about the faith and handing out Islamic leaflets on street corners. When I was 16 I stopped attending the mosque and I began to question my faith.

Mahdi Hashi was one of the young men I grew up with - another child refugee from Somalia. As a teenager he used to complain that he was being followed by the British security services. He said they wanted to make him an informant.

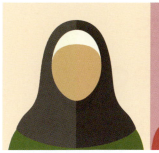   

For most newcomers, citizenship is not just confirmation of an identity, it is also about protection: that you will be guaranteed rights and treated according to the law. Hashi lost that protection. In 2009, he left for Somalia because, his family say, of harassment by the security services. In June 2012, his family received a letter informing them that he was to lose his British citizenship. Later that summer Hashi turned up in Djibouti, a tiny former French colony on the Red Sea. He was arrested. He alleges that he was threatened if he did not cooperate with authorities. In November 2012, he was taken to the US without any formal extradition proceedings. In 2016, Hashi was sentenced to nine years in prison for allegedly supporting the jihadist group al-Shabaab. He will be deported to Somalia upon his release.

The war in Syria, and the attraction that Isis and other jihadist groups hold for a small minority of British Muslims, has led to a further increase in citizenship-stripping. In 2013 Theresa May, who was then home secretary, removed the citizenship of 13 people who had left for Syria. The government has a duty to protect people, but the tool it is using will have wider, damaging consequences.

Now we are caught in a paradox, where the state is demanding more effort than ever on the part of the migrant to integrate, but your

> ## I no longer feel so safe in my status as a naturalised British citizen.

citizenship is never fully guaranteed: you are, in effect, a second-class citizen. Citizenship-stripping is now a fixture of the state. The usual caveat is that this concerns terrorists and criminals - the true purpose of such laws is to empower the state at the expense of ordinary people. The philosopher Hannah Arendt memorably described citizenship as "the right to have rights", but for people of migrant background such as myself, this is being eroded.

Today, I no longer feel so safe in my status as a naturalised British citizen, and it is not just the UK. In other liberal democracies such as Australia and Canada, moves are under way to enable citizenship-stripping – sending people like me a clear message that our citizenship is permanently up for review.

This article first appeared in the spring 2017 issue of the New Humanist
https://newhumanist.org.uk/articles/5151/
age-of-extremes-the-spring-2017-new-humanist

WHAT DO YOU THINK?

- **What are the reasons for someone becoming a citizen of a country?**
- **What things influence someone towards or away from religion?**
- **What happens if you are no longer a citizen of the country where you live?**

? Could you pass the test to become a British citizen?

A citizen of a country is someone who has rights and who belongs there - either by birth or by acquiring citizenship. As well as having rights a citizen also has a commitment to the country and its laws. So how do you go about becoming a citizen of Britain?

Most of us hardly think about our citizenship or nationality - it is just a fact of everyday life. But what if you had to go through a process to become a citizen? In Britain becoming a naturalised British citizen involves a set of conditions, tests and costs. Would you qualify?

Are you the right age and character?

You must be 18 or over (there are different conditions for children). You must also be 'of good character'. There is no clear definition of what that means but if you have been in prison in the last ten years you will automatically be refused. If you have had any sort of court sentence - even a fine - in the last three years, your application will be blocked. The decision maker can look at other features of someone's character - if a person is found to be dishonest, involved with gangs, financially unsound, has made speeches inciting violence or is known (by the community) to have caused trouble then they can be refused citizenship. Even if the person does not fit these categories, a decision maker who has doubts can still refuse the application.

Do you live here?

You have to be committed to continue to live in the UK. Before you apply you must have lived here for at least the last five years and not spent long periods of time (about three months per year) outside the UK. Obviously you must be in the UK legally and not have broken any immigration laws. (There are slightly different requirements if you are married to or in a civil partnership with a British citizen).

Do you have enough money?

The fee for naturalisation - which is due when you send in your application - is £1,282. If your application is refused you may get a part of this back.

Can you pass the tests?

Knowledge of English

Candidates have to pass a language test, which costs about £150 to take. The minimum requirement is to be able to hold a ten minute conversation with the examiner. The first five minute section is based around a topic prepared by the candidate and the second five minutes is on two topics chosen by the examiner from a list of six. People who are over 65 or from an English-speaking country or who have a degree which was taught in English, don't have to take this test.

Life in the UK

For this test, which costs £50 to take, you have 45 minutes to answer 24 questions about British traditions and customs. Some of the questions will seem fairly obvious to people who have lived here all their lives while others are more obscure.

To pass the test you must answer 18 out of 24 questions correctly, that's 75%.

After paying your money and passing the tests you can be given British citizenship at a ceremony where you must give this solemn pledge: 'I will give my loyalty to the United Kingdom and respect its rights and freedoms. I will uphold its democratic values. I will observe its laws faithfully and fulfil my duties and obligations as a British citizen.'

Here's a random sample of ten practice questions:

1 What is the name given to rented additional land which some people use to grow fruit and vegetable?

A: Allotment **B:** Garden

C: Spacage **D:** Roomage

2 What type of literature is 'The Canterbury Tales' written by Geoffrey Chaucer?

A: Novels **B:** Plays

C: Poetry **D:** Sonnets

3 What is the BBC funded by?

A: the government
B: the local council
C: advertisements
D: TV licences

4 About what percentage of people identified themselves as Christian?

A: 50% **B:** 40%

C: 60% **D:** 80%

5 You must treat everyone equally, regardless of sex, race, age, religion, disability, class or sexual orientation.

A: TRUE **B:** FALSE

6 Who was the Queen of the Iceni? She is still remembered today and there is a statue of her on Westminster Bridge in London.

A: Elizabeth **B:** Boudicca

C: Elefieta **D:** Mary

7 What is the correct order of the Patron Saints' Days? (From January)

A: St David's Day, St Patrick's Day, St George's Day, St Andrew's Day

B: St George's Day, St David's Day, St Patrick's Day, St Andrew's Day

C: St David's Day, St Patrick's Day, St Andrew's Day, St George's Day

D: St Patrick's Day, St David's Day, St Andrew's Day, St George's Day

8 Which TWO are NOT part of the UK?

A: Wales
B: the Channel Islands
C: the Isle of Man
D: Northern Ireland

9 Which charity works to preserve important buildings?

A: Age UK
B: The National Trust
C: The Red Cross
D: NSPCC

10 Which architectural style are the famous London buildings of the 19th century, such as the Houses of Parliament and St Pancras Station, associated with?

A: Roman **B:** Catholic

C: Gothic **D:** Indian

WHAT DO YOU THINK?

- **What are the 'duties and obligations' of a British citizen?**

- **What 'rights and freedoms' do you value most?**

- **What does the citizenship test prove?**

- **If you had to explain to a foreigner what was distinctive about Britain, what would you say?**

Sources: www.gov.uk/becoming-a-british-citizen, and others

Answers: 1:A, 2:C, 3:D, 4:B, 5:A, 6:B, 7:A, 8:B&C, 9:B, 10:C

'A bit of me is dying. But I can't stay': the EU nationals exiting Britain

Jon Henley

Feeling betrayed and bewildered after years in the UK, many EU citizens are leaving before Brexit. And some Britons are going too ...

They are doctors, academics, small business owners and stay-at-home parents; accountants, pensioners and IT consultants. They came to Britain from Germany, Greece, the Netherlands, Finland, Norway or France, some a few years ago, others decades earlier. Now they are leaving.

Their decisions are driven by both emotion – frustration, sorrow, anger – and hard-headed pragmatism: a conviction that, for all sorts of reasons, their families' futures are now better secured on the continent than in Britain. There are plenty of them: a request to talk on Plan B, a Facebook group, drew 40 responses in under an hour.

"We'd never thought of leaving. This was our home."

"The recruitment agency said it was quite scary, the number of applications they're now getting from EU professionals in the UK," said Alexandros, a senior academic healthcare researcher from Greece, who is moving to Frankfurt with his German wife Heidi, a medical consultant, and their two young children.

"It's difficult to exaggerate how sad and angry and disappointed we feel," he said. "We came here as teenagers, thanks to free movement. We studied here, we met here, we've spent our whole adult lives here. We'd never thought of leaving. This was our home."

According to the Office for National Statistics, 117,000 EU nationals left the UK in 2016, the year of the referendum – a 36% increase on 2015. A recent Deloitte report suggested 47% of highly skilled EU27 workers in the UK were considering leaving over the next five years, uncertain about their prospects – and those of their adopted country – once Britain exits the union.

Alexandros and Heidi, who asked not to be fully identified because they have not yet told their UK employers they are leaving, had jobs within days of posting their CVs online. After living in Britain, most recently in the north-west since 1995, both will take up senior positions with a leading German hospital company, on more than double their UK salaries.

Their decision was made easier by the fact that stones were thrown through the windows of their house barely 24 hours after the referendum, and that their six-year-old daughter came home in tears after being told in the playground by a classmate that she would soon have to "go home".

"I feel betrayed," Alexandros said. "To have worked so hard here, done those 16-hour hospital shifts, and be treated like this … with spite. Made to feel you're not valued, not wanted, not good enough for Britain. It breaks my heart, but I just want to go now. Whatever might happen, we wouldn't stay."

Betrayal is a word that comes up often. "It's hard not to take it personally," said Elina Halonen, 37, a Finn who lived in the UK for 13 years, co-founding a specialist market research firm that now employs 10 people. She moved to Amsterdam with her Scottish partner, Tane Piper, in February.

"I worked hard, paid my taxes – now it feels almost like an illusion," she said. "Like we were never really welcome. It has all been … dehumanising. Insulting, actually."

Equally keen to keep his EU rights and make sure they were not limiting their chances to live together, buy a home and start a family if they stayed in the UK, Piper pushed hardest for the move, which the couple made before article 50 was triggered – in case that became a cut-off date.

Others are still packing up. "It will be really hard, after 33 years," said Hannelore Cossens, 51, a Dutch national who will spend the summer house-hunting in the Netherlands and finding a school for her youngest child, 11. She will be joined later by her husband Peter, a retired IT specialist, once their house near Lampeter in Wales has been sold.

"Our income, my husband's pension and our investments are in pounds and worth a lot less," she said. "But it's worth it to me. And my husband doesn't like his country any more. Why would I stay, be made to feel like some faceless 'migrant'? A bit of me is dying. But I can't stay."

For Sigrun Campbell, it is for the children. From Denmark, she has lived in the UK for 23 years and has three children with her husband, a "passionate remainer" who will be abandoning a "very good job" in banking to move with the family to Copenhagen.

"Why would I stay, be made to feel like some faceless 'migrant'?"

Campbell, who lives near Tunbridge Wells in Kent, said she knew of four other Anglo-EU couples leaving this summer: two more to Denmark, one to Lithuania and one to France. "I can't see it working for the kids here," she said. "We, their parents, have lost faith in this country. I can't see this being a great place for them to be."

None of the dozen EU citizens interviewed for this article had previously applied for permanent residency in the UK – either because they thought they would be turned down owing to inadequate paperwork or because they simply did not see why they should have to. Nor did the "generous" offer made to them last month by Theresa May change their minds.

"Britain has changed," said Michaela Aumüller, who after six years in Cornwall moved to Münster, Germany, in April with her British partner, Richard. "Something has been broken. Neither of us wanted to put up with the new attitude to EU nationals. There were incidents, little things, but they make such a difference."

But the main reason, said Aumüller, was because "we don't see our relationship being protected by UK immigration law. I'm self-supporting, I don't have the paperwork, and if EU citizens' rights ever become the same as non-EU citizens' ... we couldn't be together in the UK."

Mel Scott, a French antenatal educator, has lived in Britain since 1998. She and her husband, Dan, are moving to Le Touquet with their 10- and 11-year-old sons once their house near Crowborough in East Sussex is sold. Dan will run his IT business from France, but "it will still be a huge wrench", she said.

"Britain has changed... something has been broken."

Like Ian Paterson, who hopes to join his Belgian wife Kristel, a social worker, and their nine-year-old son in Limburg in the autumn, Scott has been on an "emotional rollercoaster" since the Brexit vote. "The time before June 23 looks like some kind of ideal world now," said Paterson, 58.

"What's the best thing? You spend so much time trying to work it out," he said. "Are house prices falling? How much will we have to live on? What if we decide to come back, what rights will Kristel have? Do these Brexiters ever consider how many ordinary people's lives they have harmed?"

Brexit has even chased British couples from Britain. Sara O'Hara, 44, and her partner Doug, 41, moved to the Dordogne with their six-year-old son – and registered Doug's landscape gardening business there – just before article 50 was triggered.

O'Hara, who has kept her job as environmental permits manager for a UK waste management firm in Dorset, said the decision had in effect been made the day after the referendum. "We were both devastated, disappointed, really confused," she said. "We had friends and family falling out."

Their future, and that of their son, made the move inevitable, she said. "The idea of him not being able to go wherever he wanted ... It's not been easy. But we have no regrets."

The Guardian, 28 July 2017 © Guardian News & Media 2017

WHAT DO YOU THINK?

- **How long do you need to live somewhere before it becomes your home?**
- **Do you agree with the people interviewed when they say Britain has changed?**
- **What do you think Britain will be like in the future?**

Monarchy and money

The finances of the Queen

There are three sources of funding for The Queen, or officials of the Royal Household acting on her behalf. These are:

The Sovereign Grant:

This is used to support The Queen's official duties and the maintenance of the Occupied Royal Palaces.

It is provided by the government as **15%** of the profits of the Crown Estate.

The land and assets of the Crown Estate are not government property or the private property of the Queen - they are managed by an independent company on behalf of the nation.

The Estate includes property worth **£12 billion**, including the whole of London's Regent Street, 792,000 hectares of agricultural land and forest, more than half of the UK's foreshore, and various other traditional holdings and rights, including Ascot Racecourse.

The 2016-17 Sovereign Grant amounted to **£42.8m**, equal to 65p per person in the United Kingdom.

You can check here to see what property near you belongs to the Crown:
www.thecrownestate.co.uk/estates-map

The Privy Purse:

Money from the Duchy of Lancaster — a portfolio of land and other assets that has been in the royal family for hundreds of years and provides an independent source of income. It is used mainly to pay for official expenses of other members of the Royal Family.

The Queen's personal wealth and income:

The Queen also has a personal fortune estimated to be about **£340 million.** She outright owns Balmoral and Sandringham Estates, which she inherited from her father, and also has a valuable artwork collection.

Estimates of the Queen's wealth often mistakenly include items which are held by her as Sovereign on behalf of the nation and are not her private property. These include the Royal residences, most of the of art treasures from the Royal Collection and the Crown Jewels.

In fact, in the last two years the Queen has not ranked in the top 300 wealthiest people in Britain.

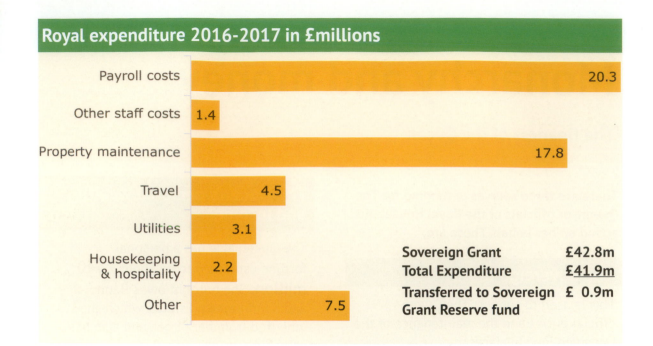

Royal expenditure 2016-2017 in £millions

	£millions
Payroll costs	20.3
Other staff costs	1.4
Property maintenance	17.8
Travel	4.5
Utilities	3.1
Housekeeping & hospitality	2.2
Other	7.5

Sovereign Grant	£42.8m
Total Expenditure	£41.9m
Transferred to Sovereign Grant Reserve fund	£ 0.9m

The official sources of funding are used entirely for official duties.

These include: Royal travel for official engagements; the maintenance of Royal residencies; funding for the work of The Duke of Edinburgh and salaries for employees of the Royal Household.

Property maintenance:

Buckingham Palace is in a bad state of repair and **£369 million** worth of work has been approved by the government. The Queen will take a larger portion of the Sovereign Grant for the next 10 years - **25%** instead of **15%**. The 2017-18 grant will be **£76.1 million**.

Travel expenses:

The Sovereign Grant covers the cost of travel between residences by the Queen, the Duke of Edinburgh, the Prince of Wales and the Duchess of Cornwall and the Duke and Duchess of Cambridge.

Safety, security, presentation, the need to minimise disruption for others, the effective use of time, environmental impact and cost are taken into account when deciding on the most appropriate means of travel.

Staff may travel with Members of the Royal Family or separately (eg to undertake reconnaissance visits or to arrive in advance).

Over 3,000 official engagements were carried out across the United Kingdom and overseas by Members of the Royal Family during 2016-17.

There were **39 journeys** by Members of the Royal Family and their staff which had travel costs of **£15,000 or more**, which came out of the Sovereign Grant.

The principal overseas visits during the year were:

- Italy, Romania and Austria by the Prince of Wales and the Duchess of Cornwall: **£154,000**;

- India and Bhutan by the Duke and Duchess of Cambridge: **£98,000**;

- Bahrain, United Arab Emirates and Oman by the Prince of Wales and the Duchess of Cornwall: **£93,000**;

- Israel for the funeral of Shimon Peres by the Prince of Wales: **£73,000**;

- Botswana and Mozambique by the Duke of York: **£56,000**.

The most expensive journey on the Royal Train was taken by Prince Charles from London to Lancashire/Yorkshire then back to London, costing **£46,038**.

Sources: Various and www.royal.uk/royal-finances-0
© Crown copyright 2017

What the public think

An Opinium survey in early 2017 found that:

- **65%** of UK adults think Britain should continue to have a monarchy in the future.

- Only **19%** hoped that Britain would become a republic at some point in the future.

- **70%** think Britain is perceived more positively abroad because of the Monarchy.

- A further **65%** think there is still a place for the Monarchy in modern Britain.

- Only **27%** thought that the Monarchy is a meaningless institution.

The three most common words or phrases Britons use to describe the Queen are:

- dedicated - **39%**;
- hard working - **36%**; and
- traditional - **34%**.

Perception of the Queen, by age group

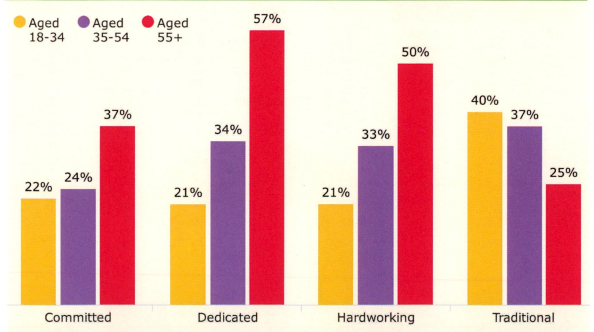

● Aged 18-34 ● Aged 35-54 ● Aged 55+

Committed: 22%, 24%, 37%
Dedicated: 21%, 34%, 57%
Hardworking: 21%, 33%, 50%
Traditional: 40%, 37%, 25%

20% of **18-34** year olds described The Queen as old fashioned compared to **7%** of those **55+**.

Source: Opinium   www.opinium.co.uk

WHAT DO YOU THINK?

- Were you surprised by any of the figures?

- Do the amounts spent represent good value for money, or would the amount be better spent on something else?

- Do you think Britain will always have a Royal Family?

Is the monarchy value for money?

People who feel we shouldn't have a monarchy have an alternative view of the costs

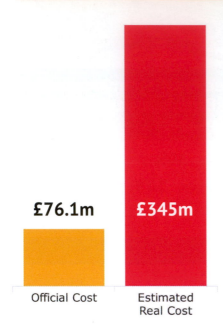

£76.1m   £345m

Official Cost   Estimated Real Cost

Republic is a membership-based pressure group campaigning for the abolition of the monarchy and its replacement with a directly elected Head of State.

Republic asserts:

"Our research suggests that the British Head of State is incredibly expensive, at around £345m a year. That's public money we could be spending on teachers, police or health services. This report shows that per head royals are the most expensive public officials, costing around £19.1m a year each.

"For £345m the government could employ 15,000 new teachers, 15,500 new nurses or fire fighter or 17,000 new police officers."

Some of their figures are taken from official sources, others are a best estimate. They include the Sovereign Grant, the amount officially allocated by the government to the Queen, but also hidden costs in lost income and lost opportunities in order to reach a broad estimate of the full cost of the royal family.

Cost breakdown

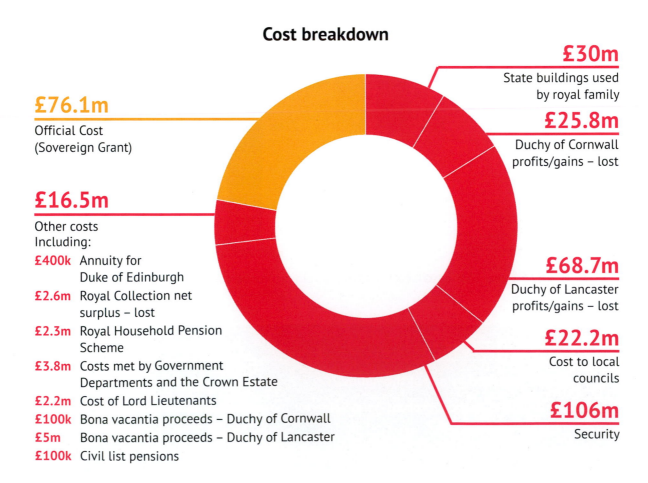

£76.1m
Official Cost
(Sovereign Grant)

£16.5m
Other costs
Including:

£400k Annuity for Duke of Edinburgh
£2.6m Royal Collection net surplus – lost
£2.3m Royal Household Pension Scheme
£3.8m Costs met by Government Departments and the Crown Estate
£2.2m Cost of Lord Lieutenants
£100k Bona vacantia proceeds – Duchy of Cornwall
£5m Bona vacantia proceeds – Duchy of Lancaster
£100k Civil list pensions

£30m
State buildings used by royal family

£25.8m
Duchy of Cornwall profits/gains – lost

£68.7m
Duchy of Lancaster profits/gains – lost

£22.2m
Cost to local councils

£106m
Security

How Republic explains the costs

Sovereign Grant

The Crown Estate is a collection of land and assets belonging to the country. A percentage of their profits is given to the Queen as the 'sovereign grant'. The amount of grant increases whenever the profits of the Crown Estate go up but, by agreement, the funding can't go down below the level of the previous year. If profits go down, royal funding remains unchanged. If the monarchy were to disappear, that portion of the Crown Estate would provide more income for the administration of this country.

Annuity for the Duke of Edinburgh

£400,000 in addition to the Queen's income.

State buildings used by the royal family

A number of royals occupy apartments in palaces for little or no rent. These would bring revenue in if the royals (or someone else) paid full rent.

Duchy of Lancaster and Duchy of Cornwall

These are not the personal property of the Queen and Prince of Wales but are crown bodies with substantial amounts of land, property and assets. If there was no monarchy the surplus would be paid to the Treasury to the benefit of all taxpayers. In addition, although the Duchy of Cornwall operates as a business it does not pay corporation tax.

Royal Collection

This is the largest private art collection in the world and is a mixture of items owned outright, as a private individual, by the Queen and others which belong to her status as sovereign, and therefore cannot be sold or disposed of.

Cost to local councils

Royal visits, to local schools and museums for example, often leave councils and other public bodies with costs for policing, road closures, time for planning, stewarding, flowers - even flags for schoolchildren to wave. The Queen's visit to Leicester in 2012 is said to have cost the Council £85,000.

Royal Household Pension Scheme

The royal household has a pension scheme for its staff. They might range from the Keeper of the Privy Purse, who is responsible for financial management, on £180,000 a year, to a live-in pot washer at Buckingham palace on £17,000 a year or a ticket seller at Windsor Castle on £8.45 per hour.

Security

About a dozen royals receive round-the-clock protection. Senior royals have multiple residences which increases security costs.

Lord Lieutenants

A Lord-Lieutenant represents the Queen in each county of the United Kingdom. It is a largely ceremonial position usually awarded to a retired notable person in the county.

Bona vacantia

Bona Vacantia means 'ownerless property'. When someone dies without leaving a will and with no identifiable relatives to inherit, their assets usually go into the general funds of the Treasury. In the Duchies of Lancaster and Cornwall, the assets go to the duchies.

Civil List pensions

These are actually small, yearly payments or grants from the monarch to people whose work is seen as outstanding and of benefit to the public. In 2012, the average pension was £2,383 and 53 people received it.

Other points made by Republic

No boost to tourism

Despite what 80% of Britons believe, there is no proof that the Royal family provides Britain with a tourism boost. In fact, they resist opening the doors of Buckingham Palace to the general public - a lost opportunity to increase tourism revenues.

Corruption

We know that Prince Charles, Prince William and others write to ministers and have regular meetings with them, no doubt with other government officials too. If they use these meetings to promote their personal ideas, agendas and interests, that is corrupt.

Secrecy

The Queen and Prince Charles pay tax voluntarily, but we have no idea how much tax. According to Republic, "One of the problems with royal funding is how it is reported and spun by the Palace. The Palace carefully manages the release of information and ensures it is couched in so much spin real abuse of public money gets glossed over."

Working Royals

A working royal is a member of the royal family who conducts public engagements and who receives public subsidy. The royal website currently lists 18 working royals, meaning they each cost the taxpayer on average £19.1m a year. Prince Charles, often said to be the busiest royal, completed 533 engagements in 2014. The average engagement lasts one hour.

Minor royals

Many minor royals receive public funding. For instance, currently Prince and Princess Michael of Kent, the Duke and Duchess of Kent and Princess Alexandra receive millions of pounds of state subsidy. Do most of us even know who they are? Even Prince Charles is said to be in favour of cutting the subsidies for minor royals like Princesses Beatrice and Eugenie.

We can have something different

The Queen is our head of state, but she is duty bound not to express any political, or controversial, opinion. In Ireland the Head of State is an elected, independent person who can speak out on behalf of the nation and, if necessary, against the government.

It weakens our democracy

Britain's political system is founded on the power of the Crown. It is the Crown's power that makes parliament, not the people, sovereign. Powers and gifts - honours and appointments for instance - are given by the queen on the instructions of the Prime Minister. This gives the PM a great deal of patronage and control. It also centralises power in London. Taking away this patronage, establishing a republic with a clear set of rules and limitations, would rebalance power.

MPs have to swear an oath of allegiance to the Queen before they can take their seat in Parliament. They must swear to "... be faithful and bear true allegiance to Her Majesty Queen Elizabeth, her heirs and successors according to law". Sinn Fein MPs, who are campaigning for a united Ireland, refuse to take the oath and therefore cannot represent their constituents in Parliament. In 2017, Richard Burgon, Labour MP for East Leeds, who is a republican, prefaced his oath by saying: "As someone who believes that the head of state should be elected, I make this oath in order to serve my constituents".

It seems unlikely that there will be a strong movement for change under the present monarch. The Queen has inspired personal affection in the country which seems to override any problems with the system. But what will come next?

Source: Royal Expenses - Counting the Cost of Monarchy Published by Republic June 2017 www.republic.org.uk

WHAT DO YOU THINK?

- **What are your personal views about the monarchy?**
- **Is it fair to include these other expenses when counting the cost?**
- **Is it reasonable to measure the cost of the monarchy against services like education and the police?**

Manchester's bike-share scheme isn't working – because people don't know how to share

There are bikes in the canal, in bins and in back gardens. You wouldn't blame Mobike for taking its remaining bicycles to a better behaved city

By Helen Pidd

I really wanted to believe that Mancunians could be trusted with nice things. Just over a fortnight ago, a Chinese company called Mobike brought 1,000 shiny new silver and orange bikes to my city. Unlockable with a smartphone and available to rent for just 50p for half an hour, they could be ridden wherever you liked within Manchester and Salford and, crucially, could be left anywhere public once you were done.

I was an immediate convert, boasting about the superiority of our new bike-sharing system over London's, pitying sadsacks in the capital who had to trundle around looking for a docking station. One sunny evening shortly after the launch, I rode a Mobike to Salford Quays, where I swam a mile in the filtered water of the glistening Lowry, reflecting as I did my backstroke that Manchester was starting to feel rather European. I had always fancied living in Copenhagen, where the cyclist is king and the harbour has been turned into a lido. Was I now living that continental dream?

Two weeks on and I fear that a dream is all it was. There are Mobikes in the canal, Mobikes in bins and I am fed up with following the app to a residential street where there is clearly a Mobike stashed in someone's garden. On launch day, the Chinese designer told me the bikes were basically indestructible and should last four years without maintenance. It took a matter of hours before local scallies worked out how to disable the GPS trackers and smash off the back wheel locks.

On Thursday, none of the eight bikes showing on the app as being near my house were actually there. I was so incensed when I reached the location of the ninth and could see it locked away in a backyard that I lost control of my senses and knocked on the door. A young man opened it and I asked nicely if I could rent the bike. He looked surprised and said, no, it was his, and anyway, he needed it later. I explained that was not how the system worked, that the bikes were public, and that if everyone was as selfish as him the whole thing would collapse. He rolled his eyes and told me I would be trespassing if I dared try to fetch it.

I decided to dob him in instead, hoping that Mobike would ban him from renting another, as is supposed to happen to anyone with the brass neck to take the bike out of circulation for their own personal use.

Steve Pyer, Mobike UK's general manager, is determined to look on the bright side. Mancunians love the bikes, he says, and are now taking 4,000 trips every day, "even when it's raining".

Responsible cyclists Eddie and Eve collecting their Mobikes outside the Bridgewater Hall, Manchester
Photo: Chas White

Fifty bikes have been trashed, he says, although only a few are beyond repair. Many more have indeed ended up on private property, and the bike redistribution team will be knocking on doors themselves to clear up "misunderstandings". He finds comfort in the Mancs recovering Mobikes missing in action: a boat owner fished one out of the canal and it will be ready to ride again soon after a bit of TLC.

He does admit that the scale of vandalism took him by surprise. It has been far worse than in any of the Asian countries where Mobike operates 5m bikes. "In Singapore we launched our scheme in March with 5,000 bikes and there have been just two reports of broken locks," he says.

I do not want to live in a country where you can get caned for graffiti, but I would like to live in a city where people know how to share. The man who wanted to have his own personal Mobike displayed an all-too common sense of entitlement. There is always someone who refuses to put

headphones on or take their feet off the seat, who won't shut up during the gig and can't be bothered finding a bin.

My Mobiking nemesis just couldn't understand why I would object to his behaviour, just as the young degenerates I have seen pulling wheelies on hacked Mobikes in my local park can't understand that they are spoiling things not just for everyone else but themselves, too. Although Pyre insists that Mobike is committed to Manchester and expects the idiocy to calm down once the novelty wears off, the truth is it is just a six-month trial. You could hardly blame the Chinese if, at the end of the pilot, they decided to wheel any remaining bikes to a better behaved city.

I hope my pessimism is ill-placed. There are some glimmers of hope: apparently after I had a go at the young man and reported his selfishness, a Mobike suddenly appeared on the street outside his house. Funny, that.

The Guardian, 16th July 2017 © Guardian News & Media 2017

Mobikes

What are they?

Mobike is the world's first and largest smart bike-sharing company. Its mission is to bring more bikes to more cities, using its innovative technology to make cycling the most convenient and environmentally-friendly transport choice for urban residents.

Using specially designed bikes equipped with GPS and proprietary smart-lock technology, Mobike enables users of its smartphone app to find a bike near them, reserve and unlock it, all using their smartphones. After reaching their destination, the user parks the bike by the roadside and locks it, automatically making the bike available to the next rider.

This automatic locking makes them different from London's Boris bikes in that they are dockless so can be left in designated areas.

What's their story?

They are the brain child of Hu Weiwei, a Chinese entrepreneur.

The company officially launched its service in Shanghai in April 2016, and Mobikes are already a key part of life in 130 cities across China and Singapore, where more than 5m bikes are now in operation.

It is said that they are 'near impossible' to vandalise and 'pointless' to steal. The company have developed a credits system where users who disobey the Mobike rules - park them in the wrong place for example - will be charged more to hire them. But 'good users' will be rewarded.

How will they work?

- To use the service, people will download the Mobike app to a smartphone and register.
- Users will pay an initial refundable deposit when they join up.
- Built-in GPS will show the user where their nearest free bike is.
- They will have 15 minutes to get to the bike, where they can unlock it by scanning its code. Usage is charged at 50p per 30 minutes. The GPS technology will also be used to collect data on bike use.
- At the end of their ride, users will leave the bike at any public bike parking area near to their destination and close the lock on the bike.

Of course, there is always room for improvement!

A user has suggested:

- Bigger bikes for taller riders. The saddles on the current crop won't go high enough for anyone much over six foot.
- Bigger, better baskets that can hold a supermarket bag of shopping without everything falling through the gaps.
- More robust mudguards. The fenders on a few of the bikes have started catching on the tyres.
- More bikes - A thousand is a good start but the scheme will only work if there are enough in circulation so that there's always one within five minutes walk from anyone who wants to use one.

Source: Various and https://mobike.com/uk/

WHAT DO YOU THINK?

- Are these bikes a good idea?
- In Singapore there have been very few acts of vandalism, in Manchester there have been a lot more. What could explain this?
- The writer suggests that perhaps the bikes should go to "a better behaved city". Is there one?

No religion

A large proportion of the British population consider themselves to have no religion

'**No religion**' has been Britain's largest religious grouping for over two decades.

Data from the British Social Attitudes and European Social Survey was analysed by The Benedict XVI Centre for Religion and Society.

Do you regard yourself as belonging to any particular religion?

(Base: 4,312 British adults)

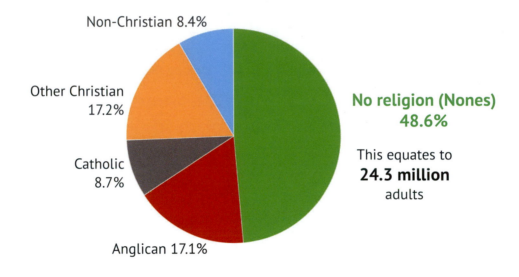

Non-Christian 8.4%

Other Christian 17.2%

Catholic 8.7%

Anglican 17.1%

No religion (Nones) 48.6%

This equates to **24.3 million** adults

Overall, **Nones** were more likely to be men than women - **55%** compared to **45%**.

Nones by age and gender

● **Male**   ● **Female**

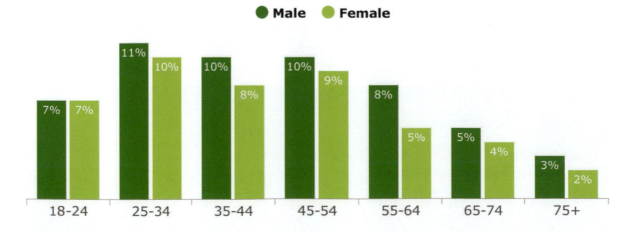

	18-24	25-34	35-44	45-54	55-64	65-74	75+
Male	7%	11%	10%	10%	8%	5%	3%
Female	7%	10%	8%	9%	5%	4%	2%

Nones by region

58% of those in the South East say they are **Nones** - this is the highest proportion. It is almost double the lowest percentage, Inner London - **31%**.

Nones make up an overall majority in seven of the regions, including Scotland and Wales, which are the areas with the most people saying they have no religion, after the South East.

Age

Nones are younger than average: **35%** are under 35, compared to **29%** of all British adult. To compare: just **6%** of adult Anglicans are under 35, and **45%** are 65 or older.

Racial diversity

Overall, **95%** of **Nones** were **White**; **1%** were **Black**; **2%** were **Asian**; and **2%** were **Mixed** or **Other**.

Upbringing

The growth of the No religion population in Britain – as in other countries – is largely the result of people who were brought up in a religion deciding later in life, to identify with none.

The 'Nones' were asked what religion they were brought up as?

(Base: 2,096 British adults who said they had no religion)

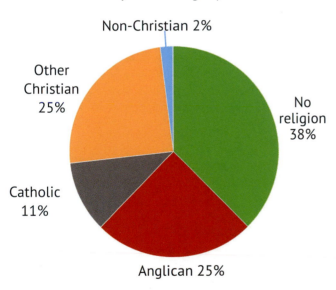

- Non-Christian 2%
- Other Christian 25%
- No religion 38%
- Catholic 11%
- Anglican 25%

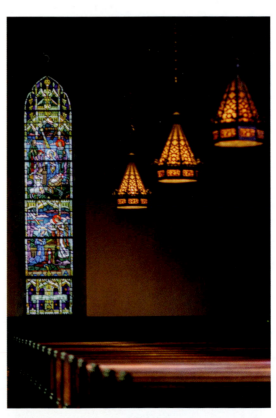

Source: The "no religion" population of Britain - Benedict XVI Centre for Religion and Society at St Mary's University Twickenham www.stmarys.ac.uk

Totals may not equal 100% due to rounding

WHAT DO YOU THINK?

- Is having no religion the same as having no beliefs?

- Do these figures point to Britain becoming a completely secular society?

- Does the fact that the majority of people in Britain are not Christian have any influence on national character or on politics?

Telling the truth

Who do we think are the most trustworthy people?

The public were asked to rate the trustworthiness of professionals

Who would you generally trust to tell the truth?

Base: 1,019 British adults aged 15+

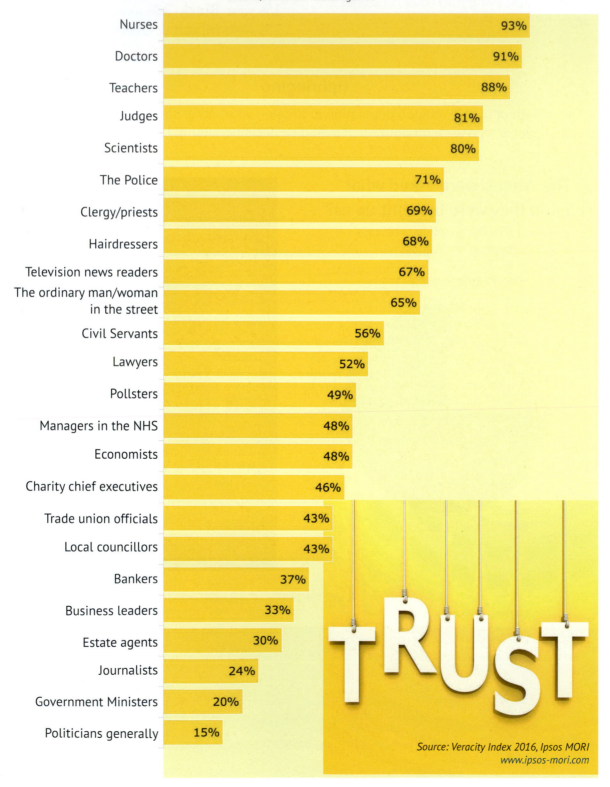

Nurses	93%
Doctors	91%
Teachers	88%
Judges	81%
Scientists	80%
The Police	71%
Clergy/priests	69%
Hairdressers	68%
Television news readers	67%
The ordinary man/woman in the street	65%
Civil Servants	56%
Lawyers	52%
Pollsters	49%
Managers in the NHS	48%
Economists	48%
Charity chief executives	46%
Trade union officials	43%
Local councillors	43%
Bankers	37%
Business leaders	33%
Estate agents	30%
Journalists	24%
Government Ministers	20%
Politicians generally	15%

Source: Veracity Index 2016, Ipsos MORI
www.ipsos-mori.com

Trust in Journalism Sinks to All-Time Low

When YouGov researched trust in the press in May 2006, they found that **37%** of the public trusted journalists at national newspapers to tell the truth.

Trust in **national newspaper journalism** has halved since then, and now stands at an all-time low of **18%** – below even the level of **19%** which was reached in July 2011 when there was the outcry over phone hacking.

1,578 GB Adults aged 18+ were asked their opinion of the British press.

Trust by type of journalism

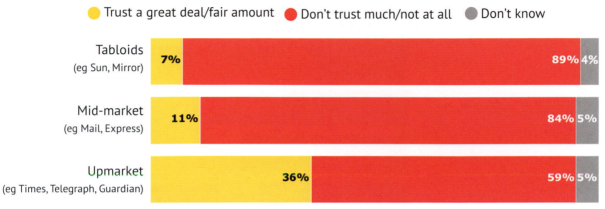

● Trust a great deal/fair amount   ● Don't trust much/not at all   ● Don't know

Tabloids
(eg Sun, Mirror)   7%   89% 4%

Mid-market
(eg Mail, Express)   11%   84% 5%

Upmarket
(eg Times, Telegraph, Guardian)   36%   59% 5%

When asked what was most important to them when deciding which newspaper to read in print or online, **50%** said '**decent standards of journalism**'.

When asked how they would describe the British press, the most common responses included words such as:

- **liars;**
- **untrustworthy;** and
- **unreliable.**

Other common answers included:

- **exaggerated**
- **sensationalist;** and
- **fake.**

Source: YouGov for IMPRESS - The Independent Monitor for the Press www.impress.press

WHAT DO YOU THINK?

- Does this list match with the type of people you think are most trustworthy?
- Can you think of a reason why the groups who score highly would be the most trusted?
- Do the groups who score lowest have anything in common?
- What sort of things might change the levels of trust from one time to another?
- What do you think fake news is? And how could you spot it?

Raising money

The UK's favourite ways to raise money for good causes

The UK Giving survey collected information about charitable giving from 1,004 adults aged 16 and over in the United Kingdom.

The ten most popular fundraising events people took part in during 2016

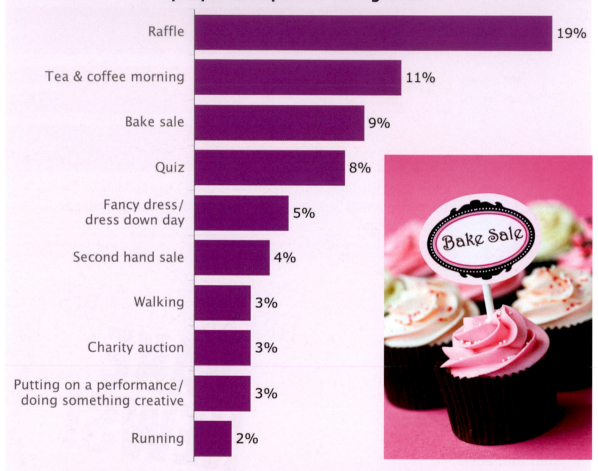

Event	%
Raffle	19%
Tea & coffee morning	11%
Bake sale	9%
Quiz	8%
Fancy dress/ dress down day	5%
Second hand sale	4%
Walking	3%
Charity auction	3%
Putting on a performance/ doing something creative	3%
Running	2%

"Raising money for charity can be a really good reason to do something you enjoy."

Susan Pinkney, Head of Research at Charities Aid Foundation

Source: Charities Aid Foundation www.cafonline.org

WHAT DO YOU THINK?

- Which fundraising activities are most successful?

- Do big national events, like Red Nose Day, put people off raising money at other times?

- Could the effort that people put into fund raising be put to better use?

Essential Articles & Facts

www.completeissues.co.uk

A *better* *way of* *giving?*

In 2016 the favourite way to raise money for charities was to take part in a raffle. It's a way to persuade people to give yet to offer something in return. The luck of the draw adds excitement and anticipation even if the prizes only consist of a soft toy, some toiletries and a box of chocolates.

But imagine if that raffle offered an experience you could never otherwise dream of, such as having breakfast at a fabulous hotel with all of the Doctor Whos. What if you could join Miranda Hart for tea? Or you could bake a cake with Mary Berry?

£5 could win you tickets to Glastonbury

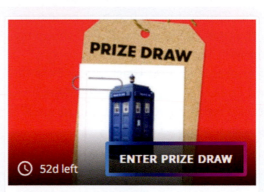

BREAKFAST WITH THE DOCTOR WHOS

These are just some of the creative ideas that have allowed a company called Givergy to raise over £45 million for more than 1,200 causes.

Founded in 2009 to help charities raise more at their fundraising events and online, Givergy organises raffles and auctions with prizes that money can't buy so that charities are able to raise more funds and reach a wider, even a global, audience.

Red Nose Day was one of the charities to benefit. Some of the priceless experiences that lucky prize winners received in return for a £5 raffle tickets for Red Nose Day included a personal session with Joe Wicks, The Body Coach, a cooking lesson with Jamie Oliver and a £1,000 shopping trip with Tanya Burr. Tickets to sought-after events such as Glastonbury, Bestival and The Cursed Child (with privileged access) were part of a stunning range of special treats.

Other Givergy auction and prize draw listings have included former One Direction star Zayn Malik's customised Marc Jacobs leather jacket which made tons of money for Mind, the mental health charity. A meeting with Wayne Rooney and the chance to lead out the Manchester United team was a great fund-raiser for the NSPCC.

Conservation charity Save the Rhino, like many charities, encourages supporters to do sponsored runs and appeals for donations, but now it also looks set to benefit from a very special prize draw - courtesy of Givergy employee and frequent fundraiser Sophie Clarke.

Most individual fundraisers still use the tried and proven methods, everything from online donation pledges to bake sales. But, it's no secret that fatigue is all too common with friends and family. There are only so many times you can ask friends to spare another fiver, especially for individuals who fundraise for multiple events throughout the year, whether it be a marathon or crowdfunding a new idea.

There are only so many times you can ask friends to spare another fiver

Sophie Clarke decided to shake things up this year and to provide an alternative for her marathon fundraiser. "I knew I had a big target to hit, but felt like I couldn't burden my friends again with another push to get me over the finish line. Luckily, I had my hands on two spare tickets to Ed Sheeran's sold out London gig and decided to get creative."

Sophie donated the much-in-demand VIP concert tickets to Save the Rhino, the charity who she is running the marathon on behalf of. Since they already had a dedicated charity page on Givergy.com, Save the Rhino made the tickets available to the general public as a prize draw. For only £5 to enter the draw, one lucky winner would get to see the famed artist, all while raising money for a good cause and helping Sophie reach her fundraising target.

"I love animals, and after recently seeing the Save the Rhino twitter feed showcasing such animal cruelty, it really brought home how much they suffer and I knew I had do something to contribute to their safety," Sophie said.

Save the Rhino's Rosie Cammock fully supports the campaign as a new way for donors to get involved. "Givergy.com is a fantastic asset for any charity looking to inspire their supporters to fundraise in new and innovative ways. Not only have we used Givergy.com for our own online auctions and fundraising campaigns, but our supporters are really engaging with the platform to raise money on an individual and group basis in support of our cause. It's incredibly easy and is a completely risk-free approach to fundraising"

It's unlikely that we have seen the end of chuggers, door to door collections, small children with dubious fairy cakes or the traditional tombola - but if you could contribute to a good cause and also have a chance to have the experience of a lifetime - surely that is win-win!

Source: Givergy.com & others

WHAT DO YOU THINK?

- **What is your favourite charity?**
- **What would be your ideal raffle prize?**
- **How do you feel when people ask you to donate to charity?**

Running for charity

Women are racing ahead of men when it comes to running for good causes

1,003 UK adults were asked whether they'd run for charity

18%
of Britons have taken part in runs to raise money for charity, ranging from fun runs to marathons.

63%
of those running for a good cause were women
37%
were men.

40%
of the 16-24 year olds asked had never run a marathon but said they'd like to one day, compared to
3%
of those over 65.

12%
of those who ran for charity had completed a marathon.

The average age of someone running for charity is
40.

"For many runners, raising money for a good cause can be one of the crucial motivating factors"

Sue Pinkney, Head of Research, Charities Aid Foundation

The average charity runner raises
£442
for their chosen causes.

In 2016 the Virgin London Marathon raised
£59.4 million
for charities.

This set a new world record for an annual single day charity fundraising event for the tenth successive year.

The race was founded in 1981 and has so far generated
over £830 million
for good causes.

Source: Charities Aid Foundation - YouGov survey, 2017

WHAT DO YOU THINK?

- Have you ever considered being sponsored to do something for charity?
- Are there better ways of supporting good causes?
- What could account for the much higher percentage of women than men?

Giving your best

How you give to charity matters as well as what you give

After the horror of the Grenfell Tower fire, the response was so great that teams had to be organised to deal with the volume of goods donated by people who desperately wanted to help. The same generous impulse drove people to donate to the various emergency funds via the JustGiving website. Many will have tried to maximise their donation using Gift Aid, which means the charities receive back 25p in tax relief for every pound that is donated.

The response broke all records for donations in a single day and by two days after the tragedy it had already reached a total of £2.6m, donated via a variety of routes, including several JustGiving pages.

JustGiving describes itself as "the world's most trusted platform for online giving." and says "Our mission is to ensure no great cause goes unfunded." It certainly makes sponsoring your friend to run a marathon or spontaneously donating after being moved by a TV advert, easy and efficient, but how many people realise that, as a business, JustGiving takes a percentage of the gifts and charges the charities that register with it?

The business takes 5% of any donation, including Gift Aid donations, and also charges a 1.25% processing fee (1.45% if you pay via PayPal). That means that by the time donations reached that astonishing £2.6m, the website was due fees of £115,000 from the total. Charities are also charged a monthly fee for registering with the site.

In 2016, £443m was donated to good causes through this enormously successful website. But it faced criticism earlier this year when it took £22,500 in administration fees from the fund set up for the family of PC Keith Palmer, who was killed in the terrorist attack on Westminster Bridge and the Houses of Parliament. In that case, as in the case of Grenfell Tower, the company was asked to waive or cap its fees. In both cases it refused, though it did donate £10,000 of the £35,500 it would otherwise have collected to PC Palmer's fund.

MoneySavingExpert.com, the site that concerns itself with all ways of getting value for money, has conducted a survey of giving sites, based only on those which host the top ten charities: Oxfam, RSPCA, The Salvation Army, Save the Children, NSPCC, British Heart Foundation, British Red Cross, RNLI, Macmillan Cancer Support and Cancer Research UK.

It found that MyDonate (mydonate.bt.com) came top, giving charities £12.35 from a £10 donation with Gift Aid. There are no charges for the charity itself, though there is a 15p card fee. It has around 9,500 charities signed up. Every Click (fundraisers.everyclick.com) had the most charities registered, 200,000. It's free for charities to use, and £11.94 of your £10 donation with Gift Aid goes to the charity.

Amount passed on by sites for a £10 spend + Gift Aid (if debit card used)

	Amount given directly to charity	Transaction fees/VAT	Charges to charity	Number of charities signed up
Donate to UK charities:				
MyDonate	£12.35	£0.15	£0	9,500
Charity Choice	£12.25	£0.25 [1]	£0	4,000
Virgin Money Giving	£12.15	£0.35	£120 - one-off	11,500
Givey [2]	£12.50 (but an extra 50p is charged on top of your £10 donation)	£0.50 [3]	£0	8,100
Every Click	£11.94	£0.56	£0	200,000+
JustGiving	£11.78	£0.72 [4]	£15 or £39 - monthly [5]	13,000
Donate to global causes:				
The Big Give	£12.00	£0.50	£0	9000+
Global Giving	£11.25	£1.25	£0	600
Donate and fundraise through online sales:				
PayPal Giving Fund	£12.50	£0	£0	8,500

[1] Donors can choose to pay the fee. If they don't, it's passed onto the charity.
[2] Givey will also allow people to donate to global causes.
[3] If you donate £10 to charity, it'll cost you £10.50 but the charity gets the full £10 donation.
[4] Including a card fee. Debit card fees are fixed - 17p for Visa and 16p for Mastercard. The credit card fee is 1.3% of the amount donated.
[5] Charities raising over £15,000 in 12 months will be charged £39/mth. Charities raising less will be charged £15/mth.

But JustGiving is not the only website to charge fees. A personal campaign on Go Fund Me will cost 7.9% of the money raised plus about 30p per donation – so that the company will have done particularly well from the more than £1.3million raised for baby Charlie Gard raised by 84,350 people in 6 months.

Site charges are not something we generally think about in that moment of spontaneous sympathy, or guilt, but the various charges and admin fees can make a huge difference to what a charity receives. So perhaps we should!

Sources: Various and Money Saving Expert
www.moneysavingexpert.com/family/charity-fundraising-sites#online

WHAT DO YOU THINK?

- Have you ever used these websites to donate?
- Does knowing what they charge make a difference to your attitude?
- Are there any better ways of donating to charity?

Trust in charities

What does the public think of charities and the role they play in society?

Overall trust and confidence in charities

How much trust and confidence do you have in charities?

On a 0 to 10 scale where **0 = don't trust them at all**
and **10= trust them completely**

(Base: 1,085 adults aged 18+ in England and Wales)

● 0 to 2   ● 3 to 7   ● 8 to 10

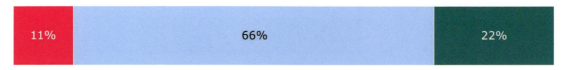

| 11% | 66% | 22% |

The average trust score is **5.7** - a significant decline from **6.7** in recent years.

Trust is **highest** among **18-24 year olds** (**6.0**) and **lowest** among those **aged 55-64** (**5.2**).

Women are slightly more trusting than **men** (**5.9** and **5.5** respectively).

Which one, if any, of these qualities is most important to your trust and confidence in charities overall?

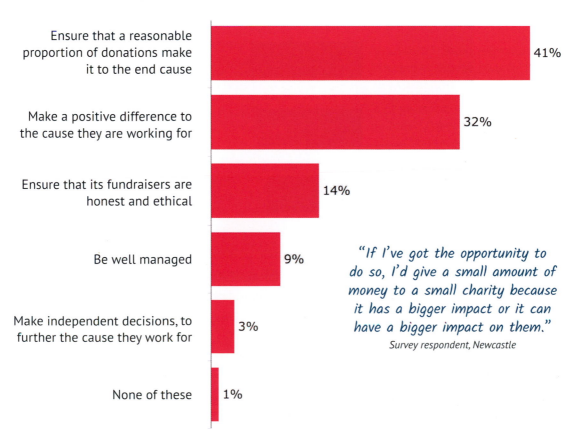

Ensure that a reasonable proportion of donations make it to the end cause — 41%

Make a positive difference to the cause they are working for — 32%

Ensure that its fundraisers are honest and ethical — 14%

Be well managed — 9%

Make independent decisions, to further the cause they work for — 3%

None of these — 1%

"If I've got the opportunity to do so, I'd give a small amount of money to a small charity because it has a bigger impact or it can have a bigger impact on them."

Survey respondent, Newcastle

How much do you agree or disagree with the following statements?

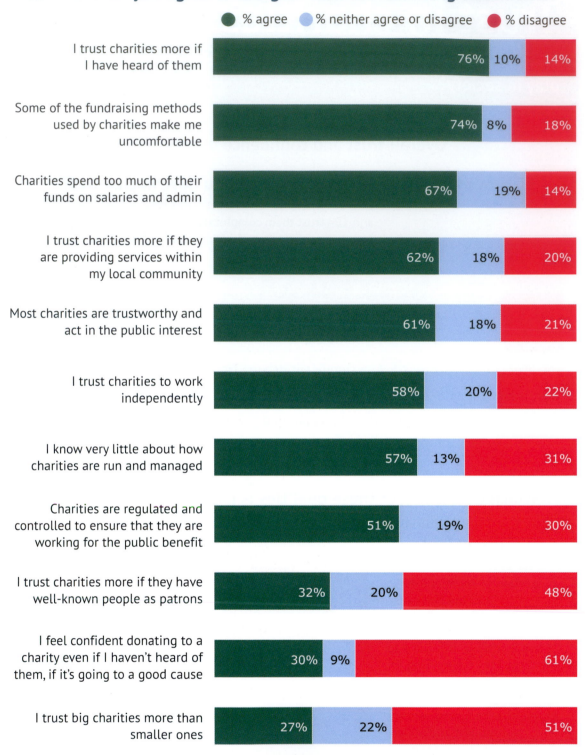

● % agree   ● % neither agree or disagree   ● % disagree

I trust charities more if I have heard of them — 76% | 10% | 14%

Some of the fundraising methods used by charities make me uncomfortable — 74% | 8% | 18%

Charities spend too much of their funds on salaries and admin — 67% | 19% | 14%

I trust charities more if they are providing services within my local community — 62% | 18% | 20%

Most charities are trustworthy and act in the public interest — 61% | 18% | 21%

I trust charities to work independently — 58% | 20% | 22%

I know very little about how charities are run and managed — 57% | 13% | 31%

Charities are regulated and controlled to ensure that they are working for the public benefit — 51% | 19% | 30%

I trust charities more if they have well-known people as patrons — 32% | 20% | 48%

I feel confident donating to a charity even if I haven't heard of them, if it's going to a good cause — 30% | 9% | 61%

I trust big charities more than smaller ones — 27% | 22% | 51%

QUICK FACTS

Amongst those who say their trust and confidence has decreased:

- 33% think this is due to general media stories about a charity or charities;
- 32% think it is due to media coverage about how charities spend donations, for example, expense claims, bonuses etc;
- 21% say their confidence has decreased because they don't trust charities or don't know where the money goes;
- 18% say that their trust has declined because of charities using high pressure tactics to elicit donations.

The charities people trust most...

When asked, unprompted, to name the particular charities or the types of charities they trusted the most, the top three most trusted charities named are some of the bigger ones: Cancer Research UK, Macmillan Cancer Support and the British Heart Foundation.

Familiarity and transparency were the reason they trusted these charities in particular.

...and least

The charities that the public trusts the least are international aid charities in general (12% of responses), followed by Oxfam specifically (11%), animal charities (6%) and less established charities (5%).

International aid charities are trusted less than other charities because the public believe that the money doesn't go to where it needs to and they can't see the outcome of donating.

"I'd like to donate to charities where I can see the end product. When you're just putting money in a bucket you don't know if it's actually helping."
Survey respondent, Cardiff

While the public realise that charities do need to fundraise, they are tired of 'incessant' phone calls asking for money, adverts that they feel deliberately manipulate the emotional responses of donors, and street fundraising ('chugging').

"I subscribe to Save the Children. I did used to do one for deaf children, but they just kept phoning and asking for more money all the time. It was £8, and wanted me to go up to £17 a month, and they were just quite irritating."
Survey respondent, London

Source: Populus for Charity Commission - Public trust and confidence in charities © Crown copyright 2016
www.populus.co.uk   www.gov.uk/government/organisations/charity-commission

WHAT DO YOU THINK?

- Which charities would you support?
- Do you agree that sometimes charities put too much pressure on people?
- Should the government really provide the services that charities provide?
- Should senior managers who work for a charity be paid the same rate as senior managers who work in other industries, or should they take less?

Giving to charity is selfish – and that's fine

David Shariatmadari

As I recently found out, donating money is as much about making ourselves feel good as it is helping others. But it's something that we should embrace

Last year, moved by a particularly upsetting news story, I decided to make a big donation to charity. Christmas was approaching, and I thought: what if I cut back on presents, and deploy a bit of belt-tightening elsewhere – surely I can manage to find £300 to help a group of people whose lives are falling apart?

It was the largest amount I'd ever given in one go. I don't know if that's impressive or embarrassing – research reported in today's Times suggests that the British public regards £278 as a generous donation – but it's hardly big-time philanthropy. I'm lucky, of course, to be in the position where I can even consider parting with that much money on a whim. But it was still a significant chunk out of my monthly budget.

My charitable habits are modest. I give a small amount to two organisations each month, and almost never make one-off donations. I have never been the type to raise money via feats of physical prowess. I once abseiled down a castle wall as part of a school charity event, but since I'd neglected to find any sponsors at all, no one was any better off for my vertigo.

One reason, I think, is that I feel a bit uncomfortable giving money away. That's convenient, I hear you say. But it's true: I suspect my motives. I reckon that I'm only really doing it to feel good about myself, and that makes me uneasy. But if the price of my purity is that good causes miss out, maybe I should just get over it?

As it happened, my £300 donation was an interesting study in the psychology of giving. I posted a link to the charity on Facebook, telling my friends what I was doing (I didn't specify the amount), and suggesting they did the same. Sacrifice some Christmas presents for a gift that might really make a difference. I was hoping for a multiplier effect. I even tweeted it. Maybe someone huge would RT me and a cascade of giving would ensue. I was proud of myself. I thought of the people I was helping and imagined them in my mind's eye receiving clean water, bedding, shelter. I felt a warm glow.

This warm glow is a very real, physiological phenomenon. In one study, researchers used functional magnetic resonance imaging to look at the effect of donation on the brain. They found increased activity in the ventral striatum during acts of voluntary giving. This is a region associated with reward, one of the areas that bursts into life under the influence of addictive stimulants like cocaine. Charity can get you high.

It's easy to imagine why helping others has become linked with reward pathways in the brain: a tendency to pitch in to ensure the survival of members of the group (and we're often more motivated to give to those we identify closely with) has obvious evolutionary advantages.

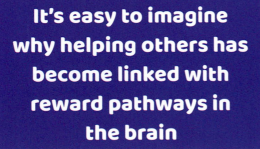

> ## It's easy to imagine why helping others has become linked with reward pathways in the brain

For some reason, with this cause, I managed to override my wariness at feeling smug. This crisis was bigger than me. What I was actually doing, I told myself, was putting my own feelings aside, making a sacrifice for something that felt urgent and worthwhile.

Well, almost. A month later I was confronted with the flimsiness of my commitment. I hadn't realised it, but when I made the first donation, I had clicked a box that meant it would recur. When I checked my bank statement in January, I was horrified to see that another £300 had flown out of my account and landed in the charity's coffers. I gulped. My first thought was: can I get it back?

Of course I couldn't. The loss of that money would be a serious inconvenience to me. But there was no way I could pretend I was worse off than the people I had wanted to help before Christmas. I was stuck with an act of generosity I hadn't intended, and it felt very strange.

My initial donation had, despite what I thought, been motivated by that warm glow. If it were pure altruism, I would have been pleased the extra money had found its way to those in need. Instead, I felt tricked. Well, for a moment anyway, until I realised it would be morally indefensible to act like I was the one who was hard done by.

It was instructive to be exposed in this way, if only to myself. I'm a human being, and the good feeling I get from being generous isn't something I can rise above. Better to acknowledge that giving to charity is selfish, and keep on giving, all the same.

The Guardian, 7 April 2015
© Guardian News and Media

WHAT DO YOU THINK?

- **What motivates you to give to charity?**
- **Is it right to describe that 'warm glow' as selfish?**
- **How can charities encourage people to give more?**

World Giving Index

A snapshot of the scope and nature of giving around the world

The World Giving Index is taken from a survey of **over 148,000 people** in **140 countries**, which represents around **96%** of the world's population.

People aged 15+ were asked about three aspects of giving:

In the past month have you ...

 ...donated money to charity?

 ...volunteered your time to an organisation?

 ...helped a stranger who needed help?

The responses from the three key questions were averaged. Each country was given a percentage and then ranked in order based on their score.

Top 10 most giving nations	World Giving Index Ranking	World Giving Index score (%)	Donating money Ranking	Average (%)	Volunteering time Ranking	Average (%)	Helping a stranger Ranking	Average (%)
Myanmar	1	70	1	91	2	55	27	63
USA	2	61	13	63	5	46	9	73
Australia	3	60	3	73	11	40	14	68
New Zealand	4	59	5	71	6	44	31	61
Sri Lanka	5	57	17	61	4	49	36	61
Canada	6	56	11	65	14	38	20	65
Indonesia	7	56	2	75	3	50	104	43
UK	8	54	7	69	22	33	33	61
Ireland	9	54	10	66	10	40	47	56
United Arab Emirates	10	53	14	63	61	21	5	75

NB Where two or more countries seem to have the same percentage, but are not placed equally, this is due to rounding,

Donating money

Highest-ranked countries by PERCENTAGE of people who donate money to charity in a typical month

Myanmar — 91%
Indonesia — 75%
Australia — 73%
Malta — 73%
New Zealand — 71%
Iceland — 70%
UK — 69%
Norway — 67%
Netherlands — 66%
Ireland — 66%

NUMBER of people donating money

Highest ranked country	People (millions)
India	203
USA	165
Indonesia	139
China	66
Brazil	48
Germany	41
Pakistan	38
UK	37
Myanmar	36
Thailand	35

QUICK FACTS

- Myanmar is top of the World Giving Index because of the high percentage of people who give money.

- 80% to 90% of people in Myanmar are practising Buddhists. Almost all of them donate to support those living a monastic lifestyle.

- Giving in this way carries significant religious meaning and small, frequent acts of giving are the norm.

Volunteering time

Highest-ranked countries by PERCENTAGE of people who volunteer time in a typical month

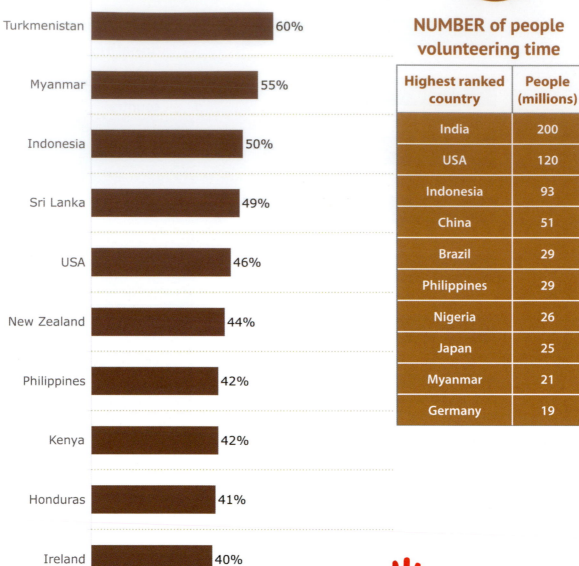

Country	Percentage
Turkmenistan	60%
Myanmar	55%
Indonesia	50%
Sri Lanka	49%
USA	46%
New Zealand	44%
Philippines	42%
Kenya	42%
Honduras	41%
Ireland	40%

NUMBER of people volunteering time

Highest ranked country	People (millions)
India	200
USA	120
Indonesia	93
China	51
Brazil	29
Philippines	29
Nigeria	26
Japan	25
Myanmar	21
Germany	19

QUICK FACTS

- Globally, volunteering time has increased this year.

- 23.4% of the world's men said they had volunteered in the last month - this was the highest level recorded in the last 5 years.

- 19.9% of women said they had volunteered in the last month - although women show lower levels of volunteering than men, it is still on an upwards trend over the years from 17.9% in 2011.

Helping a stranger

Highest-ranked countries by PERCENTAGE of people who helped a stranger in a typical month

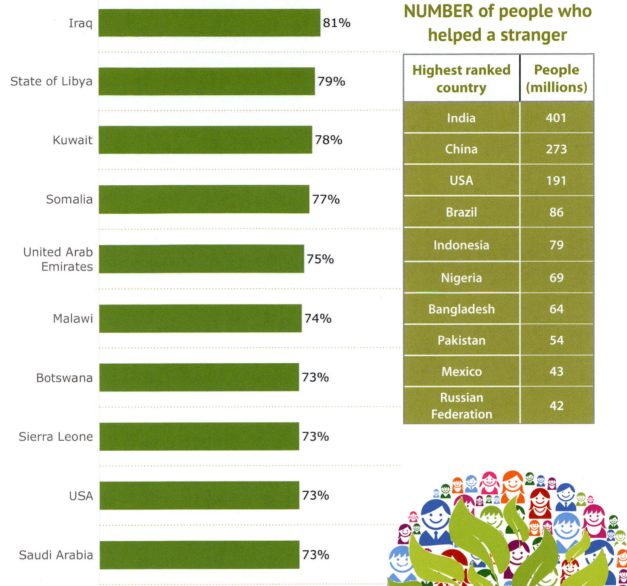

Iraq	81%
State of Libya	79%
Kuwait	78%
Somalia	77%
United Arab Emirates	75%
Malawi	74%
Botswana	73%
Sierra Leone	73%
USA	73%
Saudi Arabia	73%

NUMBER of people who helped a stranger

Highest ranked country	People (millions)
India	401
China	273
USA	191
Brazil	86
Indonesia	79
Nigeria	69
Bangladesh	64
Pakistan	54
Mexico	43
Russian Federation	42

QUICK FACTS

- For the first time since the World Giving Index began, more than half the world's population, 51.4%, said that they'd helped a stranger in the last month. This is also the highest figure ever recorded for any of the three measures of generosity.

Source: World Giving Index 2016, Charities Aid Foundation
www.cafonline.org

WHAT DO YOU THINK?

- Does an index like this tell us anything about national characteristics?
- Is the survey a good indicator of how generous people are with their money and time?
- Which sort of help is most important?

Autism

A hidden disability

What is autism?

Autism Spectrum Disorder (ASD) is a lifelong disability which affects a person's communication and interaction with other people, their interests and behaviour.

'Spectrum' means range. People are affected in a variety of ways and to different extents.

For example, children with ASD can find it hard to understand other people's emotions and feelings, and have difficulty starting conversations or taking part in them properly.

They can have difficulty with eye contact, facial expressions, body language and gestures.

They may also lack awareness of and interest in other children and tend to play alone.

Over 700,000 people - **more than 1 in 100** - in the UK are autistic. Together with their families, this means autism is a part of daily life for **2.8 million** people.

Awareness & understanding

There is a lack of understanding about autism. Often there are false or negative perceptions of the condition which can make it difficult for people to have their condition recognised and to get access to the support they need.

Misconceptions can lead to some autistic people feeling isolated and alone. In extreme cases, it can also lead to abuse and bullying.

More than 99% of the public said they have heard of autism – yet only **16%** of autistic people and their families think the public have a good understanding of the condition and how it can affect behaviour.

Myths & Facts

Myth:

People tend to 'grow out' of autism in adulthood.

Fact:

It's a lifelong condition – autistic children become autistic adults. There's no "cure" for ASD, but speech and language therapy, occupational therapy and educational support can be helpful.

Myth:

Autism is a mental health problem.

Fact:

Autism is a difference in how your brain works. Autistic people can have good mental health, or experience mental health problems, just like anyone else.

Myth:

All autistic people are geniuses.

Fact:

Just under half of all people diagnosed with autism also have a learning disability. Others have an IQ in the average to above average range. Abilities like extraordinary memory are rare.

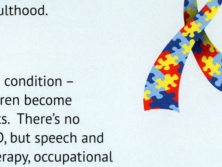

Myth:

There is a popular misconception that autism is simply a male condition.

Fact:

Autism affects both boys and girls. Although more males than females are diagnosed with autism, recent research suggests that the number is far more equal than previously thought; the problem is that professionals often don't understand the different ways autism can show itself in women and girls.

Myth:

Everyone is a bit autistic.

Fact:

Just having a fondness for routines, a good memory or being shy doesn't make a person 'a bit autistic'. To be diagnosed with autism, a person must consistently show behaviours across all the different areas of the condition.

Processing time

Sometimes people with autism feel like they're getting 'too much information' and need a few moments to filter through it all.

"Not having enough time to process information can feel very confusing for an autistic person. In my case, I've always compared it to a computer crashing."

Dana, Young Campaigner, The National Autistic Society

Sensory overload

People with autism can be sensitive to lights, sounds, smells and sights, eg for someone who is over-sensitive to touch and sound, people brushing past them and a loud announcement at a train station could cause pain and sensory overload, leading to a meltdown.

"If I get sensory overload then I just shut down; you get what's known as fragmentation...it's weird, like being tuned into 40 TV channels."

Anonymous

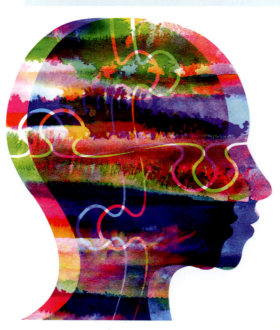

Meltdown

This is when an autistic person becomes overwhelmed by everything around them, and may begin to shout, scream, cry or lose control.

28% of autistic people have even been asked to leave a public place because of their autistic behaviour.

75% of parents said their children on the autism spectrum had been labelled "naughty" or "strange".
72% said that people avoid them;
74% said people make disapproving noises; and
87% said people stare.

Unexpected changes

The world can be an unpredictable, confusing place for autistic people, and that makes a set routine crucial but when something unexpected happens, it can feel like the whole world is spinning out of control.

Social anxiety

Trying to understand what others mean and how to behave can be exhausting and stressful for autistic people, causing many to end up feeling excluded and isolated.

"By the second year in Secondary School, I was feeling different from other children. This was mainly because some children used it as an excuse to bully me. The bullying escalated and became physical as well as verbal and made me feel very low."

Danny

Harassment

44% of people on the autism spectrum said they stay at home because they are afraid of being abused or harassed – **49%** said they have been abused by someone they thought of as a friend.

"I was bullied but I didn't always know this was the case. I didn't like being called names, but I enjoyed the attention and often mistook the bullies' actions for friendship."

Karen

Friends

22% of young people on the autism spectrum said they had no friends at all.

10% said their friends were mainly adults.

50% said they would like more friends.

Support

70% of autistic adults say that they are not getting the help they need from social services. **70%** of autistic adults also said that with more support they would feel less isolated.

At least **33%** of autistic adults are experiencing severe mental health difficulties due to a lack of support.

Children

There are an estimated **120,000** school-aged children on the autism spectrum in England, the vast majority - **73%** - in mainstream schools.

75% of children on the autism spectrum of secondary school age say they have been bullied at school.

34% of children on the autism spectrum say that the worst thing about being at school is being picked on.

63% of children on the autism spectrum are not in the kind of school their parents believe would best support them.

17% of autistic children have been suspended from school;
48% of these had been suspended three or more times;
4% had been expelled from one or more schools.

Work

Only **15%** of autistic adults are in full-time paid work.

53% of people on the autism spectrum say they want help to find work, but only **10%** get the support to do so.

43% of those who have worked have left or lost a job because of their autism.

Source: The National Autistic Society www.autism.org.uk
NHS Choices www.nhs.uk

WHAT DO YOU THINK?

- Did you believe any of the myths about autism before reading these facts?
- Do you know about any efforts that are being made to help people with autism?
- What changes would help autistic people cope with school or college better?

Making a new start

By Peggy

From a young age, I almost relished my brother's autism.

People would say to me: "You're so mature, you cope so well, you're so brave". I thought his autism was a gift for me that would help me develop as a person and it hadn't crossed my mind that his autism would ever become something I was ashamed of. I loved my brother from the bottom of my heart, included him in everything and introduced him to all my friends. I talked about him all the time and spent every waking moment caring for him.

When I was about eight years old, it began to dawn on me that people did not understand my brother's special needs. Whenever we went out together as a family, people would give us strange looks, point their finger at us and giggle, sometimes making impressions.

This was when I slowly began to resent my brother. Nonetheless, I couldn't help protecting him, sticking up for him and even getting into fights with people who made fun of him.

My increasing awareness of people's misconceptions of autism seriously affected my confidence. I was withdrawn and shy and no longer told people that my brother had autism. I knew they would say things like "spastic", and "retard", which actually physically hurt me.

One weekend I went bowling with my family, and to my horror, a good male friend from my class at school was there too with his family. I was terribly embarrassed and concerned that he would pick up on my brother's strange habits and tendencies. When I went to school on Monday I had completely forgotten about it but was welcomed by a class mimicking my brother's OCD-like behaviour, pretending to lick tables and dribbling – this was the first time I'd cried in 6 years (I find it difficult to cry as it distressed my brother, so trained myself not to, even under the most dire circumstances).

Relentless bullying continued until I left for secondary school, where I kept my brother's autism to myself – I wanted to escape from being my brother's sister, I just wanted people to know me. I would come home every day and see my brother's autism grow worse and I would often sit and wonder 'why me?'. I wished for a normal family, and thought this was God's way of punishing me for something I did in a past life.

I had many sleepless nights worrying about what would happen when my parents died. I had an image in my head of me living in a grotty flat, with my only money coming from the government, spoon-feeding my brother and dressing him, at the age of 40. It terrified me, and I gradually distanced myself from my brother and the rest of my family. I no longer made an effort at school as I couldn't see the point of preparing for a working life when I had no life or career ahead of me.

I would consider my brother's autism moderately severe. He has difficulty with speech, and only started grasping basic literacy and numeracy at the age of 17. He also suffers severe OCD and anxiety, which often results in him becoming violent. He is physically very able, which can make his violent outbursts quite frightening.

I only told my new friends about my brother's autism after he had become exceedingly violent which left me emotionally distressed and I had to take a few weeks off school. As soon as I explained my situation to them, they all shared stories with me about their relatives with autism, or their knowledge of it - I instantly knew that I'd finally met a lovely group of people who would fully accept me and my brother, and not treat his autism as a problem, but a way of life.

Since I started regaining my faith in people who were looking at my brother's autism from a positive and mature perspective, I have only once had another negative experience. My first serious boyfriend spouted some nasty insults about my brother when I broke up with him, but his disgraceful comments were only harmful to himself and made me realise who he really was.

Now, at the age of 16, I still notice the giggling and the comments, but I've begun to rebuild my relationship with my brother. We've made a new start and I now dedicate a lot of my free time to helping other people with autism by raising money and volunteering for various events. It's one of the very few things I feel extremely passionate about and openly stand up against anyone who makes remarks about mental health.

> **I wanted to escape from being my brother's sister, I just wanted people to know me.**

I love watching him experience new things and grow up, just like any normal boy.

I don't know why or when this change of attitude occurred, it may simply be emotional maturity and the fact that I have realised that others do not necessarily have any knowledge of autism. I can't expect everyone to know what it means to have autism or live with someone who is autistic in the same way that I do not know about other conditions or illnesses people might have.

Seeing my brother grow up and accepting that he is not going to get better or change, has helped me become a stronger person. I sometimes feel almost indestructible, that I can take on any challenge that comes my way and that's because of my brother, it has nothing to do with me.

I love him more than anyone in the whole wide world. When I'm not with him I wonder what he's doing and I love watching him experience new things and grow up, just like any normal boy. He's the reason I smile when I wake up in the morning.

Source: The National Autistic Society www.autism.org.uk

WHAT DO YOU THINK?

- How much do you know about autism and where do your ideas come from?

- Can you sympathise with how Peggy felt when she wanted to escape from her situation?

- What factors helped to change her point of view?

Photo: Alessandra D'Innella

The way I see it:
living with partial blindness
Annalisa D'Innella

Of all those registered blind or partially sighted, 93% retain some useful vision – often enough to read a book or watch a film. But this can lead to misunderstanding and confusion.

Two young men are in my way. Their laughter echoes off the houses opposite as I move quickly to skirt around them on the narrow pavement. As I pass, they fall silent. I am a few inches away now, my white cane skimming the uneven paving stones, when one of them shouts to the other. His voice is confused, angry. He is shouting: "She's not blind."

You can't be a bit dead. It's a binary thing. You either are or you aren't – same goes for pregnancy. But what about blindness? Can you be a bit blind? Is that allowed? And how does that work? What does it look like?

It looks like a woman seeing two men in front of her and using her cane to navigate around them. It looks like a man folding up his cane outside the cinema and going in to enjoy a movie. It looks like a girl on a train reading a newspaper while her guide dog rests his chin on her lap.

I have a genetic eye condition called retinitis pigmentosa (RP). One in 3,000 of us have it. People with RP begin losing their night vision and peripheral vision any time from infancy to their early 20s and, in many cases, lose their central vision entirely in later life. Many of us

Can you be a bit blind? Is that allowed? And how does that work?

struggle in bright light as well as low light. Many of us wear sunglasses in the rain. But what most of us contend with for a good few decades is tunnel vision.

Imagine looking through a fogged-up window with a tiny dot of clarity in the middle. Now imagine the dot as a cursor on a screen. I can move my eyeballs around to get a sense of the big picture. This is why I am able to see a train arrive at the platform, walk to the doors and get in without needing help. I can also find a seat, get out my Kindle and read this summer's bestseller. But there are a multitude of situations where my scanning technique isn't up to the job. Playgrounds, revolving doors, pavements – most outdoor places, really.

So I can enjoy lunch in a cafe. I can get the bill and type in my PIN. All this will be fine until I get up, walk into a chair and fail to locate the exit. Once I have found the door, I will probably have to scrabble around to find the handle. I will be that person, hesitant and slow, standing on the pavement outside until my eyes adjust to the sun. I will get in your way. I will hover at the top of the stairs gripping the railing. I will apologise constantly, even though I won't have actually seen what I have done wrong. I will crash into you as you queue up at the turnstiles at the tube station. When I get home, I will cry from nothing more than sheer physical exhaustion. My head

will ache. My neck will ache. I will check my new array of flowering bruises and will decide to cancel all further social engagements because it has just been too bloody hard. But when I am reading my Kindle on the train, I look normal. I feel normal.

Lately, as my central vision has begun to worsen, my scanning technique has become less effective. My eyes do not clasp on to those crucial details – facial features, for example – with the ninja-like speed they used to. I am missing more. The misty mazes around me feel thicker and more befuddling. So, last year, I decided to abandon the art of being sighted. It was a decision made with surprising ease. I called social services and was put through to a man called Andy who offered me mobility training and the gift of a shining white cane.

When I say I made the decision "with surprising ease", I mean that it wasn't with tooth-gnashing resistance. I waited for Andy's first visit with the enthusiasm of a condemned woman. The surprising ease came later. Andy showed me three different canes. The symbol cane looks like a conductor's baton. It doesn't reach the ground. It is there merely for show – to let other people know you cannot see very well. I had never heard of a symbol cane before. Andy showed me two other canes that touch

When I am reading my Kindle on the train, I look normal. I feel normal.

Photo courtesy of RNIB

And, as I glided around, my daughter and I chatted about the window displays. With the cane, I could free my eyes to admire my surroundings. And people kept apologising to me. All the time.

And then it happened. That pang, that familiar summoning of resilience, that surprise arrow of shame. I neared a doorway and stopped, because I saw a man approaching and I decided to wait for him to open the door rather than open it myself. I did this because, in that split second, I felt compelled to "play blind". In that split second, I felt like a fraud.

"Who cares what people think?" It's always angry, that statement. I have had it said to me a lot recently. I have also seen the expression of genuine incomprehension from Andy. "The cane is here for you," he said, exasperated. "You are not a fraud. You are exactly who it's here for."

I talk to people about my condition as much as possible.

We all feel the need sometimes to explain ourselves to strangers. We all want to present a coherent picture, to make sense. Psychotherapist and cane-user Rachael Stevens has RP. She spoke about it on BBC Radio 4's Today programme and was flooded with positive responses from visually impaired listeners. One caller spoke of a nasty encounter in which he was accused of being a "benefits fraud". Stevens herself once told me about a time she had been confronted outside her son's nursery by a man who had planted himself directly in front of her, smirking, as if to test her.

In order for guide canes and symbol canes to be effective, they need to be understood. Somehow, some time ago, the people who came up with these valuable low-vision solutions only did half the job. They didn't put the resources needed into raising public awareness and, as a result, the cane has become symbolically too blunt an instrument.

I took the decision that I had to find the best way I could to present myself as partially sighted. I had to be me in the world. I unfold my cane whenever I need it. When people move out of my way, I thank them. I use different canes for different situations. I don't use a cane when I am with my toddler as I have not yet found a way to hold a cane and push a buggy simultaneously.

the ground, thereby giving the user "feedback". We decided I needed feedback. My heart was thumping as we left the house together with my new cane. I felt sick with misplaced, wrongheaded and overwhelming shame.

And yet, a few days later, I was swanning through Canary Wharf shopping centre, my cane sweeping the shining floor in front of me, my daughter skipping alongside. I wanted to dance and shout. My eyes didn't ache. My back was straight. My stomach was unclenched. I felt amazing. I felt free. I felt as though I had got my sight back. I realised so much on that day – what it felt like to be in the world and not feel stressed; why my friends and family are never as exhausted as I am all the time; how mad and wrong I had been to expect myself to be able to keep up with everyone else; that I had to forgive myself for not being able to keep up.

I felt compelled to "play blind". In that split second, I felt like a fraud.

Also, I have found that the buggy itself (as well as the yelps from my son) provide adequate feedback. Some days, the light conditions are just right and I can operate without a cane. Other days, I stand at the front door and can't take two steps forward.

I talk to people about my condition as much as possible. "Are you allowed a guide dog?" asks a friend. Good question. Yes. Jessica Luke, an RP friend with a guide dog, came with me to give a talk to my daughter's class at school. We put up slides showing the different ways people see.

Visually impaired people come in many different variations.

We got one teacher to wear RP-simulation specs and we threw her a ball. She dropped it and the kids screamed with laughter.

The Royal National Institute for Blind People (RNIB) website tells me that 93% of people who are registered blind or partially sighted in the UK retain some useful vision. So why isn't there better understanding of visual impairment? Is it because it is easier for sight-loss charities to raise money if they present a more simplistic, pitiable image of blindness? Or is it because it is thought too complex an issue to explain? Dyslexia is a complex condition, but nowadays a child with dyslexia can grow up in a world that (largely) understands their needs. I believe passionately that the same must be done for partial sight.

Blindness is not binary. It is a rich and fascinating spectrum. Visually impaired people come in many different variations. Some of us have central vision but no periphery. Some have periphery but no central. Some see the world through a window stained with blobs. For others, it is all a blur. We could form a zombie army. But we will probably just quietly get in your way on staircases.

Photo courtesy of RNIB

And, given the chance, many lovely people do understand – such as the man who saw me holding my cane, squinting up at a noticeboard at St Pancras station. As I sat down next to him, taking my Kindle from my bag, he leaned over: "Did you get all the information you needed from that board?" I replied that I wasn't 100% sure but I thought the Sevenoaks train was arriving in 10 minutes. He got up, checked the board and confirmed I was right. "Well done," he said. "Thank you," I replied, and we both got on with reading our books.

To find out more about the RNIB's #howisee campaign, visit:
rnib.org.uk/howisee

To find out more about RP, visit
rpfightingblindness.org.uk

The Guardian, 14 November 2016
© Guardian News & Media 2016

WHAT DO YOU THINK?

- **What did you already know about different types and levels of sight problems?**

- **Do you think enough has been done to educate sighted people about how to help (if help is needed)?**

- **If this author had the same regular journey as you do, what problems would she face?**

Different canes explained

Symbol cane

For people with low but useful vision. This is carried to let other people know that someone is partially sighted. It's particularly useful in busy places.

Guide cane

This is used to find obstacles such as kerbs or steps. It is held across the person's body .

Long cane

For people who have extremely restricted vision or none at all, Once people have been trained to use a long cane, they roll or tap it from side to side as they walk, to find their way and avoid obstacles.

Red and white banded cane

Red and white banded canes of all types show that the person has a hearing impairment as well as sight loss.

www.rnib.org.uk/cane-explained

To see how the different canes are used:
www.youtube.com/watch?v=69gDygNlP0c&feature=youtu.be

I ran my first marathon
after going blind

Gillian Bailey

Every year I would watch the London Marathon and feel a thrill as the runners crossed Tower Bridge. But two years ago, as I stood on the sidelines with my daughter Hazel and watched them pass by in their jaunty fancy-dress costumes, I felt sad and unable to cheer with any enthusiasm. I said to Hazel, 'My one regret is not having run the Marathon. I'll never do it now.'

I was feeling low because I was losing my sight. It happened almost overnight. One morning at work, several years earlier, I noticed a strange blob on my computer screen.

'I'll never do it now.'

I popped into the opticians to get a check-up – but was immediately rushed to hospital. I was diagnosed with age-related macular degeneration, a relatively common condition among people in their 60s and 70s. Only I was 49.

It was such a shock to hear that I would never see properly again, and I lost my confidence immediately. I took voluntary redundancy from the homeless charity where I worked. Shopping and travelling became difficult, and reading was especially frustrating as the words were often out of focus. I also stopped running – until then I'd been doing fairly short distances, usually about four miles, a few times a week.

We spent the first seven miles running between a Womble and a man carrying a washing machine on his back

By the time I came to watch that London Marathon in 2015, my eyesight had deteriorated so badly that I couldn't make out the runners' features, just their shapes.

But as I lamented, Hazel, now 29, was defiant. 'Yes, you could run it,' she said. 'We'll run it

Hazel spent most of the time shouting, 'Debris! Debris!' so that I didn't trip over discarded water bottles. But I loved it

next year together!' We got a charity place through Guide Dogs UK and that was it.

Hazel had just had a baby and neither of us was fit, so we devised a strict training regime. We also had to learn to run in tandem: blind runners attach themselves to their guide by the wrist using a strip of material. There is no standard rope so we adapted a pair of tights because they're soft and stretchy.

For the first few weeks, I thought there was no way it would work. Everything was a blur when I moved and it was hard to run in rhythm. But Hazel was very patient, and I was determined not to disappoint her. By April, I knew we could complete the 26.2 miles.

Finally, the big day arrived. At the starting line I was overwhelmed as the crowds cheered and bands played. We spent the first seven miles running between a Womble and a man carrying a washing machine on his back.

At mile 19, in Canary Wharf, my family was waiting with a flask of tea. After that, I thought, 'The race is ours.' And I was elated when we finished in four hours and 46 minutes.

Afterwards we were swept off to a reception at the Houses of Parliament with Guide Dogs UK, who we raised almost £2,800 for. All I could think was, 'I'm desperate to run it again next year.'

'The race is ours.'

We've had to postpone, however, as Hazel is pregnant again – but I've suggested signing up for a triathlon after the birth. I enjoy swimming, there's less running and we could ride a tandem bike. After all, nothing will stop me now.

Interview by Laura Silverman

Source: The Sunday Telegraph, 23 April 2017
© Telegraph Media Group Limited 2017

WHAT DO YOU THINK?

- What is the attraction of marathons and other gruelling events?
- Do you admire marathon runners, and this one in particular?
- How could we improve opportunities for disabled people in sport and in everyday life?

Sign language

12.7 million people in the UK would like to learn sign language

British Sign Language (BSL) is a language in its own right and uses handshapes, facial expressions, gestures and body language to convey meaning.

It is the first language of some deaf people and is used in addition to spoken English by others.

Nearly 80% of deaf children in England attend mainstream schools where they may be the only deaf child enrolled.

There are more than 45,000 deaf children in the UK.

A survey of 1,155 UK adults aged 16-55+ for the National Deaf Children's Society found:

- **24.5%** of people in Britain said they wanted to learn sign language;

- The other two languages in the top three that people said they would like to learn were:
  Spanish **28.8%**;
  French **23.2%**;

- **61%** of people felt embarrassed they couldn't communicate well with deaf people and wished they could do better;

- **66.8%** of people think that sign language is more impressive than speaking a foreign language.

The top ten phrases Brits would most like to learn in sign language are:

Thank you **57.9%**

Can I help **42.4%**

Sorry **32.8%**

Please **32.6%**

I don't understand **30.3%**

Their own name **29.9%**

Excuse me **19.6%**

I love you **18.1%**

Happy Birthday **11.2%**

Where are you from **9.9%**

Source: National Deaf Children's Society © NDCS 2017 www.ndcs.org.uk

WHAT DO YOU THINK?

- **When have you seen sign language being used?**

- **What would be attractive and useful about knowing British Sign Language?**

- **Should BSL be offered as a school subject?**

Photo: Flickr/Jørgen Schyberg used under Creative Commons

'No excuses!'

INSIDE BRITAIN'S STRICTEST SCHOOL

Katharine Birbalsingh's Michaela school in north London has a formidable reputation thanks to its emphasis on discipline – but opinion is split on its approach to teaching

Richard Adams

It is billed as the strictest school in Britain – but the headteacher says its biggest challenge is not keeping pupils in line, but with critics from outside.

At the Michaela community school in Brent, north London, the emphasis on discipline has earned it a formidable reputation, with the headteacher, Katharine Birbalsingh, touted as "Britain's strictest teacher" by the Sunday Times. But some educationalists are less enamoured: almost every evening on social media sees skirmishes between pro- and anti-Michaela factions.

Sometimes, according to Birbalsingh – one of the small number of black or ethnic minority women heading a secondary school in England – the debate turns sour. The emails are the worst, she says.

"They wish us cancer and things like that, because they don't like what we are doing," she says. "People ask me, what's your biggest challenge running the school? It's the detractors on the outside. On the inside there are daily challenges. But the detractors on the outside are very time-consuming, emotionally draining. And they are obsessive."

Photos: Michaela School

"They learn so much here, it's quiet, they are not being bullied"

At the school, a group of pupils prepare to end their break and move to their next lesson. They line up quietly under the eye of their teacher – who stops to ask one of them to pick up a grape from the floor.

"Do you see that?" Birbalsingh tells a group of visiting teachers. "In other schools that would never happen. You'd never see a teacher ask a pupil to pick up a grape, because they'd go mad."

She says one of the things that is different about Michaela, the state secondary school she founded three years ago, is its unwillingness to let even a single pupil – or grape – go astray.

"It's about habit change, and constantly reminding pupils to be respectful," Birbalsingh says. "We have made it unacceptable not to pick that grape up."

The year 7 pupils file out to their next class, illustrating another Michaela principle: silent corridors. The children walk between classrooms without speaking, in single file, moving quickly. Anyone who does not gets a demerit, leading to a detention.

The reason, says Birbalsingh, is that corridors in schools are where bad behaviour often takes place: pushing and fights breaking out as large groups of children mill around. By moving in a straight line, the children stay calm and focused for their next lesson.

Michaela's staff are mostly young and active on Twitter and the education blogosphere, and Birbalsingh and the school have just published a book, Battle Hymn of the Tiger Teachers. It carries an endorsement from the philosopher Roger Scruton, who says Michaela is a model "that all our schools should imitate".

One of the staff, Joe Kirby, has detailed Michaela's "no excuses" policy: detentions are awarded for arriving one minute late to school, for not completing homework, for scruffy work, for not having a pen or ruler, for reacting badly to a teacher's instruction by tutting or rolling eyes, and even for "persistently turning round in class" after being told not to.

Photo: Michaela School

Detention for not having a pen sounds harsh – until you learn that Michaela provides pens to all pupils at the start of the year, that there is a school shop selling cut-price ones each morning, and that parents are given persistent reminders about the equipment their children need to bring every day.

Michaela hit the headlines in 2016 when it emerged children whose parents had not paid for school lunches were made to eat in a separate room. But Birbalsingh was unmoved by the criticism. She says: "At other schools if their parents didn't pay they wouldn't get any lunch at all. Here they still get lunch, a good lunch."

Birbalsingh herself has been in the news since she spoke scathingly about the state of England's schools at the 2010 Conservative party conference. After her appearance, she left her job as vice-principal of an academy in south London.

The launch of free schools gave her an opportunity to open Michaela in 2014, in an old college building close to Wembley stadium.

In her office, Birbalsingh briefs the visitors – teachers and officials from Abu Dhabi's education council – on the school, starting with its discipline.

"The children love it here because they know that in comparison to their primary schools or schools where they were before, that they learn so much here, it's quiet, they are not being bullied," she tells them.

"They can go to the toilet here and not be worried about being bullied. At other schools you will find children who train themselves not to go to the toilet all day because they are so scared of the bullying that takes place. So they just don't go to the loo. That isn't the case here."

The second big difference, Birbalsingh says, is the school's traditional style of teaching.

> ## Detentions are awarded for arriving one minute late to school.

"We have the teacher standing at the front and imparting knowledge. We believe the teacher knows more than the children. Most teachers in Britain do not believe that. They believe that the children and teachers all know pretty much the same stuff, which is why the children just need to be guided by the teacher as opposed to being taught by the teacher."

But the third reason is more arresting. "We teach kindness and gratitude, because we think children should be kind to each other and to their teachers and be grateful for everything we do for them."

Being a teacher and a parent, Birbalsingh explains, is "the most exhilarating, most exciting, most important job in the country". Instead, she says, teachers in Britain were "driven into the ground".

"In other schools children are not kind at all, they are horrible."

She adds: "Teachers and parents need support and appreciation. That doesn't happen in this country. Teachers are constantly being vilified in the press, they are constantly being attacked. There are actual examples of teachers getting attacked in the street, and nothing really happens to the assailants.

"If I'd have had those children in this school, they wouldn't be attacking anybody. They would be different human beings when they grow up, and that is because they would have learned kindness and gratitude here."

"You will find in other schools children are not kind at all, they are horrible. And they are horrible because nobody has taught them how to be kind," Birbalsingh says.

There is an element of hyperbole in Birbalsingh's depiction of other schools. Sir Michael Wilshaw, the outgoing Ofsted chief inspector, made his name with a strict regime as head of Mossbourne academy in Hackney. And the Ark academy chain's King Solomon academy in Paddington uses similar techniques.

"I think all schools should be like this."

The stakes for Michaela are high: it is awaiting its first Ofsted inspection, and in two years' time will produce its first GCSE results.

What is particularly striking is the school's attention to detail. The corridor carpet has a black line woven into it for the pupils to follow. The classrooms have hooks on the back wall to stow jackets and bags, to stop them getting in the way. Pupils must use a school-issue pencil case made of clear plastic.

The pupil's bathrooms don't have mirrors, and makeup is banned. The staff bathroom has a framed letter of praise from a government minister in one of the cubicles.

Every detail, and the silent corridor routine, has a single purpose: to maximise the pupils' time in front of a teacher so that learning takes centre stage.

Even lunch, a spirited affair starting with pupils loudly reciting the poem If, includes exhortations from the deputy head about pupils completing the homework over Christmas. "Don't make the wrong choices," he warns the pupils, underlining a Michaela theme.

Birbalsingh, meanwhile, is applying to open another free school, this time an "all-through" school from reception to sixth form.

But would Michaela need to be strict if it was in a wealthy suburb such as Hampstead rather than deprived Brent, where 30% of pupils are on free school meals?

"I don't think it would need to be. But I think all schools should be like this," Birbalsingh says.

The Guardian, 30 December 2016
© Guardian News and Media

WHAT DO YOU THINK?

- **Would you do well in a school like this?**

- **How do you learn best?**

- **What would you change in your own school in order to improve your education?**

Teachers as 'guides':
inside the UK's first Montessori secondary school

The Montessori Place has no year groups, no assessments, and students work in partnership with mentors to decide what to study   **Ryan Wilson**

One student is completing a project on the rise of the emoji in modern culture. Another is making notes on the incubation of duck eggs, in anticipation of a hatching the next day. Others are outside in the garden, tending to basil, which will later be sold in a local shop.

This is an unusual place to learn, and the first Montessori school for adolescents in the UK to be endorsed by AMI (Association Montessori Internationale), although there are others that teach in the Montessori style. There are no year groups, no subject departments, no timetables and no assessments. There are also no teachers in the traditional sense: adults are "guides", mentors who meet with students weekly or fortnightly to review their work and set a programme of learning. Students study in mixed age groups, learning from each other and working on topics that interest them.

Montessori pre-school and primary schools have become popular in the UK – with around 700 early years and primary institutions, four of which are state-funded.

Outside the curriculum

The Montessori Place is a converted conference centre in East Sussex with an extensive walled garden, "the living laboratory", where students spend a large part of their time learning how to grow vegetables and tend to animals.

The school opened its doors to adolescents in September and although there are currently only seven students, it plans to expand to 60 in the coming years. Paul Pillai, the softly spoken and intellectual head guide, describes the partnerships between students and guides as "a different relationship" to the usual teacher-student dynamic: "I'm more of a coach, or a line manager. I meet with the students individually, we discuss goals and how we'll achieve them, and then we meet again and see how they've got on."

Deciding what each student will work on is about looking for "a spark", says Pillai: "What fires this student up? If we don't find that, we are wasting our time." From there, they work together to plan a series of activities loosely covering recognisable curriculum areas such as the humanities, arts and maths. And then the students more or less get on with it.

"Real work" and looking after the community are other vital elements of the student experience. So they help with cooking, cleaning and the maintenance of the building, as well as running a bed and breakfast for visitors.

Students will take GCSEs in English and maths with the option to take science and other subjects by request, but qualifications aren't the main focus. "There is a point at which a qualification is valuable and that's A-level," says Pillai. "Before that, we just want to feed a passion. There's a joy to studying a subject without curriculum constraint."

Elitist?

During sessions, students are also encouraged to take time out to reflect and "just be". Dr Robert Loe, director of education consultancy and research organisation Relational Schools, believes it's an approach that has value: "One of the biggest issues we face is that schools these days are time poor. Time is the currency of relationships, and relationships precede learning and success."

But the Montessori approach is not without its critics. They say that it's too individualistic in its approach at the expense of group work and social interaction; that it focuses too much on the practical; and that it's elitist, with most schools only being available to those who can afford the private fees.

Life in Montessori schools starkly contrasts with that in many UK secondaries, where budget constraints and performance measures see extracurricular activities cut and creative subjects sidelined.

Since the Montessori Place is a private school, such education doesn't come cheap. So does that investment lead to better results? There's been little research into the academic results among adolescent Montessori students, but there is evidence to suggest improved motivation and engagement among Montessori middle-schoolers, and better academic performance among younger children in the US.

And what about after they've taken their A-levels, when these students are applying for jobs, or for university courses? Will they be disadvantaged? Christine Doddington, fellow emerita of educational philosophy at the University of Cambridge, doesn't think so. "These students may not have as many GCSE results, but they'll have advantages in other ways," she says.

"In recent years, universities have been talking about how many students they get who don't have the ability to think for themselves. So I think students who have had different experiences could be very attractive in that context."

She questions, though, whether so much independence is always positive. "There's a real need to mediate learning for adolescents so that it is not remote, inert and dry but instead has the urgency, warmth and intimacy of a direct experience. This requires great artistry and skill as a teacher, and I'm not sure the idea of teacher as guide does justice to that."

What the future looks like for this first cohort of students from the Montessori Place remains to be seen. But in the context of increasing focus on academic subjects in secondary education more broadly, the school is perhaps one worth watching.

The Guardian, 15 June 2017,
© Guardian News and Media 2017

WHAT DO YOU THINK?

- **Would this way of learning suit you?**
- **Could traditional schools learn anything from this approach?**
- **What do you think the advantages and disadvantages will be for these students?**

Behaviour in school

What teachers and students think

Surveys conducted by behaviour consultants Pivotal Education (pivotaleducation.com) asked teachers and pupils about discipline.
Teachers believe that managing behaviour in school is an important part of their job.
Only **11%** see themselves as purely subject teachers, who should leave the management of behaviour to others.

How confident teachers feel about dealing with pupil behaviour

 ●% agree ●% disagree

	agree	disagree
Behaviour management is an important skill for a teacher	98%	2%
I am personally responsible for my learner's behaviour	89%	11%
I feel confident in handling learner behaviour in the classroom	90%	10%
I feel confident in handling learner behaviour around the school in general	80%	20%
Behaviour is well managed in my school	69%	31%
Staff in this school deal effectively with behavioural issues around the site	61%	39%

72% of teachers believe that "Learners in this school have a clear understanding about rules and expectations" and **67%** of pupils feel the same way.

Only **7%** of secondary pupils say they don't understand school rules, but **25%** can sometimes be unsure.

However, it seems teachers are frequently having to deal with behavioural problems. **45%** reported an **unpleasant experience** with a pupil within the last week, rising to **60%** within the last month.

28% reported that they had had to **remove a pupil** from class within the last week, rising to **43%** within the last month.

82% of teachers believe that the short term benefit of removing a pupil has long term disadvantages.

Secondary school pupils were asked:

How often are your lessons disrupted?
(per week)

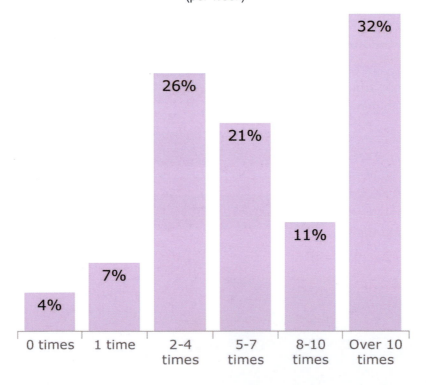

4%	7%	26%	21%	11%	32%
0 times	1 time	2-4 times	5-7 times	8-10 times	Over 10 times

82% of secondary pupils believe that it is the disruptive ones who get the most attention rather than those who try hard.

91% believe that some pupils enjoy the attention they get from bad behaviour.

Most teachers would consider the start of lessons a crucial moment to establish class atmosphere. Secondary students reported that very few lessons started on time.

How long does the lesson usually take to start?

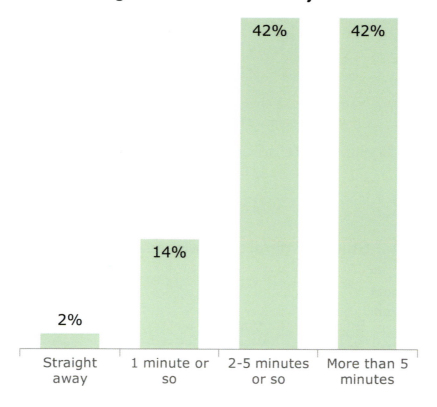

Straight away	1 minute or so	2-5 minutes or so	More than 5 minutes
2%	14%	42%	42%

Most teachers are already in the room when students arrive. **33%** greet them as they come in and **27%** are preparing for the lesson.

21% of teachers are reported to be waiting for everyone to sit down, **13%** are doing something else.

7% usually arrive after the students.

36% of **students** who arrive late apologise and take a seat. **35%** explain and discuss their lateness with the teacher before sitting down. For **14%** of students there is a punishment for lateness while for **12%** nothing happens. **3%** are not allowed into the classroom if they are late.

75% of secondary students said that there are things they can get away with in front of some teachers and not others.

41% adjust their behaviour according to different teachers.

Student interactions with teachers

Secondary school students were asked:

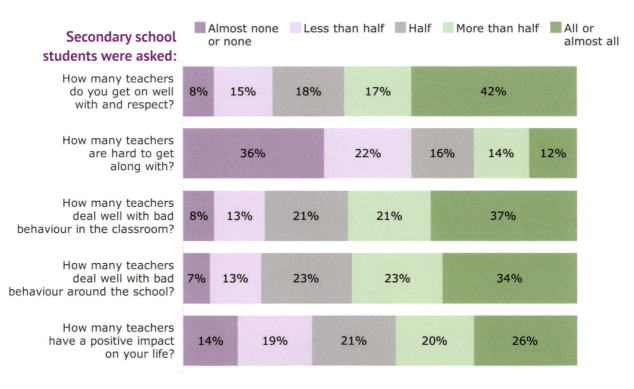

	Almost none or none	Less than half	Half	More than half	All or almost all
How many teachers do you get on well with and respect?	8%	15%	18%	17%	42%
How many teachers are hard to get along with?	36%	22%	16%	14%	12%
How many teachers deal well with bad behaviour in the classroom?	8%	13%	21%	21%	37%
How many teachers deal well with bad behaviour around the school?	7%	13%	23%	23%	34%
How many teachers have a positive impact on your life?	14%	19%	21%	20%	26%

Source: Pivotal Education, a company specialising in training teachers in methods to change behaviour, conducted surveys with 2,900 staff, 2,400 primary learners and 4,000 secondary learners
https://pivotaleducation.com

WHAT DO YOU THINK?

- Do you agree that disruptive pupils get the most attention?
- What are the best methods for dealing with or preventing disruption?
- How much do good relationships between students and teachers matter?

Holidaying in Disney World isn't a human right

JULIA HARTLEY-BREWER

Every parent thinks they're the most qualified person to decide what is best for their child. Jon Platt is one of those parents.

He has spent two long – and very expensive – years fighting his local council after he was fined £120 for taking his daughter out of school during term time for a week's family holiday to Disney World, Florida.

> **More and more parents flout the law, regarding the £60 fine as a small price to pay in return for a cheaper flight**

Yesterday, Mr Platt lost his Supreme Court appeal, despite his insistence that he, rather than the state, is best placed to decide what would most benefit his daughter and her two brothers: a week of boring maths lessons or an exciting one riding rollercoasters. Just because parents think they know best doesn't mean that they actually do.

Indeed, the empirical facts suggest that, with widespread child obesity, a couch-potato lifestyle spent on gadgets and shockingly poor behaviour of so many youngsters, I would hazard a guess that far too many parents blatantly don't know what's best for their children.

That's why I applaud both the Supreme Court decision and the law allowing schools to fine parents who take their children on unauthorised holidays when they should be studying at their school desks.

More and more parents are choosing to flout the law, regarding the £60 fine as a small price to pay in return for a cheaper flight or cut-price hotel out of season.

Indeed, prosecutions of parents like Mr Platt for child truancy leapt by over 60% in just four years after the tough new rules banning unauthorised term-time holidays were brought in.

Mr Platt boasted in court that he does comply with the law because his daughter has a 92% attendance record and therefore attends school "regularly". Yet, that figure means she misses at least a week of school a term – every term. My 10-year-old hasn't missed a full week of lessons over her entire six years at primary school; those occasional days that she has been absent have been thanks to illness, not to her parents' holiday whims.

As much as I cherish our family holidays, I've never taken my daughter out of school for a vacation because, the last time I looked, the right to a term-time break in the sun was not one of the fundamental entitlements listed on the UN Charter of Human Rights.

And even if it was, I have a funny feeling parents who think it should be might feel differently if it was the teacher disappearing off for a week's holiday mid-term, not their own child.

While many parents feel understandably aggrieved at the higher cost of hotels and flights the moment school holidays start, I'm afraid that's just the laws of supply and demand in a free market economy.

Some countries, such as Germany, have sought to tackle this by staggering school holidays by region, to spread out the demand over the year and reduce costs. There's no reason our Government couldn't do the same.

Many parents, like the Platts, also have children at different schools with clashing holiday dates. Again, this could be easily resolved by local councils requiring all schools in their area to synchronise calendars. Likewise, parents who work in the emergency services, who can often struggle to both get time off during school holidays, could be guaranteed an annual week's family break without too much fuss.

Whatever measures are taken, parents like Jon Platt will continue to flout the law because they think their child losing a week here or there of school won't matter. They are wrong.

And term-time holidays don't just damage their own child's education, it affects their classmates, too. If a child misses the week their teacher introduces new concepts such as fractions to the whole class, when that child returns, Miss has to spend her time getting that child up to speed – and that's time she is not spending teaching others.

Anyway, if it's okay for one child to take a week off during term time, then why not two weeks, or three – and why not every child?

Crucially, though, it's not just the lessons that a child doesn't learn while they're on holiday that matter. It's also the lesson they do learn.

School teaches us more than merely the three Rs. It teaches us about life: how to get along with other people, follow rules and prepare for the world of work and adult responsibilities.

Platt boasted in court that his daughter has a 92% attendance record at school. Meanwhile, my 10-year-old hasn't missed a full week of lessons over her entire six years at primary school

Teaching your child that school is optional, something you only do when you fancy it, is all very well, but when they venture out into the big, bad world, they will learn to their cost that remarkably few employers take the same view when it comes to turning up to work.

The crackdown on term-time holidays isn't about undermining parents or hurting families, or putting the State in charge of our lives. It's simply about putting the right of children to their education ahead of their parents' right to a cheap package holiday to Disney World.

Source: The Daily Telegraph, 6 April 2017
© Telegraph Media Group Limited 2017

Term-time holidays don't just damage their own child's education, it affects their classmates, too

In June 2017 the case went back to the Magistrates' Court. Jon Platt was convicted of failing to secure his child's regular attendance. He was given a 12-month conditional discharge and ordered to pay £2,000. The case cost taxpayers £140,000.

At a glance: What are the rules about term-time holidays?

- According to guidelines, you can only allow your child to miss school if they are ill, or if you have received advanced permission from the school.

- Getting permission from the school requires making an application to the head teacher in advance, who will decide if your request will be granted.

- Where, previously, head teachers could grant 10 days of authorised absence, now they are unable to grant any, except in exceptional circumstances.

- If you take your child out of school without permission, you risk receiving a fine of £60, which rises to £120 if not paid within 21 days.

- If you don't pay the fine after 28 days you may be prosecuted for your child's absence from school, and could be fined up to £2,500 or receive a jail sentence of three months.

Source: www.gov.uk

WHAT DO YOU THINK?

- The writer says, "far too many parents blatantly don't know what's best for their children." Do you agree?

- Do you agree that absence during term time damages others and gives out a bad message?

Absence from school

Stricter rules have been applied and fines have been imposed on parents

Local councils and schools in England can use various legal powers if a child is missing school without a good reason. (These rules and fines do not apply in Wales, Northern Ireland and Scotland).

A local council can give parents a fine - sometimes known as a **penalty notice** - of **£60**, which rises to **£120** if they don't pay within 21 days. If they don't pay the fine after 28 days they may be prosecuted for their child's absence from school.

Prosecution: Parents could get a fine of up to **£2,500,** a community order or a **jail sentence** up to 3 months. The court also gives them a **parenting order**.

There were **15,828 prosecutions** in 2015/16 following non-payment of penalty notices.

- If a local authority decides not to bring legal proceedings when a penalty notice remains unpaid after 28 days, the notice is **withdrawn**.

- **22,394 penalty notices** were **withdrawn** in 2015/16 - an increase of **30.9%**, from 2014/15.

Parents can be fined for taking their child on holiday during term time without the school's permission.

Number of penalty notices issued to parents

From September 2013, regulations stated that term time leave could only be granted by headteachers in exceptional circumstances. There has been a sharp increase in penalty notices issued since that date.

QUICK FACTS

- The region with the greatest number of penalty notices issued was the **North West of England** with **27,542 penalty notices** issued in 2015/16.

- The region with the fewest penalty notices was the **North East of England**, with **4,576** penalty notices issued in 2015/16.
  NB the pupil population in the North East is much smaller than the North West.

Year	Penalty notices
2009/10	25,657
2010/11	32,641
2011/12	41,224
2012/13	52,370
2013/14	98,259
2014/15	151,125
2015/16	157,879

Another way to deal with unauthorised absence from school is for the courts to issue a **parenting order** - this means a parent has to attend parenting classes. They also have to do what the court says to improve their child's school attendance.

There were **192 parenting orders** made in 2015/16.

Parenting contract: This is a voluntary agreement between parents and schools or local authorities.

Ways are found to improve the child's attendance. If a parent refuses to make a contract or doesn't stick to it, this can be used as evidence if the local council decides to prosecute them.

Number of parenting contracts offered

72.8% of parenting contracts were accepted by parents during 2015/16.

25,862

19,511

20,019

18,958

18,828

19,885

18,319

| 2009/10 | 2010/11 | 2011/12 | 2012/13 | 2013/14 | 2014/15 | 2015/16 |

Source: Department for Education © Crown copyright 2017

WHAT DO YOU THINK?

- **What are 'exceptional circumstances' which would justify absence?**

- **Are there circumstances in which fines and parenting orders are appropriate?**

- **Are there other ways of dealing with the problem of term time absence?**

Is it too easy to get a first class degree?

One in four students at top universities now receive top honours.

Harry Cockburn

The number of first class degrees being handed out to graduates at British universities has soared to make up almost a quarter of all degrees awarded.

Since 2010, when the cap on tuition fees was raised to £9,250 by the coalition Government, numbers of firsts have risen at almost all universities so that a third of institutions now pass one in four students with top honours.

The new analysis by the Press Association has fuelled renewed debate about grade inflation as well as the structure of the grade classification system that has been in place in the UK for centuries.

Nick Hillman, director of the Higher Education Policy Institute (HEPI), told PA: "Some rise is not unreasonable, given that schools have got better and some universities have increased their entry tariffs so they're getting better quality students."

But he also said greater focus on university league tables may also be a cause for institutions awarding students higher grades in a bid to prevent the university moving down the rankings.

Mr Hillman suggested the system in which external examiners are recruited from other institutions could be open to abuse.

"There are people who think the system isn't as robust as it might be. It can all be a bit cosy - you ask someone you know to be an external examiner."

In addition, many universities mark students' work themselves.

"A comparison would be if schools could decide how many A grades to give in A-levels - it's a big incentive for grade inflation," he said.

Essential Articles & Facts   www.completeissues.co.uk

The PA analysis shows:

- At 50 UK universities - roughly a third of the total - at least 25% of degrees awarded in 2015/16 were a first, while at 10 institutions, more than a third were given the highest award. By contrast, in 2010/11 just 12 institutions gave at least one in four degrees a first, and only two gave more than a third the top honour.

- On average, across all institutions there has been around an eight percentage point rise in firsts in the last five years, the analysis of Higher Education Statistics Agency (HESA) data shows.

- Just seven institutions have seen a fall in the proportion of firsts.

- Five universities and colleges have seen the proportion of top honours rise by at least 20 percentage points, while 40 institutions have seen at least a 10-point hike.

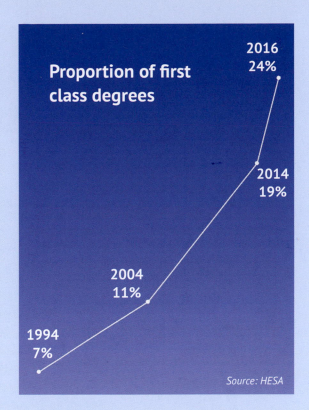

Proportion of first class degrees

2016 24%

2014 19%

2004 11%

1994 7%

Source: HESA

"Many universities mark students' work themselves ...it's a big incentive for grade inflation"

The figures, for the academic years 2010/11 and 2015/16, are based on 148 universities and colleges for which there is comparable data, and exclude degrees rated as "unclassified".

Another factor in the apparent improvement in performance could be a growing work ethic among students.

Mr Hillman said that while grades had risen, contact hours with teachers had not, and students themselves may be working harder now than in recent history.

He said: "As you wander round universities, the student union bars are empty and the libraries and working environments are full.

"They're not putting in more hours, but they are more productive in the hours they are doing."

A spokeswoman for vice-chancellors' group Universities UK told PA degree classifications are a matter for individual institutions.

"Every one of our universities is unique, with a different subject mix, student body, faculties and departments and, of course, different course curricula and content, which makes comparison difficult, but this diversity is valued by students and staff and this is a strength of the UK sector," she said.

"The sector has changed significantly since 2010, with universities putting more emphasis on the quality of teaching and investing in learning support, alongside the fact that with higher fees, students may be working harder to achieve higher grades."

The Independent, 19 July 2017 www.independent.co.uk

WHAT DO YOU THINK?

- **What is your reaction to these figures?**

- **Does it take away value from a top degree if a larger proportion can achieve it?**

- **How much does a degree matter?**

A degree of deceit

Wholesale copying, buying essays and using spy devices in exams; universities are struggling to beat the cheats

It's never a completely level playing field in education. Some kids start off with an advantage and get more help along the way from parents and tutors. But we like to think that in the end hard work and intelligence pay off and only the brightest earn the best marks at university. Yet the internet has spawned a whole industry dedicated to aiding not the most intelligent but the most devious to achieve top marks.

Plagiarism is the practice of passing off someone else's work as your own. It is a form of theft - stealing someone else's ideas, language and work and taking the credit for it. For some years universities and other academic institutions have had strategies in place to detect cheating by students who copy whole passages from sources, especially from the internet. Tutors look out for inconsistencies, a sudden change in writing style or an increase in vocabulary level. Most universities have software in place to help detect examples of students copying.

But a minority of students see nothing wrong with their attempts to obtain a qualification by deceit and a whole industry has grown up around helping them to cheat.

One example is the growth of essay-mills. These are firms which specialise in supplying ready-made essays, theses and dissertations to students who, for whatever reason, are failing to produce the goods themselves. Some justify their existence by saying they are supporting over-stretched students, supplying them with the tools they need to complete their work when they are too stressed. The appeal of the websites, though, is blatant: 'Simply send us your essay question, and we'll locate an expertly qualified writer to create an answer like no other. At university, every essay is your chance to impress - get it right first time and learn smarter today.' says UK Essays. It offers delivery of 1,000 words in 7 days at the level of a first class degree for £275, though you can reduce your costs to £122 if you only aspire to a 2:2!

Education

"Learn smarter today" says one essay-writing firm.

EssayMania has a different appeal - to the cash strapped student: 'Find Us By Your Side When You Ask, "Can Someone Write My Essay For Me Cheap?" Try Us As We Are Professionals." The language of their website certainly calls their professionalism into question: 'We have access number of top class online libraries as we believe to deliver only authentic and latest information to the client.'

More than 20,000 university students are known to have engaged in this contract cheating, a disproportionate number of them from top universities. It is likely that the true figure is higher since this particular form of cheating cannot be detected by plagiarism software so many will have used this method undetected.

Ironically, bright students in difficult financial circumstances can sometimes earn money by working for the essay-mills - who openly tout for candidates - while wealthier students make use of their efforts in a sort of educational serfdom!

New Zealand has acted against the companies engaged in this academic fraud by making the practice illegal. As a result, contract cheating has been reduced - students think twice about cheating when the consequences can be a criminal charge.

Cheating in exams is probably as old as exams themselves. All the 'traditional' methods - the sort you would see in the Beano or old-fashioned school stories - still occur - writing the answers up your arm, sneaking in bits of paper, copying over someone's shoulder, hiding answers that you can access in a toilet break. More modern adaptations include making a facsimile of a drinks label so that cheat material can be written on the back (obviously the drink has to be something opaque, not water). Examiners have found notes written on the soles of shoes, inside jackets, on tiny scrolls of paper within a watch casing and even formulae incorporated into a design on false nails.

But technology presents a whole new range of techniques for fraud - and there is a whole industry dedicated to methods of cheating. One website offers fake glasses so that you can communicate with a partner who feeds you answers. Advertised as "INNOVATIVE SPY DEVICE FOR SUCCESSFUL EXAM" the glasses come with a tiny earpiece to receive information and contain a microphone. The earpiece is tiny enough to be undetectable and the glasses look sufficiently authentic. The top of the range "professional" set costs £374. There is a video demonstrating their use but it does not explain how a cheating student would conceal from an invigilator their need to read out the questions throughout an exam.

The website helpfully contains tips - perhaps we should call this a cheat sheet - on how to assist in the cheating because: "There are situations when your friend cannot get ready for an exam because of some personal reasons. And the best solution to the problem can be cheating in exam with the help of a spy earpiece." It also suggests that the assistant needs to have all the study materials to hand and to familiarise themselves with the subject - in other words to do what a sensible student would have done before the exam.

"The best solution to the problem can be cheating with the help of a spy earpiece"

There are technical variations, too, on the older methods: a pen which can hide an A4 page worth of notes which will be visible only to the student, smart watches which can display exam notes on-screen, but have an "emergency button" to switch the screen display back if the cheating is likely to be detected, an "exam calculator" which can double-up as a screen for stored notes and formulae.

Although some of these methods sound laughably elaborate, there have been genuine attempts to use 'spy' methods to cheat. In its latest annual report the Office of the Independent Adjudicator, which rules on complaints against universities, reported its judgement on one appeal. A law student appealed to the office because her university failed her in all her modules for the year after she was caught cheating in an exam. She had a law book with her, which she was allowed to do, but it contained 24 pages of notes in invisible ink.

She had also brought a UV light into the exam to enable her to read the notes. Not surprisingly she was spotted both by the invigilator and by other students. The cheating student had appealed to the OIA on the grounds that the reaction of the university was an excessive punishment. The OIA judged that the university had acted appropriately.

There is some sympathy for students who find themselves overwhelmed but are desperate to succeed. A little less, perhaps, for those who are desperate because their parents have spent so much to send them to a UK university. It may be that examinations which rely heavily on memory, rather than analysis are more likely to encourage cheating behaviour. There are now calls for the UK to follow New Zealand's example and outlaw essay-mills. It may prove necessary to counter cheat-tech by having airport style searches of students entering exam rooms.

The Law student had notes in invisible ink and a UV light.

In addition to the sheer unfairness of such dishonest practices, the fact that below-par or lazy students can succeed by cheating could eventually undermine the status, value and reputation of degrees from UK universities. For the sake of those students who have earned their marks, we can hope that fear of detection might persuade cheats that the amount of time spent researching, setting up, disguising and, hopefully, regretting cheating tactics might more fruitfully have been spent on revising, learning and even appreciating the value of knowledge.

Sources: Various

WHAT DO YOU THINK?

- Are some forms of cheating worse than others?

- If someone is caught cheating, what should happen?

- What do you think will happen to those students who cheated once they graduate?

Climate extremes

Climate change is reaching disturbing new levels across the Earth

Information from 80 national weather services is used in a report, The State of the Global Climate 2016, to give a more complete picture of the year's climate data.

2016 was the warmest year on record and it saw carbon dioxide (CO2) in the atmosphere rise to a new high, while Arctic sea ice recorded a new winter low.

Temperature: +1.1°C

2016 was the warmest year on record, **1.1 °C** above the pre-industrial period - ie the time before human activity began to have an impact on the climate.

But not all the world warmed at equal speed in 2016

- In the Arctic, temperatures were about **3 °C** above the 1961-1990 average.

- In Svalbard, a Norwegian island high in the Arctic circle, the yearly average was **6.5 °C** above the long-term mark.

Temperatures in 2016 were "substantially influenced" by El Niño - a complex weather pattern resulting from changes in ocean temperatures in the Equatorial Pacific.

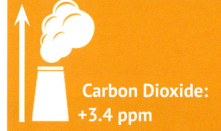

Carbon Dioxide: +3.4 ppm

CO2 reached a record annual average concentration of **400 ppm** (parts per million) in the atmosphere.

The CO2 rise in 2016 was the fastest on record - **3.4 ppm** per year.

Sea-surface temperature: +3°C

Higher sea-surface temperatures, as much as **3 °C** above average in some areas, are thought to be the cause of dramatic changes to the physical, chemical and biological state of the marine environment with great impacts on food chains and marine ecosystems, as well as important fisheries.

When sea temperatures rise the algae that live on coral and give it its colour cannot be sustained (coral bleaching). The coral begins to die off - with consequences for the marine environment.

The very warm ocean temperatures contributed to major coral bleaching in some tropical waters. Among the areas greatly affected was the Great Barrier Reef, Australia, where there were record high sea-surface temperatures.

Sea ice: -4m square km

The extent of global sea ice dropped more than **4 million square km** below average.

Scientific research shows that changes in the Arctic and melting sea ice are leading to a shift in the way the oceans and the atmosphere move. This is affecting weather in other parts of the world because of waves in the jet stream – the fast moving band of air which helps regulate temperatures.

Sea-levels: +20cm

Globally sea levels have risen by **20 cm** since the start of the twentieth century. This is mostly due to the oceans warming and expanding and the melting of glaciers and ice caps.

Global sea levels rose strongly during the 2015/2016 El Niño, rising about **15 mm** between November 2014 and February 2016.

Weather:

Severe **droughts** affected agriculture in many parts of the world, particularly in southern and eastern Africa and parts of Central America, where several million people experienced food insecurity and hundreds of thousands were displaced internally.

Hurricane Matthew in the North Atlantic was one of the most damaging **weather-related disasters**, responsible for the deaths of at least 546 in Haiti and 49 in the USA.

Hurricane Matthew hits Haiti

NASA Earth Observatory image by Joshua Stevens

"...we are seeing other remarkable changes across the planet that are challenging the limits of our understanding of the climate system. We are now in truly uncharted territory,"

World Climate Research Programme Director David Carlson

Statement on the State of the Global Climate © World Meteorological Organization, 2017
https://public.wmo.int/en

WHAT DO YOU THINK?

- Do you think you have directly experienced any of the effects of climate change?
- What concerns you most about these facts?
- What do you think could be done to stop or slow down climate change?

'Luxury water' for £80 a bottle? It's ignorant, insensitive and irresponsible

Katherine Purvis

Limited edition water harvested from melting polar icebergs, is now on sale at Harrods. It's just another ugly indicator of our world's many inequalities

We've reached peak bottled water. From today, for a sweet £80, Harrods will sell 'luxury water' harvested from icebergs off the coast of Svalbard.

Svalbarði is the brainchild of Jamal Qureshi, a Norwegian-American Wall Street businessman who visited the archipelago in 2013, and returned with melted iceberg water as a gift for his wife. He then, it seems, decided to bring this water to more people.

Astonishingly, the governor of Svalbard has approved Qureshi's venture. He charters an icebreaker to make two expeditions a year, in the summer and the autumn when icebergs calve away from glaciers that run into the sea. One-tonne pieces of ice are carved from these floating bergs at a time. Using a crane and a net, they are lifted onto the boat and taken to Longyearbyen to be melted down into bottles of "polar iceberg water" which has "the taste of snow in air". On each expedition, Qureshi plans to harvest 15 tonnes of ice to produce 13,000 bottles.

The environmental sustainability of the venture is the first concern of many people, Qureshi told the Guardian. "But we're carbon neutral certified, and we're supporting renewable energy projects in East Africa and China," he said. "We also only take icebergs that are already floating in the water and would usually melt in a few weeks, and that can't be used for hunting [by polar bears]."

Some may argue that if you can afford to drink melted ice caps, who should stop you? Your money, your choice. Depleting 30 tonnes of iceberg a year is, arguably, not that much in the grand scheme of things. But Qureshi's venture is not the first of its kind. Tibet has already approved licences for dozens of companies to tap Himalayan glaciers for 'premium' bottled drinking water. Ten major rivers that flow into South Asia depend on the Qinghai-Tibet Plateau. Disrupting their source could have devastating impacts for water security across the region.

And this is not the only problem. First, sea ice is already melting. The extent of Arctic

sea ice shrank to its second lowest record last year and scientists have warned this could have devastating impacts across the rest of the world, such as shifts in snow distribution that warm the ocean and change climate patterns as far as Asia, as well as the collapse of key Arctic fisheries, which could impact other ocean ecosystems. Icebergs don't need yet more human interference – no matter how small the scale – to speed up the melting process.

Second, the bottled water industry is already giving us enough of a headache. It is estimated that 3l of water are need to produce just one 1l plastic bottle of water, which is more likely to be discarded and end up in landfill than recycled. Beside the fact that our planet is slowly silting up with plastic, it also takes huge amounts of fossil fuels to make water bottles – plastic or glass – and transport them around the world. In the US, for example, 1.5 million barrels of oil are needed per year to meet the demand of the country's water bottle manufacturing.

But surely the most problematic aspect of this product is the sheer insensitivity of exploiting one of the world's last wildernesses, and charging such a high price for its product? This, while 663 million people currently live without safe water. Consider the extremes: one person pays £80 to drink water, never before touched by humans and preserved by micron filters and UV light, while another – one of 159 million– depends on surface water, vulnerable to contamination by faeces, parasites, pesticides and more. The emergence of luxury water is just another ugly indicator of our world's many inequalities.

For so many of the things we buy, there is a flashier, pricier, more luxurious alternative for those who can afford it. Why travel in economy if you could travel first class? Why buy from the high-street when you could buy designer clothing? Water, it seems, is just the next in a list to receive this divisive treatment; why, if you live somewhere it is clean and safe, drink water from a tap when you could drink bottled water from "pristine peaks", "artesian aquifers" and now "from the top of the world"?

The wheels are in motion. Precedents have been set. Will more wealthy entrepreneurs now eye up other precious natural resources to create yet another "must-have" item?

We already live beyond our means. Our lifestyle choices see us using the equivalent of 1.6 Earths to provide the resources we consume, and absorb what we throw away. At such a time, Svalbarði seems insensitive,

ignorant and irresponsible. It's time to live sustainably and consume responsibly, not promote mindless habits just because some people can afford it.

For some time, water has been thought of as a commodity, and even the former UN special rapporteur on the human rights to safe drinking water and sanitation believes it doesn't have to be free. But something so precious, so essential to all life – human, animal and mineral – should never be marketed as a luxury.

Source: The Guardian, 15 February 2017
© Guardian News & Media 2017

A million plastic bottles are bought around the world every minute

QUICK FACTS

- More than **480bn** plastic drinking bottles were sold in 2016 across the world, up from about **300bn** a decade ago - if placed end to end, they would extend more than halfway to the sun.

- By 2021 this will increase by **20%** to **583.3bn**.

- Fewer than half of the bottles bought in 2016 were collected for recycling and just **7%** of those collected were turned into new bottles. Instead most plastic bottles produced end up in landfill or in the ocean.

- Between **5m** and **13m** tonnes of plastic leaks into the world's oceans each year to be ingested by sea birds, fish and other organisms, and by 2050 the ocean will contain more plastic by weight than fish.

- In the UK **38.5m** plastic bottles are used every day – only just over half make it to recycling, while more than **16m** are put into landfill, burnt or leak into the environment and oceans each day.

Sources: Various

WHAT DO YOU THINK?

- 'Your money, your choice.' Do you agree?
- Why has bottled water become so popular and what are the alternatives?
- Do we all have a right to safe drinking water for free?

Climate change

People around the world are concerned

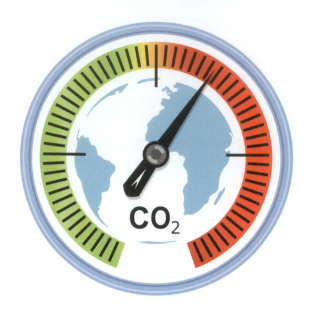

The Pew Research Center surveyed 45,435 adults aged 18 and over in 40 nations about their climate change concerns.

The majority thought global warming was a serious problem but the level of concern varied.

People in the US and China were least concerned despite their countries having the highest overall carbon dioxide (CO2) emissions.

Those who thought global warming was a VERY SERIOUS problem

(Regional medians*)

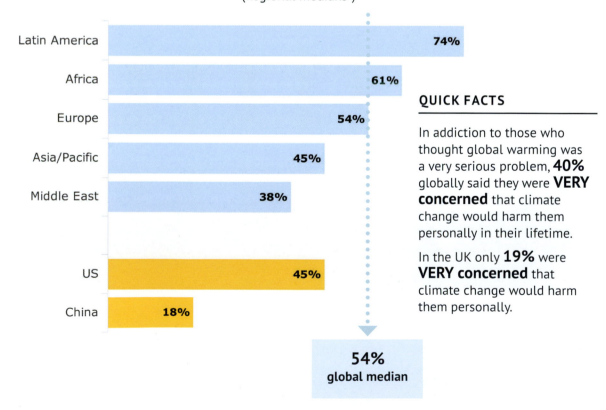

Region	%
Latin America	74%
Africa	61%
Europe	54%
Asia/Pacific	45%
Middle East	38%
US	45%
China	18%

54%
global median

QUICK FACTS

In addiction to those who thought global warming was a very serious problem, **40%** globally said they were **VERY concerned** that climate change would harm them personally in their lifetime.

In the UK only **19%** were **VERY concerned** that climate change would harm them personally.

*Median - The middle value when a range of values are put in order lowest to highest
NB Russia and Ukraine not included in any European medians

The consequences of climate change

Those surveyed were given a list of four potential effects of global warming and asked which **ONE** most concerned them.

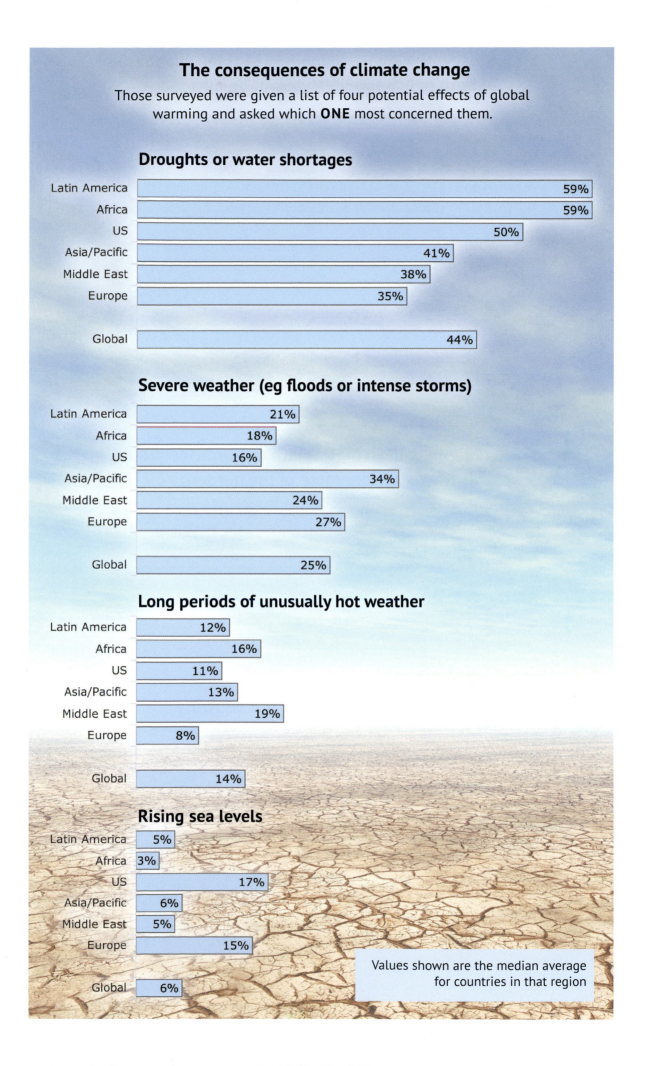

Droughts or water shortages

Latin America	59%
Africa	59%
US	50%
Asia/Pacific	41%
Middle East	38%
Europe	35%
Global	44%

Severe weather (eg floods or intense storms)

Latin America	21%
Africa	18%
US	16%
Asia/Pacific	34%
Middle East	24%
Europe	27%
Global	25%

Long periods of unusually hot weather

Latin America	12%
Africa	16%
US	11%
Asia/Pacific	13%
Middle East	19%
Europe	8%
Global	14%

Rising sea levels

Latin America	5%
Africa	3%
US	17%
Asia/Pacific	6%
Middle East	5%
Europe	15%
Global	6%

Values shown are the median average for countries in that region

To deal with climate change, most think changes in both policy and lifestyle will be necessary.

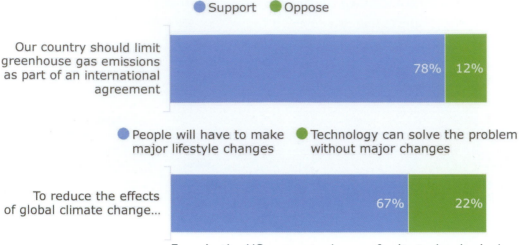

● Support   ● Oppose

Our country should limit greenhouse gas emissions as part of an international agreement

78%   12%

● People will have to make major lifestyle changes   ● Technology can solve the problem without major changes

To reduce the effects of global climate change...

67%   22%

Even in the US, a country known for its technological advances, only **23%** believe technology alone can solve climate change.

People believe that wealthier countries should shoulder more of the burden:

● Rich countries should do more   ● Developing countries should do just as much

To address global climate change...

54%   38%

Source: Global Concern about Climate Change Report – Pew Research Center

Paris Climate Agreement

In 2015, 195 countries joined a groundbreaking deal to keep global temperatures from rising more than 2°C. Scientists warn that a rise above this would be disastrous for our planet.

Each country is allowed to decide its own contribution to reducing greenhouse gas emissions.

At the end of May 2017, the US withdrew from the Paris agreement.

WHAT DO YOU THINK?

- Do you view climate change as a serious issue?

- What action should be taken to deal with climate change?

- People were asked if climate change would affect them in their lifetime. Why is this a good question to ask? What other questions could be asked?

Biological Annihilation

Chris Graham

The Earth is undergoing a sixth mass extinction, with scientists warning that the "biological annihilation" of wildlife is "more severe than perceived".

Researchers from the National Autonomous University of Mexico and from Stanford University in the US have published a stark warning about the risks to animal species and how little time is left to act.

Blaming the overpopulation and over-consumption of humans, the researchers said the world had a window of about 20-30 years at most to tackle the crisis.

"Earth is experiencing a huge episode of population declines and extirpations" - when a species is wiped out in a particular location - "which will have negative cascading consequences on ecosystem functioning and services vital to sustaining civilisation," the researchers wrote in the journal Proceedings of the National Academy of Sciences.

"We describe this as a 'biological annihilation' to highlight the current magnitude of Earth's ongoing sixth major extinction event."

In the study, researchers from Stanford University and the National Autonomous University of Mexico examined the population trends of 27,600 vertebrate species such as birds, amphibians, mammals, and reptiles, including a detailed analysis of 177 species of mammals.

They found that as much as 50% of the number of individuals animals that once shared Earth with us have already disappeared and billions of populations of animals are gone.

The detailed study of 177 species found most of them have lost more than 40% of their geographic ranges over the years, and almost half have lost more than 80% of their ranges in the period between 1900–2015.

Among the species found to be in danger were cheetahs, with only 7,000 left alive in 2016. There were fewer than 5,000 Borneo and Sumatran orangutans and populations of the African lion had dropped 43% since 1993.

"We emphasise that the sixth mass extinction is already here and the window for effective action is very short, probably two or three decades at most," the scientists wrote.

The main factors behind these losses are human overpopulation and continued population growth, and overconsumption, especially by the rich.

This swift decline in wildlife has "is already damaging the services ecosystems provide to civilisation", the study found.

"The serious warning in our paper needs to be heeded because civilisation depends utterly on the plants, animals, and microorganisms of Earth that supply it with essential ecosystem services ranging from crop pollination and protection to supplying food from the sea and maintaining a livable climate," Prof Paul Ehrlich, one of the scientists involved in the study, told the Guardian.

The scientists conclude: "The resulting biological annihilation obviously will have serious ecological, economic and social consequences. Humanity

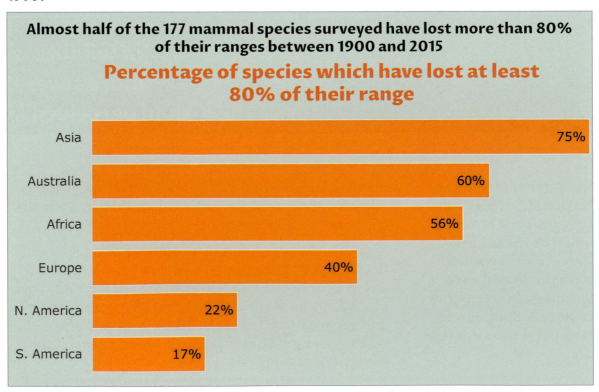

Almost half of the 177 mammal species surveyed have lost more than 80% of their ranges between 1900 and 2015

Percentage of species which have lost at least 80% of their range

Asia	75%
Australia	60%
Africa	56%
Europe	40%
N. America	22%
S. America	17%

will eventually pay a very high price for the decimation of the only assemblage of life that we know of in the universe."

"All signs point to ever more powerful assaults on biodiversity in the next two decades, painting a dismal picture of the future of life, including human life," they wrote.

While the world has seen five extinctions in its history, the current one is unfolding much quicker.

Noting that the Earth had lost 200 species of vertebrates in the past 100 years alone, the researchers said that if it had followed the trends of the past two million years, those losses should have taken place over 10,000 years.

Top twelve mammals under risk of extinction

Clouded leopard (Neofelis nebulosa)
Tiger (Panthera tigris)
Marbled cat (Pardofelis marmorata)
Bactrian camel (Camelus ferus)
Takin (Budorcas taxicolor)
Nilgiri tahr (Nilgiritragus hylocrius)
Long-beaked echidna (Zaglossus bruijnii)
Giant ground pangolin (Smutsia gigantea)
Aye aye (Daubentonia madagascariensis)
Madagascan fruit bat (Pterofus rufus)
Collared brown lemur (Eulemur collaris)
Sulawesi giant squirrel (Rubrisciurus rubriventer)

Elizabeth Kolbert, author of "The Sixth Extinction", said humans were leaving the world "a much, much poorer place".

"An extinction should be something that's very unusual," Ms Kolbert told CBS News. "When you can identify lots of species that have gone extinct or are on the verge of extinction, that's actually a very unusual time in the Earth's history and a very dangerous one."

Daily Telegraph, 11 July 2017 © Telegraph News & Media Ltd 2017

Earth's five previous mass extinctions

- **443 million years ago - Ordovician:** A severe ice age led to sea level falling by 100m, wiping out 60-70% of all species which were prominently ocean dwellers at the time. Then soon after the ice melted leaving the oceans starved of oxygen.

- **About 360 million years ago - Late Devonian:** A messy prolonged climate change event, again hitting life in shallow seas very hard, killing 70% of species including almost all corals.

- **About 250 million years ago - Permian-Triassic:** The big one – more than 95% of species perished, including trilobites and giant insects – strongly linked to massive volcanic eruptions in Siberia that caused a savage episode of global warming.

- **About 200 million years ago: Triassic-Jurassic:** Three-quarters of species were lost, again most likely due to another huge outburst of volcanism. It left the Earth clear for dinosaurs to flourish.

- **65 million years ago - Cretaceous-Tertiary:** A giant asteroid impact on Mexico, just after large volcanic eruptions in what is now India, saw the end of the dinosaurs and ammonites. Mammals, and eventually humans, took advantage.

You don't need a scientist to know what's causing the sixth mass extinction

Paul R Ehrlich

It's simple. It's us. The more people there are, the more habitats we destroy. Human civilisation can only survive if the population begins to shrink

One should not need to be a scientist to know that human population growth and the accompanying increase in human consumption are the root cause of the sixth mass extinction we're currently seeing. All you need to know is that every living being has evolved to have a set of habitat requirements.

An organism can't live where the temperature is too hot or too cold. If it lives in water, it requires not only an appropriate temperature range, but also appropriate salinity, acidity and other chemical characteristics. If it is a butterfly, it must have access to plants suitable for its caterpillars to eat. A lion requires plant-eaters to catch and devour. A tree needs a certain amount of sunlight and access to soil nutrients and water. A falciparum malaria parasite can't survive and reproduce without Anopheles mosquitos in its habitat and a human bloodstream to infest.

The human population has grown so large that roughly 40% of the Earth's land surface is now farmed to feed people – and none too well at that. Largely due to persistent problems with distribution, almost 800 million people go to bed hungry, and between one and two billion suffer from malnutrition.

As a consequence of its booming population, Homo sapiens has taken much of the most fertile land to grow plants for its own consumption. But guess what? That cropland is generally not rich in food plants suitable for the caterpillars of the 15,000 butterfly species with which we share the planet. Few butterflies require the wheat, corn or rice on which humans largely depend. From the viewpoint of most

Photo: Comma butterfly by Debbie Fuller

Human demands cause both habitat destruction and outright extermination of wildlife.

of the Earth's wildlife, farming can be viewed as "habitat destruction". And, unsurprisingly, few species of wildlife have evolved to live on highways, or in strip malls, office buildings, kitchens or sewers – unless you count Norway rats, house mice, European starlings and German roaches. Virtually everything humanity constructs provides an example of habitat destruction.

The more people there are, the more products of nature they demand to meet their needs and wants: timber, seafood, meat, gas, oil, metal ores, rare earths and rare animals to eat or to use for medicinal purposes. Human demands cause both habitat destruction and outright extermination of wildlife. So when you watch the expansion of the human enterprise; when you see buildings springing up; when you settle down to dinner at home or in a restaurant; you are observing (and often participating in) the sixth mass extinction.

The expanding human population not only outright destroys habitats, it also alters them to the detriment of wildlife (and often people themselves). The more people there are, the more greenhouse gases flow into the atmosphere, and the greater the impacts on wildlife that require specific temperature ranges.

And the more people there are, the more cities, roads, farm fields, fences and other barriers preventing wildlife from moving to areas of more favourable temperature or humidity in a rapidly changing climate. Less recognised, but perhaps even more dangerous to both people and wildlife, is the increasing toxification of the entire planet with synthetic chemicals. Growing populations want myriad more items of plastic that often leak toxic chemicals: more cosmetics, cleansing compounds, pesticides, herbicides, preservatives and industrial chemicals. Many of these novel chemicals mimic natural hormones, and in tiny quantities can alter the development of animals or human children, with potentially catastrophic consequences. As with climate disruption, this is one more case of human overpopulation threatening civilisation.

So we don't really need the evidence meticulously gathered and analysed by the scientific community showing the unusual and accelerating extermination of wildlife populations – and ultimately, species – to know that human population growth is a major and growing driver of the sixth mass extinction, just as it is with the related accelerating climate disruption. It will take a long time to humanely stop that growth and start the gradual shrinkage of the human population that is required if civilisation is to persist. All the more reason we should have started a half century ago, when the problem first came to public attention.

Paul R Ehrlich is a professor of population studies at Stanford University and the author of The Population Bomb (1968)

The Guardian, 11 July 2017 © Guardian News & Media 2017

WHAT DO YOU THINK?

- Do you agree that human beings are wholly to blame for this problem?
- What are the first steps that should be taken to control the impact of human life on the planet?
- Does it really matter if species die out?

FROZEN ARK
FREEZING EARTH'S FUTURE

What does the word 'ark' mean to you? Almost certainly a picture from childhood of a great wooden ship with pairs of animals walking calmly up the gangplank while Noah casts a worried glance at the threatening clouds. It's actually a picture of hope, since after the flood Noah is able to repopulate the natural world with the animals he has saved from extinction. There's another ark, a modern interpretation of Noah's vessel, based in land-locked Nottingham and relying on science to save endangered creatures.

The Frozen Ark Project, a UK charity based at the University of Nottingham, focuses on animals threatened with extinction and tries to collect genetic material both to help in the conservation of species and to ensure that attributes, that we may not even be aware of but which could benefit society and life on earth, are not lost. Conservationists are doing their best, but thousands of species, across all animal groups, are becoming extinct. The loss of a species destroys the results of millions of years of evolution. If cells are preserved, precious information about the species is saved - information which could be vital in saving species or developing new medicines.

The project's mission is summed up on its website: "Time is running out for many species. Conservation efforts will undoubtedly save some but we must preserve the genetic record of all endangered species for our future."

The source of the problem - mankind

Animal species are dying out at an unprecedented rate and mankind is responsible. The increase in human populations and the demands we make on the planet have caused a rise in extinctions. Our increasing requirements for land, food, water, raw materials, access and leisure put pressure on animal populations and their habitats. Human intervention, even when it is well-meaning, can disrupt the balance of nature, with disastrous consequences. Global warming is also a major contributor to the destruction of species.

GIANT AFRICAN LAND SNAIL   Photo: Ventura/Flickr

Can grow to over 20cm long

ROSY WOLF SNAIL   Photo: Scot Nelson/Flickr

Adults are typically 7-10cm long

PARTULA SNAIL   Photo: John Slapcinsky/Flickr

Up to 2.5cm long

What the Frozen Ark does

The Frozen Ark Project is not a substitute for conservation, but a backup of genetic material for the good of future generations. Samples are taken from captive breeding programmes, from zoos and from wild populations. It is hoped that no more animals will be allowed to approach extinction without such material being conserved. An international group of museums, zoos, aquaria and research laboratories, are all committed to the long-term preservation of genetic material.

The Ark has 48,000 samples from 5,000 species stored in a variety of ways. The ambition is to "save the genetic heritage of just about everything" according to Professor Ed Louis, one of the trustees of the project. The samples include material from the scimitar horned oryx (extinct in the wild), and from endangered species such as the snow leopard and Malayan tapir. On a smaller scale, but possibly even more crucially, the Ark has a collection of honey bee samples free from the varroa mite which has been causing such destruction to honey bee colonies.

The Frozen Ark initiative was inspired by research conducted by Professor Bryan Clarke, his wife Dr Ann Clarke and their colleagues. The story of how the Ark began illustrates the effect mankind can have - even with the best of intentions - on a population of creatures, and why the Ark matters.

Starting small - and slow! The story of some snails

In the 1940s the Giant African Land Snail was deliberately brought into the islands of the South Pacific with the intention that it would become a cheap and sustainable source of protein for the islanders. These snails are adaptable, fast growing and produce hundreds of young. However, they were not popular as food for people who had never included snails in their diets. The molluscs escaped from their containers and soon became pests, eating so many crops that they were damaging the economy of the islands.

A carnivorous snail - the Rosy Wolf Snail - was brought into the islands in an attempt to control the African Land Snail. The Rosy Wolf Snail, which is a native of the southern part of the United States, follows the trails of other slugs and snails and devours them. These cannibal snails were supposed to solve the problem but instead they (or rather the humans who introduced them) were responsible for the extinction of almost all of the 58 species of the smaller Partula tree snails which only live in those islands.

Professor Clarke was among the people responsible for collecting the few remaining Partula snails for a breeding programme and sending them to zoos around the world, with the intention that they would eventually be re-introduced to the islands around Tahiti. He also collected tissue samples to preserve their DNA.

Both Professor Clarke and Doctor Clarke presumed that someone must be doing similar work for all endangered species but they found that there was no project which was looking at all animal species and that invertebrates - the uncuddly but vital creatures - were particularly neglected.

There were people working separately in museums and universities but the Clarkes and their colleagues were concerned that the methods of preservation would not be suitable in the long term and that these efforts were not targeted at endangered species. They resolved to set up a centre for collaboration, cooperation and the sharing of samples and expertise - and so the Frozen Ark Project came into being.

The Ark is not without its critics. To some people it seems like an admission of defeat - that collecting tissue samples means giving up on preserving populations of living animals. But the Ark's supporters believe that conservation may very well depend on its store of genetic material. The project is intended to reach out - to educate, inform, collaborate and develop new methods.

The threats to the earth's diverse animal population require a response in the same life-preserving style as the Biblical one. The Frozen Ark website sums up its mission:

"We won't know what we've lost if we don't have a record. Can we restore the beauty we have enjoyed for our children's children? Can we find new materials, new medicine, new solutions from what Nature has already tried and tested?"

Sources: https://frozenark.org and others

WHAT DO YOU THINK?

- **How necessary do you think this project is?**

- **How important is it that we preserve traces of all animals, even the less 'attractive' ones?**

- **The Frozen Ark is a charity. How much support should it get from governments?**

Wolves and brown bears could return to the British countryside to 'naturally cut the deer population'

Sarah Knapton

They are the snarling beasts of fiction and folklore, but conservationists are hoping to bring back wolves to the British countryside within the next 20 years.

The Wildwood Trust, which has successfully helped reintroduce beavers, water voles, pine martins and dormice to parts of the UK where they had become extinct, now wants to start 'rewilding' the country with larger creatures.

In March, the Trust brought a pack of six wolves from Sweden to its 200 acre parkland site in Escot, East Devon, where their behaviour is being monitored as part of an ongoing research project into animal domestication, and to see how they adapt to living in Britain.

Experts believe that introducing wolves back into the countryside could help control the burgeoning deer population which now stands at around 1.5 million animals, the highest it has been for 1,000 years.

Deer have no natural predators, and cause destruction to woodland habitat which provides food and shelter for native species. They also are responsible for around 50,000 traffic accidents and the death of 20 people each year.

Peter Smith, CEO of the Wildwood Trust, said the charity wants to reintroduce lynx in the next few years, followed by wolves in around two decades, and brown bears within 50 years. But they first must meet rewilding protocols set out by the International Union for Conservation of Nature (IUCN) and then gain a licence from Natural England.

"These animals were all once native to Britain, and the benefits they could bring to the ecology of Britain would be immense," he said

"Wolves and lynx will change the behaviour of the deer, causing populations to drop naturally, which helps plants and trees to flourish.

"There are wolves all over Europe and they don't cause problems. When was the last time you heard of someone being killed by a wolf?

"Statistics show that you have more chance of being killed in a car going to visit a wolf in captivity than you have of being attacked by one in the wild. And no lynx has ever killed a child or a human. Reintroducing them could allow our children the chance to enjoy our amazing natural heritage which has been wiped out by upland sheep farming."

Wolves have not existed in Britain for around 300 years after they were hunted to extinction to allow sheep farming to expand at the height of the wool trade.

Calls for their reintroduction dates from 1999 when Dr Martyn Gorman, a senior lecturer in zoology at Aberdeen University suggested they should be brought back to deal with the 350,000 deer in the Scottish Highlands which were damaging trees. However the idea was shelved following an outcry from sheep farmers.

The issue was raised again following a study in 2007 by Imperial College London which concluded wolf reintroduction into the Scottish Highlands and English countryside would aid in the re-establishment of plants and birds currently hampered by the deer population.

"When was the last time you heard of someone being killed by a wolf?"

It followed the successful introduction of wolves to Yellowstone Park, Wyoming, in 1995, which radically improved the ecosystem. With a new predator to worry about, populations of elk were forced to roam further afield to avoid being hunted, allowing trees and bushes to recover and native species to flourish.

The Lynx Trust has also been campaigning for the reintroduction of the wild cats in Scotland and Kielder Forest in Northumberland for several years.

The lynx was once native to the British Isles but the last British lynx was hunted to extinction for its fur around 700AD.

Calls for the introduction of lynx follow successful breeding programmes in Europe which have seen numbers of the Iberian lynx triple in 15 years. The Iberian lynx, which is the type campaigners are hoping to introduce, mostly eat rabbits and are around the size of a large dog.

The Trust has applied for a licence from Natural England and Scottish Natural Heritage to reintroduce the animals and is waiting to find out if the request will be granted.

But the National Farmers Union has raised concerns that predators like lynx and wolves would hunt highland sheep, pet dogs and may even attack ramblers.

The Iberian lynx mostly eat rabbits and are around the size of a large dog

NFU countryside adviser Claire Robinson said: "The arguments for rewilding appear idealistic and ignore the economic impacts.

"Any species introduction, particularly if it has not been in this country for hundreds of years, would also have a massive impact on the many benefits that the countryside delivers and we do not know how such animals would behave in the current environment.

"We also have concerns over the impact on farm animals particularly lambs, given that many examples of rewilding focus on upland locations."

However Mr Smith said: "Actually it may be beneficial for farmers because when lynx and wolves are around there are fewer foxes and badgers. There is evidence to show fox populations drop to a quarter when lynx are present."

The Wildwood Trust is hoping that the new wolves, named Elvis, Sting, Lemmy, Moby and their sisters, PJ and KD, will help rehabilitate their reputation in the eyes of the public.

The Daily Telegraph, 30 June 2017
© Telegraph Media Group Limited 2017

Deer are responsible for around 50,000 traffic accidents and 20 deaths per year

WHAT DO YOU THINK?

- What is your first reaction to the idea?

- Who should have a say in this decision?

- If wolves, lynx and bears were brought back into Britain, would that change how you felt or behaved in the countryside?

Social relationships

Having friends and feeling part of a community is really important for our health and wellbeing

Our relationships with friends

83% of people said they had good relationships with their friends and for **47%,** these relationships were said to be very good.

Gender: 86% of women said they had good relationships with their friends compared to **80%** of men.

Age: Older people are more positive about their friendships than younger people. **90%** of those who were **65 or older** said they had good relationships with their friends, compared to **80%** of those aged **16-24** and **25-49**. Possibly older people having more time to spend with their friends, without pressure from work and the demands of bringing up children.

Quality of friendship: 45% of people with very good relationships with their friends said they felt good about themselves often or all the time, compared to **20%** of people with average friendship quality.

The better the relationships we have with our friends, the more likely we are to feel good about ourselves, and the less likely we are to feel down.

Percentage of people who had one or more close friends

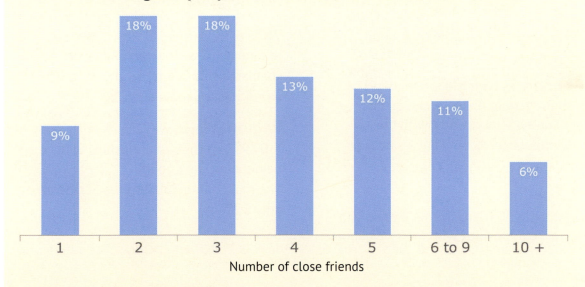

Number of close friends

QUICK FACTS: NO CLOSE FRIENDS

- **13%** of those surveyed in 2015 had **no close friends**. This was an increase from **10%** in 2014 and **6%** in 2010.

- **45%** of them said they felt lonely at least some of the time, and **18%** said they feel lonely often or all of the time.

- **40%** said they never or rarely felt good about themselves.

Friends might be the most important **social** (not family or couple) relationships we have, but they are not the only wider social relationships we have. Those surveyed were also asked about their relationships with their neighbours.

Our relationships with neighbours

60% of people said they had good relationships with their neighbours.

Gender: As with friends, there was a slight gender divide in the quality of people's relationships with their neighbours. **62%** of women said their relationship was good compared to **57%** of men.

Age: As with friends, older people had better relationships with their neighbours.

78% of those aged **65 or older** said their relationships with neighbours were good, compared to **50%** of people aged **25-49**, and **35%** of people aged **16-24**.

Region: Wales was the most neighbourly – **67%** said their relationships with neighbours were good.
The most un-neighbourly was **London** at only **52%**.

Source: YouGov survey of over 5,000 people in the UK for Relate.
The Way We Are Now – The state of the UK's relationships www.relate.org.uk

WHAT DO YOU THINK?

• **How many friends and how many close friends would you say you have?**

• **What qualities make a good friend?**

• **What qualities make a good neighbour?**

Families

A snapshot of family structures and relationships within them

In 2016 there were **18.9 million** families in the UK.

A family is a defined as: a married, civil partnered or cohabiting couple with or without children, or a lone parent, with at least one child, who lives at the same address. The children can be dependent - aged under 16 or 16-18 and in full time education, or non dependent -aged over 18 but still living in the family home.

Families have changed a lot over the years and continue to change.

A family relationship survey of more than 5,000 people aged 16+ across the UK found that, on the whole, relationships were good within families.

How UK families were made up, 2016
(in millions of families)

Married or civil partner couple family with dependent children	4.8
Married or civil partner couple family without dependent children	7.9
Cohabiting couple family with dependent children	1.3
Cohabiting couple family without dependent children	2
Lone parent family with dependent children	1.9
Lone parent family with non dependent children only	1

QUICK FACTS

- There were **12.7 million** married or civil partner couple families with or without dependent children. This was the most common type of family

- Cohabiting couple families were the fastest growing family type, more than doubling from **1.5 million** families in 1996 to **3.3 million** families in 2016.

- Around **25%** of young adults aged 20 to 34 were living with their parents, an increase from **21%** in 1996.

- Around **7.7 million** people lived alone, the majority were women.

Relationships with immediate family

- **81%** had a good relationship with their mum.

- **75%** had a good relationship with their dad.

- **Gender:** Relationships with mums didn't differ by gender but relationships with dads did - **77%** of daughters said they had good relationships with their dad compared to **72%** of sons.

- **Age:** Relationships with dads also appeared to improve with age in a way that those with mum didn't - **72%** of those aged **16-30** said they had a good relationships with their dad but among those aged **31-50** this was **76%**.

- **Siblings: 70%** said they had good relationships with their brothers and sisters.

- **91%** said they had a **good** relationship with their children - **73%** saying the relationship was **very good**.

- Dads had slightly lower levels of **good** relationships with children than mums - around **93%** for mums and **88%** for dads.

- The difference between mums and dads who said they had **very good** relationships with their children was bigger at around **78%** for mums and **67%** for dads.

Relationships with grandparents

Grandparents have always played an important role in family life. Increasingly they provide essential childcare to help parents to return to work and are becoming even more central to family life in the 21st century.

- **88%** of grandparents said they had good relationships with their grandchildren.

- But a lower proportion of grandchildren said they had a good relationship with their grandparents - **71%**. This might be because the value of our family relationships increases as we get older.

- **Gender:** As with relationships with children, there was a gender difference - **92%** of grandmothers said they had good relationships with their grandchildren compared to just **84%** of grandfathers.

As parental relationship breakdown has increased over the years, this has created a rise of the 'blended family' as parents form new relationships.

Family relationships after separation

- **89%** of parents who were divorced or separated said they had **good** relationships with their children - **69%** said they were **very good**.

- Relationships with stepchildren, however, were of a lower quality than with parents' own children - **61%** of step-parents said they had good relationships with their stepchildren – compared to the **91%** who had reported good relationships with their own children.

- The proportion of people who said they had a good relationship with their step-parents, was lower than for relationships with parents - **49%** said they had a good relationships with step-parents.

- **By gender:** Men were more likely to say they had a good relationships with their stepchildren than women: **65%** of stepdads compared to **57%** of stepmums.

Source: Office for National Statistics - Families and households in the UK: 2016 © Crown copyright 2016
www.ons.gov.uk
YouGov survey for Relate, The Way We Are Now - The state of the UK's relationships
www.relate.org.uk

WHAT DO YOU THINK?

- **How many different types of family do you know?**

- **What qualities and attitudes help a family to get along well with each other?**

- **How important is the extended family - aunts, uncles, cousins and so on?**

Why race has no place when a child needs a home

Jenny McCartney

Once again, race has proved a bar to adoption in the UK. This time, Sandeep and Reena Mander, a British-born Sikh couple living in Berkshire, have reportedly been told that by their local adoption agency that they need not apply, because only white children are available.

The Manders, who are in their thirties, are taking the agency to court with the help of the Equality and Human Rights Commission. They say that they were judged suitable parents, but advised instead to adopt from India, a country with which they have no close links.

There seems little doubt that the Manders are highly sincere about adoption. They have tried for seven years to have a child, through 16 gruelling IVF attempts. They made it clear that they would be very happy to provide a loving home for a child of any ethnic background. Yet because they are classed under their "cultural heritage" as Indian/Pakistani, it seems that – in Berkshire, at least – they don't stand a chance.

One can only imagine their frustration, yet the Manders are far from the first to experience such feelings. When Britain had a strict policy of "same-race" adoption, before legislation in 2014, it was more often white families that were denied the chance to adopt a child from a different ethnic group. The theory was that it was better for the child's self-image to be placed with people from the same "cultural heritage".

The reality was that black children in particular spent a far longer time stuck in the care system than white ones. This was not because white families didn't want to adopt them – often they did, very much – but because the system demanded an ethnic match which wasn't always available. The prioritising of ethnic identity above all other concerns was having a negative effect on actual children in real life.

Although I think such a policy was deeply short-sighted, I can partly see how it came about. Stories had trickled back from much earlier adoptions in which some black children growing up in white families reported feeling confused about their identity.

Sometimes they were the only black child in a white family and a largely white area, in an era when children were broadly expected to be grateful and get on with things. In those days, personal feelings about race often weren't

openly discussed, but racist taunts from strangers were more widely tolerated.

If an alternative was adoption by a loving black family, I can see why this would have been preferable. Yet many transracial adoptions had also been great successes, and what the ban overlooked – as pristine theories often do – was that in cases where no racially appropriate match was available, that child would instead grow up in care, deprived of the assured love of any family at all.

This official elevation of theory over humanity happened to my own family, in Northern Ireland in the mid-sixties – a place in which, with a few exceptions, the ethnic mix was almost exclusively white. My parents, who then had two girls of their own, had home visits from a little boy of mixed African and white ethnicity, who was nearly two and in a care home. They loved him and wanted to adopt him, but the young social worker ruled against it.

Her reason wasn't openly connected to race, but some theory of sibling rivalry whereby she decided that my two sisters were more intelligent than him and the placement wouldn't work.

My parents reported that he showed a lively curiosity when in their house, but nothing could alter the decision, not even appeals to their MP. Further contact was discouraged. Decades later, my parents discovered that he had remained in the children's home, a place with a terrible reputation, until he was 16. The thought of the loving childhood he could have experienced instead is upsetting to contemplate.

> **Because they are classed under their 'cultural heritage' as Indian/Pakistani, it seems that – in Berkshire, at least – the Manders don't stand a chance**

The current policy is that "cultural heritage" should be a consideration when placing a child, but that they should not be kept waiting for a "perfect match". The website of Adopt Berkshire, for example, interprets this by saying that it will look first of all for prospective adopters that "reflect the child's religion and culture of heritage".

This means that if a child was nominally white and Christian, say, with a large number of similar families on the waiting list, adoptive parents from another religious or ethnic group might not get a look-in.

Yet I wonder if even this policy always makes sense in a UK that has changed enormously. There are so many factors in each individual child's needs. As a nation, we are increasingly tricky to categorise: our fastest growing ethnic group is now mixed race, a group that includes my own children.

I am a white Northern Irish woman married to a man of Punjabi origin who grew up in the Midlands. His father is Hindu, his mother is Sikh. Our children celebrate Christmas and Diwali, eat potato bread and parathas, and seem perfectly happy growing up in London. All around me I see other mixed-race families, in their different combinations, doing the same thing.

Mixed-race marriage is not the same as transracial adoption, of course. Adopted children do need to learn about their "cultural heritage", whereas most adults already know it.

But the adoption process is now so demanding that surely education around these issues must be an important part of the package. And I can't help thinking that a child of any background would be fortunate to have the Manders as parents. Such a child would at least experience what so many lonely children in our erratic care system never, ever get to feel – the confidence that they were, and are, dearly loved and wanted.

The Daily Telegraph, 27 June 2017
© Telegraph Media Group Limited 2017

> As a nation, we are increasingly tricky to categorise:
> our fastest growing ethnic group is now mixed race,
> a group that includes my own children

In numbers: Adoption statistics in England

- **4,690 children were adopted from care during the year ending 31st March 2016, compared to 5,360 in 2015.**

- **53% (2,490) of children adopted in this period were boys and 47% (2,200) were girls.**

- **The average age at adoption was 3 years 5 months.**

- **83% (3,880) of looked after children adopted during the year ending 31st March 2016 were white**

- **48% (1,190) of the children with a placement order waiting to be placed at 30 June 2015 were part of a sibling group.**

Source: adoptionuk.org

WHAT DO YOU THINK?

- **What do you think of this decision by the council?**

- **How important is it to fit in with your family and neighbourhood?**

- **What are the most important things to consider when a child goes into care?**

TEARS OF JOY AND SORROW

Two families, and an eighteen year old in turmoil

The date was January 2017, the scene a courtroom in Walterboro, South Carolina, USA. 18 year old Alexis Manigo was crying as she saw her mother being escorted in handcuffs from the courtroom. "I love you, Mom," she told Gloria Williams, who blew her a kiss from behind a metal screen. Alexis promised to pray for her mother and later defended her "My mother raised me with everything I needed and most of all everything I wanted," she wrote on Facebook. "My mother is no felon."But Gloria was accused of a very serious crime with the prospect of a long prison sentence, a crime so serious that she was denied bail. The 51 year-old was being committed for trial on charges of kidnapping and interfering with custody. The offence had been committed 18 years previously and the victim was her 'daughter' Alexis.

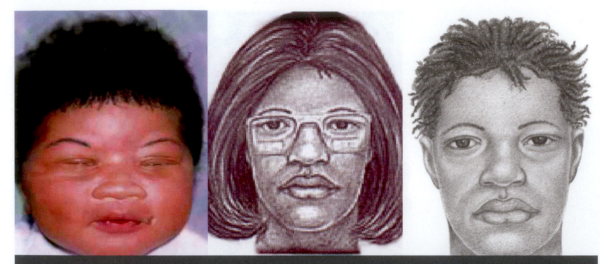

Composites of what Kamiyah Mobley (left) and her abductor (centre & right) would look like.

Jacksonville Sheriff's Office

It started in Florida

Change the time to 10 July, 1998 and the scene to University Medical Center, Jacksonville, Florida. Shanara Mobley, aged 16, had given birth to a daughter to be named Kamiyah Teresiah Tasha Mobley. The child's father, Craig Aiken, aged 19, was not present, he had been jailed for having intercourse with a minor, since Shanara had been fifteen at the time of conception.

Baby Kamiyah was only eight hours old when a woman dressed in a blue smock and with surgical gloves came into the room and told Shanara that the baby had a fever and would need to be checked. Shanara believed that the woman, who had been in the hospital for some hours, was a member of staff, and expected to have her baby back in her arms in a short while. Staff thought the woman, who had been asking questions about the baby, was a relative of Shanara's. Nobody challenged her as she disappeared with Kamiyah.

Once the kidnapping was discovered, it triggered a major police operation. The hospital and grounds were searched, helicopters were brought in, roadblocks were set up and a distraught Shanara pleaded on TV for the return of her daughter saying,

"Please bring my baby back. If you were faking a pregnancy or you just can't have no kids, how do you think I feel... That's my first child." The hunt extended right across the nation and a reward of $250,000 was offered. But there were difficulties. There were no photographs of Kemiyah taken in the brief eight hours since her birth and the CCTV footage was too grainy to be of any use in identifying her kidnapper.

In South Carolina

Three hours drive away, Gloria Williams showed a new baby, that she named Alexis Kelli Manigo, to unsuspecting friends and family. She had been pregnant so her appearance with a newborn was not questioned, seemingly no one knew that she had suffered a miscarriage. She told her husband, Charles Manigo, that she had given birth while he was away.

Meanwhile 175 miles away, a family could not come to terms with their loss. Every year for 18 years there was a birthday cake for the missing Kamiyah. Shanara spoke to a newspaper in 2008, on the tenth anniversary of the abduction: "It's stressful to wake up every day knowing that your child is out there and you have no way to reach her or talk to her. The main thing that beats you up the most is ... you don't know nothing. I wonder, What does she like? What kind of food? What kind of colours? How smart is she? Does she have long, pretty hair? Does she have my eyelashes?" Kemiyah's grandmother Velma Aiken, said that she had never even had the chance to hold the baby, "I just pray to God that one day I will see her before I die."

A normal childhood

As far as Alexis Manigo was concerned, hers was a normal childhood. She and her siblings were brought up by their mother Gloria, with limited contact with her father. Her Facebook page shows her happy and smiling alongside her mother. Friends recall them being "always happy, always together", and that "growing up [Alexis] had the fanciest clothes and she had everything given to her that she wanted." Her mother was a social worker and a volunteer for good causes, who attended church on Sundays. But this happy, respectable family life was based entirely on a lie.

'My mother is no felon.'

A shocking revelation

The problem came when Alexis wanted to apply for a job. She needed a birth certificate, which her mother could not give her. At that point Gloria told the girl at least part of her story, that she had been born in another place, to another woman, but it is not clear how much she revealed. Alexis, it seems, did not act on the information, though she may have told a friend.

Over the 18 years in which the authorities had been, at least in theory, searching for the missing child, they had received about 2,500 tip-offs - none of which had led to finding the baby. But in summer 2016 and then again in November they received specific information that the victim in one of Florida's longest-running kidnap

Kamiyah Mobley (Left), pictured with the woman she thought was her mother

Facebook

cases was living under the name of Alexis Kelli Manigo in South Carolina. A comparison of Alexis' DNA to baby Kamiyah's provided the proof and Gloria Williams was arrested.

In between

The traumatic courtroom parting for Alexis was followed, in due course, by an emotional reunion with her birth parents. "The first meeting was beautiful," her father Craig Aiken said "It's a feeling that you can't explain. I always hoped and prayed this day would happen. I always felt she was alive. I always felt she would find us. Now we have the rest of our lives together."

> **"I just pray to God that one day I will see her before I die."**

It is, of course, not a matter of pure joy for Kamiyah. She is caught between two families and two lives. She currently has no legal identity or documentation. Without legal documents she can't have a driving licence, or work at a job that requires proof of citizenship and the payment of taxes. It also means that she can't get into the jail to visit the woman, who for 18 years, she lovingly called Mom.

In an interview with the TV programme 'Good Morning America' she spoke with calmness and maturity about being called Alexis or Lexi her whole life and then suddenly being known, nationally, by a different name. She said that while she felt she had a duty to get to know her birth parents, and hoped that finding a second family would just mean more love, she forgave Gloria completely: "From that one mistake I was given the best life... I had love especially. She loved me for 18 years, she cared for me for 18 years" and she pleaded "I know what she did was wrong, but don't just lock her up and throw away the key."

Sources: Various

WHAT DO YOU THINK?

- **Who has your sympathy in this story?**
- **Can you suggest any solutions or ways to move forward for Kamiyah?**
- **How should Gloria be punished for her crime?**

Traditional & liberal views

A snapshot of modern family life

17,180 adults aged under 65 in 22 countries were surveyed for the Ipsos MORI 2017 Global Trends Survey.

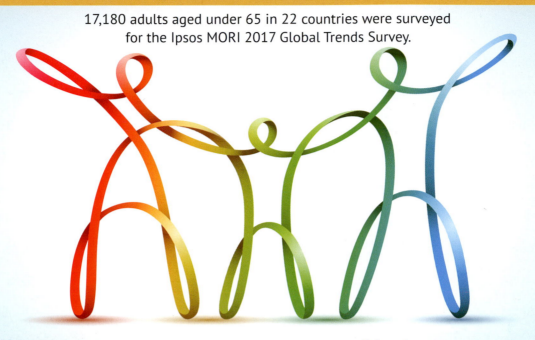

The survey found that people still tended to favour **traditional** social structures.

MARRIAGE

Overall, **57%** agreed that it was **better for parents of children to be married rather than unmarried.**

Religious belief:
62% of those with religious faiths **agreed**, compared to **42%** of non-believers.

Country who agreed most:
- Indonesia **85%**;
- India **78%**; and
- Turkey **77%**.

Countries who disagreed most:
- Spain **65%**;
- France **55%**; and
- Belgium **52%**.

51% in Great Britain **agreed**.

Gender:
61% of **men agreed**, compared to **52%** of **women**

Marital status:
67% of those who were **married agreed**, compared to **38%** of those living together or in domestic partnerships, and **45%** of people who were divorced.

PARENTING

77% agreed that **parents today do not take enough responsibility for the behaviour of their children**.

The countries who agreed most:
South Africa - **89%**;
United States - **87%**; and
Great Britain - **85%**.

HOME AND CHILDCARE

Overall, **69%** of people agreed that **men now have greater responsibility for the home and childcare than ever before**. **76%** in Great Britain agreed.

73% of men think they are taking up the burden but only **64% of women** feel the same way!

They were asked whether they agreed that
the role of women in society is to be good mothers and wives.
Overall 37% agreed and 58% disagreed.

NB: Figures do not add up to 100% due to rounding, and the exclusion of don't knows or not stated responses

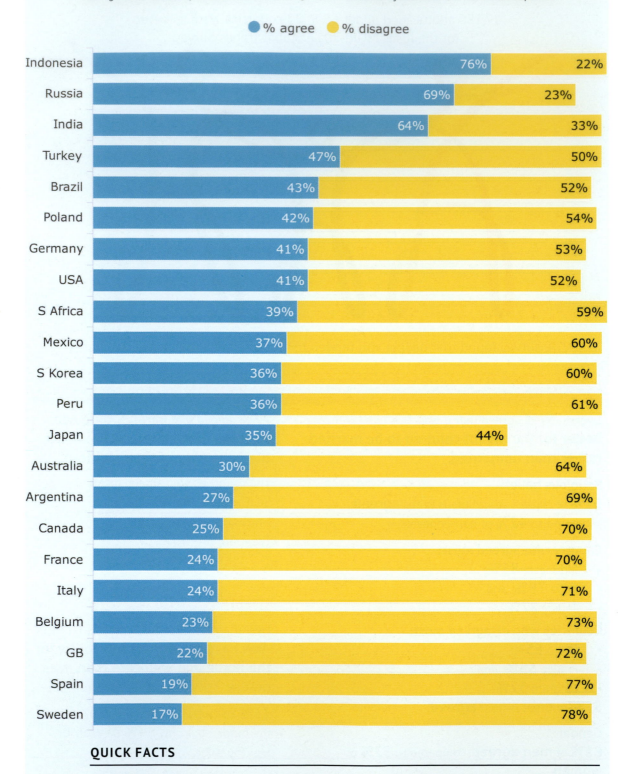

● % agree   ● % disagree

Country	% agree	% disagree
Indonesia	76%	22%
Russia	69%	23%
India	64%	33%
Turkey	47%	50%
Brazil	43%	52%
Poland	42%	54%
Germany	41%	53%
USA	41%	52%
S Africa	39%	59%
Mexico	37%	60%
S Korea	36%	60%
Peru	36%	61%
Japan	35%	44%
Australia	30%	64%
Argentina	27%	69%
Canada	25%	70%
France	24%	70%
Italy	24%	71%
Belgium	23%	73%
GB	22%	72%
Spain	19%	77%
Sweden	17%	78%

QUICK FACTS

- **41%** of men thought women should be wives and mothers - compared to **34%** of women.

- **42%** of those with religious beliefs took the traditional view on gender roles compared to **24%** of those who describe themselves as agnostic or atheist.

When it came to **individual freedoms** such as gay rights people are becoming more **liberal**.

People were asked whether they agreed that

gay men and lesbians should be free to live their own life as they wish

Overall **74%** agreed and **20%** disagreed

● % agree ● % disagree

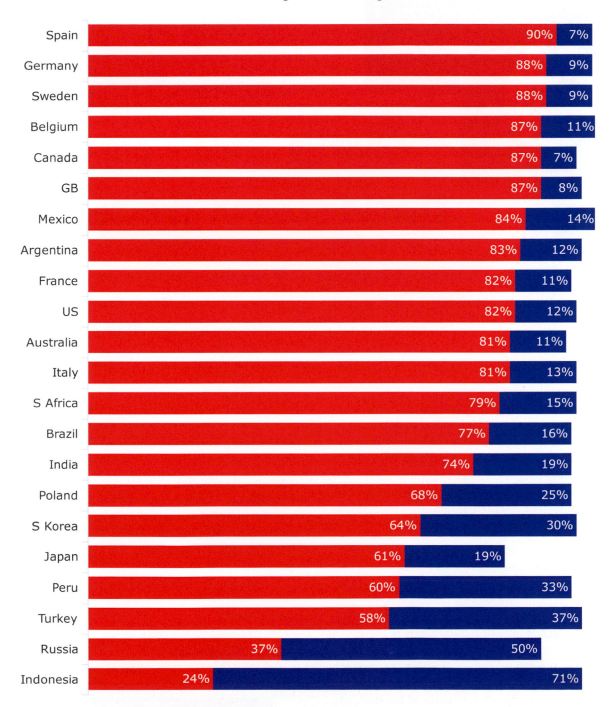

Country	% agree	% disagree
Spain	90%	7%
Germany	88%	9%
Sweden	88%	9%
Belgium	87%	11%
Canada	87%	7%
GB	87%	8%
Mexico	84%	14%
Argentina	83%	12%
France	82%	11%
US	82%	12%
Australia	81%	11%
Italy	81%	13%
S Africa	79%	15%
Brazil	77%	16%
India	74%	19%
Poland	68%	25%
S Korea	64%	30%
Japan	61%	19%
Peru	60%	33%
Turkey	58%	37%
Russia	37%	50%
Indonesia	24%	71%

Source: Ipsos MORI Global Trends Survey 2017 www.ipsosglobaltrends.com

WHAT DO YOU THINK?

- **Does it make a difference to children whether their parents are married or not?**
- **What are the responsibilities of parents?**
- **How are gender roles changing?**

Michio Hirano, MD
- Professor of Neurology
- Chief, Division of Neuromuscular Disorders
- Director, H. Houston Merritt Clinical Research Center
- Medical Director, Laboratory of Molecular Genetics
- Laboratory of Metabolic and Mitochondrial Disease
- Over 30 years experience

Honors & Awards
- America's Best Doctors

US medic is coming to see Charlie as he believes there's a 56% chance of 'meaningful improvement'

THE WORLD STANDS WITH CHARLIE GARD

Support our Charlie

#istandwithcharliegard
#charliesarmy

#letcharliegohome

https://www.facebook.com/michelle.johnston.37/posts/10155150212066888

Charlie Gard's parents: Our last hours with our son

The instincts of Charlie Gard's parents should echo in the courts

Connie Yates and Chris Gard wanted to take their child abroad for treatment they saw as a last resort – UK courts and the European Court of Human Rights have judged it right to intervene and turn off his life support

Mary Dejevsky

Few over the past few weeks can have been unaware of the plight of Charlie Gard. The peaceful face of this 10-month old has graced many a front page, as have the words and pictures of his devoted and determined parents. They have fought through the courts to be allowed to take their desperately ill child to the US for experimental treatment that they believe could have a chance of saving him.

All the courts in the UK, up to and including the Supreme Court, have said no. Now, their journey – and Charlie's – appears to have come to an end with this week's ruling from the European Court of Human Rights in Strasbourg. On Tuesday it upheld the decisions of the British courts and declined to intervene. One day in the not too distant future, Charlie's life-support will be switched off and he will receive only palliative care for what remains of his short life.

As an outsider, taking what I flatter myself to be a rational perspective, I have no quarrel with these rulings. Some of the best qualified paediatricians in the land identified a rare genetic condition that doomed Charlie's existence from the start.

There are countries where life support would have been withdrawn much sooner or never given at all. Other

very sick children with a better chance of life, it might have been argued, had a greater claim to a finite and expensive resource. Charlie's parents were entirely within their rights to challenge the doctors, but, quite simply, there was no hope.

And yet, and yet... I don't think it is only Charlie's winsome face or the very public anguish of his parents that leave misgivings. While accepting the final verdict, I have two questions to throw into the mix – questions that may simply have no answers but should at least be asked. The first concerns parental rights; the second, the state of public trust in doctors.

Charlie Gard's parent walk out of court hea

Chris Gard and Connie Yates leave af disagreement with judge during hea determine critically ill baby's future

#letcharliegohome

Photo: REUTERS / PETER NICHOLLS

Charlie's parents, Connie Yates and Chris Gard wanted to take their child abroad for treatment they saw as a last resort. It would not have been any expense to the public purse. They had raised the £1.3m themselves. But money was not the point at issue. The judges had to rule on the welfare of the child. The judgment of the UK Supreme Court was that taking Charlie to the US would cause him additional and unnecessary suffering. The ECHR, also by a majority, did not demur.

England's Children Act of 1989 – updated in 2004 – was hailed then, and is still regarded now, as a landmark piece of legislation. At its core is the principle that the child's welfare is always, and in all circumstances, paramount.

Where litigation is concerned, a child is required to have his or her own representation – an advocate who is separate from parents or guardian, and who argues in the interests of the child alone.

Where a child has been harmed, or is judged to be at risk of harm, that principle is unimpeachable. Nor is there anything wrong with the principle that a child should have separate legal representation. But does it make sense for a court to overrule the wishes of the parents of such a very young child – wishes of parents who so patently want their child to flourish?

One downside of the Children Act, or at least with its application, has been that it has made some parents wary of having any dealings with officials at all, lest their own view of their child's welfare conflicts with that of the state. There have been instances where a request for help or a visit to A&E has turned into a contest for custody. Obviously, there are times when care orders are necessary, and there are plenty of examples where doing nothing has been more dangerous – even fatal – to the child than intervention.

But in this case? Should the parents not be allowed, at their own expense, to take what they see as that last chance for their child – even if, as seems to the rest of us inevitable, their hope turns out to be misplaced?

And for the parents, the welfare of the child here is not just a matter of medical judgment, it is also a matter of trust. There was a time when most of us would have been content to take those in authority at their word, but that trust – long gone in relation to bankers, politicians and, alas, journalists – has also been seeping away to an extent from medics.

This is partly because other (not always quack) sources of information are available, and partly perhaps because patients are more demanding, more aware of mistakes and readier to sue. This month the British Medical Journal reported that three-quarters of the babies stillborn or brain-damaged during labour could have been saved with better foetal heart monitoring. These truly horrendous figures concerned NHS hospitals in England in 2015. Add the notorious patient neglect at Mid Staffs, the incidence of hospital infections, and is it any wonder trust in the medical profession is not what it was?

Nor are patients always wrong in their challenges. In 2014 the parents of 12-year old Aysha King spirited their son from a Southampton hospital and took him to Spain and then to Prague for cancer treatment. The precise rights and wrongs of this case remain blurred; there was clearly a breakdown of trust between the family and the doctors. But the Kings – Jehovah's Witnesses – had researched their options and insisted that Aysha would benefit from proton-beam therapy – tried and tested elsewhere, but unavailable in Britain.

Their argument was that proton beam treatment had less risk of side-effects for a child than standard radiotherapy. In the end, the NHS funded Aysha's treatment in Prague. He is back at school, his parents say his cancer has gone, and – lo and behold – the UK's first proton beam machine has just been delivered to Newport in South Wales, as a new study shows that this treatment is indeed less harmful to children with certain types of cancer.

So far, Aysha King's story is a happy one in a way that Charlie Gard's, alas, will probably not be, and their two conditions are anyway quite different. But the two cases both raise the same serious questions about what happens when doctors and parents clash over a child's treatment, and whether – just sometimes – the parental instincts might have the edge over medical expertise.

The Independent, 28 June 2017 www.independent.co.uk

The story of Charlie Gard

Who decides?

Court Continues On Thursday 13th July

Charlie Gard's parents walk out of court hearing

Chris Gard and Connie Yates leave after disagreement with judge during hearing to determine critically ill baby's future

I NEED YOU!!!

LIVE: 'If he's still fighting, we're still fighting' say Charlie Gard's parents

10:49, UK, Thursday 13 July 2017

Who should have the final say in the life of a child? The tragedy of Charlie Gard – a child with a rare, incurable condition – raises major questions

Charlie Gard was born in August 2016. When it became evident that he was not developing at the rate he should and was becoming ill, he was referred to a specialist hospital where he was diagnosed with a rare hereditary condition which his doctors considered was terminal.

Doctors at Great Ormond Street Hospital for Children (GOSH) who had been treating Charlie concluded that his condition was irreversible, his quality of life was negligible and that he was possibly in pain. As a result they wanted to stop treating him, with the inevitable result that Charlie would die.

Charlie's parents disagreed. They felt that there was a slim chance that an experimental treatment available in America would improve Charlie's life. They were prepared to raise the money for the trip and the treatment.

The doctors at GOSH felt that intervention would not be in the child's best interests.

Why were the courts involved?

As there seemed to be no way to reconcile these opposite views, GOSH applied to the courts for permission to stop treating Charlie.

The task of the judge was to examine the evidence and to decide what was best for the child. Parents have responsibilities for their children but they do not have 'ownership' of them, they cannot always have the final decision.

Outside influences

The case gathered so much publicity that it became a topic of heated discussion worldwide. People felt emotionally involved and free to comment. There were purely ignorant interventions claiming that the fundraising was a scam. There was opportunism - people who used the case to push their own agenda, often religious. There was abuse directed at staff of the hospital. There were US politicians who linked the case to their opposition to 'socialised healthcare'.

Medical ethics

In a submission to the court on 13th July 2017, the hospital said that their view was that Charlie had no quality of life and no real prospect of any quality of life. The treatment team had sought second opinions from three different specialists, who had all assessed Charlie and agreed. In addition, the parents had called in their own specialist who had assessed the child and also agreed with GOSH that palliative care was the best option.

However, the hopes of the parents were kept alive by the US neurologist, Michio Hirano, who offered an experimental treatment with, he estimated, a 10% chance of success. But he had never seen Charlie, or his medical records, and, it transpired, he had a financial interest in the therapy on offer.

Timeline of events

2016

4th August

Charlie Gard was born, at full-term and a good weight.

September

His parents noticed that he was less able to lift his head and support himself than babies of a similar age. Charlie was diagnosed with mitochondrial DNA depletion syndrome (MDDS), a rare inherited disease which affects cells responsible for energy production and respiration. This left Charlie unable to move or breathe without a ventilator. The condition causes progressive muscle weakness and brain damage.

11th October

Charlie was taken ill and transferred to Great Ormond Street Hospital for Children (GOSH) in London.

2017

January

Charlie's parents set up a GoFundMe page to raise money to take Charlie to America for experimental treatment. They said "It hasn't been tried on anyone with his gene before (he's only number 16 in the world ever reported) but it's had success with another mitochondrial depletion syndrome called TK2 which is similar". In time the page raised the full £1.3m needed.

The hospital said the experimental nucleoside therapies were "unjustified" and the treatment was not a cure. At this point the hospital had concluded that Charlie should receive only palliative care.

3rd March

GOSH asked the High Court to rule that life support treatment should stop.

11th April

The judge said doctors could stop providing life-support treatment and that a move to a palliative care regime would be in Charlie's best interests.

3rd May - 27th June

Charlie's parents took their case through the Court of Appeal and the UK Supreme Court with no success. They appealed to the European Court of Human Rights but European judges refused to intervene. A Great Ormond Street spokeswoman said there would be "no rush" to change Charlie's care.

2nd July

Pope Francis sent a message of support to Charlie's parents, saying that life support must not be turned off until Charlie died of natural causes.

10th July

US President Donald Trump sent a message of support to Charlie's parents offering help for treatment in the US.

17th July - 21st July

Dr Michio Hirano, the New York neurology professor who offered to treat Charlie, came to London to discuss the case with GOSH doctors and to testify in court. The lawyer representing GOSH said the new scan made for "sad reading".

24th July

Charlie's parents ended their legal fight. Their barrister said: "The parents' worst fears have been confirmed, it is now too late to treat Charlie."

28th July

Charlie died

The story of Charlie Gard

How the two sides saw each other

Extracts from the parents' statement outside the High Court

"The last 11 nearly 12 months have been the best, the worst and ultimately life changing months of our lives but Charlie is Charlie and we wouldn't change him for the world. All our efforts have been for him.

Had Charlie been given the treatment sooner he would have had the potential to be a normal, healthy little boy.

This has also never been about 'parents know best'. We have continuously listened to experts in this field and it has raised fundamental issues, ethically, legally and medically - this is why the story of one little boy from two normal everyday people has raised such conflicting opinions and ferocious arguments worldwide."

Extracts from GOSH statements to the court

13th July 2017

"Charlie is a beautiful, tiny baby afflicted by one of the cruellest of diseases. His depletive genetic disorder leaves him with no muscle function at all now and deprived of his senses, unable to breath and, so far as can be discerned after many months of encephalopathy, without any awareness.

In one respect, Charlie is immensely fortunate and that is in having parents of great fortitude and devotion. All at GOSH wish to pay tribute to their dedication to their only child and their tireless pursuit of a cure for him.

Charlie's parents fundamentally believe that they alone have the right to decide what treatment Charlie has and does not have.... They believe that only they can and should speak for Charlie and they have said many times that they feel they have been stripped of their rights as parents. "

27th July 2017

The final statement from the hospital is worth reading in full, but particularly important are their comments on Professor Hirano, whose offer of aid was central to the parents' case: "Throughout, his parents' hopes have been sustained by advice received from overseas." The statement makes it clear that the professor was invited to GOSH in January, but he did not come until 13th July and in that time he had not read any of the medical notes and second opinions or seen any brain scans. He had, nevertheless continued to offer advice - and hope - for a treatment which had never been tested on humans or animals.

www.gosh.nhs.uk/news/latest-press-releases/latest-statement-gosh-patient-charlie-gard

Sources: Various

WHAT DO YOU THINK?

- **Is it right that the courts have the final say in a child's life?**

- **Where do your sympathies lie in this case?**

- **Should anyone be blamed for the way Charlie's short life progressed?**

Where food comes from

How much does it matter?

Do you agree or disagree with the following statements?

(Figures may not add up to 100% due to rounding)

■ Agree/tend to agree ■ Neither agree or disagree ■ Disagree/tend to disagree

I would be prepared to pay more for food and drink that is produced in Britain/the UK and Ireland

48% | 25% | 28%

Food produced in Britain/the UK and Ireland tends to be more expensive than food imported from overseas

39% | 44% | 16%

It is important to support British farmers and food producers in the UK and Ireland
89% | 8% | 3%

Food produced in Britain/the UK and Ireland tastes better than food imported from overseas

25% | 47% | 28%

I have greater trust in the quality of food produced in Britain/the UK and Ireland compared to food imported from overseas
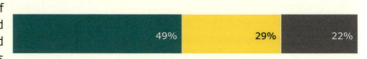
49% | 29% | 22%

Where possible I prefer to buy food produced in Britain/the UK and Ireland

53% | 21% | 26%

When buying food I check to see where it was produced

38% | 17% | 45%

QUICK FACTS

- Women were more likely to check where food was produced than men - **41%** compared with **34%**.
- Younger respondents were less likely to check where food was produced - **53%–55%** of those aged 16 to 34 compared with **35%–39%** of those aged 65 and over.

Survey of 3,118 adults aged 16+ in England, Wales and Northern Ireland for The Food & You Survey Combined Report Wave 4 © Food Standards Agency 2017 www.food.gov.uk

WHAT DO YOU THINK?

- **How aware are you about where your food comes from?**
- **What reasons are there for favouring locally produced food?**
- **Could you buy all your food from British and Irish producers?**

Would you eat a 3D printed PIZZA?

By Deborah Lupton, Centenary Research Professor & Bethaney Turner, Assistant Professor in International Studies, University of Canberra, Australia

Could you imagine serving a 3D printed turkey for Christmas lunch? Or munching on a 3D printed pizza for an afternoon snack?

This is not as far fetched as it sounds. While 3D printers have mainly been in the news for their ability to manufacture inedible goods, they are increasingly being used for culinary endeavours.

3D food printers extrude soft liquid edible matter through nozzles that build up layer by layer in patterns directed by a computer program. They can pump out everything from to chocolates, confectionery, biscuits and pancakes, to pasta, pizza and other savoury snacks.

News reports and industry blogs are very positive about what 3D food printing can offer. They have covered such events as Michelin-starred chefs experimenting with 3D food printers in pop-up restaurants in Europe.

The media have also reported on the potential for 3D printing to cater for astronauts, air travellers and people in emergency situations.

Nursing homes in Europe are offering 3D printed food with jelly-like texture for residents with chewing and swallowing difficulties. Developers of 3D food printers claim that people will soon have these devices in their kitchens, helping them prepare tasty and healthy foods at home.

Although substances such as insects and algae are natural, people thought they were disgusting.

But that's not all. There's also the radical idea of using insects and laboratory-grown meat in 3D printed food as a sustainable alternative to traditional protein sources.

Meat and Livestock Australia also recently announced that it is looking into ways to use 3D printing to produce new meat products to extract the most value from animal carcasses.

So it is not far-fetched to imagine serving a Christmas lunch with 3D printed food made from red meat and poultry, or decorative edible items made from fruit or vegetable purees, sugar or chocolate.

But would you eat it?

What do you think about 3D printed food? Would you try it, or offer it to family members or guests? Despite industry enthusiasm and investment in research and development, few studies have actually asked these questions of consumers.

To investigate these issues, we conducted our own research with 30 Australians, using an online focus group. The results highlight some interesting complications in the way many people perceive 3D printed foods, and what might tempt them to try some.

First of all, we found that none of the participants had heard of using 3D printing technology to make food products. As 3D printing technologies were usually associated with inedible objects made from substances such as plastic, plaster or metal, it was difficult for our participants to understand how they might work with foodstuffs.

They were initially incredulous that this technology could be used for making food and couldn't imagine what kinds of foods would be produced. This manner of food processing was viewed as highly unnatural, with several assuming that the resulting food would be somehow "plastic" and therefore inedible.

Our participants were far more positive about 3D printed carrots, pasta, pizza, chocolate and a meal with chicken and vegetables (made from "real" whole food purees) than they were about 3D printed sugar confections, meat and food made from food waste and alternative food sources such as algae and insects.

Cultural beliefs about what kinds of matter are considered tasty and appropriate to eat were central in our participants' responses. While substances such as insects and algae fit consumers' preferences for natural ingredients, these foods were considered disgusting by nearly all of the participants.

> **3D printers can pump out chocolates, confectionery, biscuits, pancakes, pasta, pizza and savoury snacks.**

They could not imagine eating them or serving them to others. These materials were considered to be inedible according to the cultural norms of our participants, no matter how they are prepared or processed. So it wasn't that they were 3D printed per se, but what they were printed from that affected their attitude to the food.

Those participants who had ethical misgivings about eating conventionally grown meat liked the idea of 3D printed meat products. But most of the participants considered the process to be a little too much like "Frankenfood", particularly if it involved using laboratory-cultured meat. Here it was the process of making the ingredient that was considered "unnatural".

> **People may soon have these devices in their kitchens.**

Building familiarity

Many participants' lack of familiarity with the 3D printing process underpinned their reservations about the safety of using food materials that would otherwise be discarded as waste. They were unsure about how the risks of food contamination and preservation would be dealt with.

Many of them also considered the healthiness of foods to be an important factor. Our participants had no problem viewing 3D printed sugar confections, pizza or chocolate as potentially edible. But they did express concern about the healthiness of these foods, given their ingredients and current status as junk food.

So, if our results can be generalised to the broader population, it seems many people are interested in novel food products. They will try them if they can be assured of their edibility, healthiness and safety, and have an understanding of how these products are processed and what they are made from.

But our study shows that those wishing to promote 3D printed food might have several challenges on their hands. First of all, they may need to familiarise the public with how this process works and reassure them that it is safe.

Then they might need to emphasise that 3D printed food is tasty, even if it looks unusual or is made from ingredients that are not normally considered edible by cultural standards. Only then might consumers consider the possibility of including 3D printed food as part of their lives, including at the Christmas lunch table.

Source: The Conversation, 22 December 2016
theconversation.com/uk
THE CONVERSATION

> ## WHAT DO YOU THINK?
>
> - **Would you eat food produced by a 3D printer?**
> - **Do you believe that these devices will soon be in people's kitchens?**
> - **What makes food more or less attractive to you?**

The jellyfish tastes better with music

Sight, sound and touch

Nick Curtis explores the scientific eating hacks that change how food tastes.

It is a cold, clear spring morning, and I am sitting in a double-height studio on the top floor of a former dental-goods factory in Barnet, London, eating crunchy ribbons of jellyfish from what look like a pair of surgical tweezers.

I can't talk to my dining companion, because we are both wearing cordless headphones, and I am hypnotised by how the soundtrack of sea noises - not to mention the underwater footage projected onto the table in front of us - enhances both the taste and the texture of the gelatinous flesh.

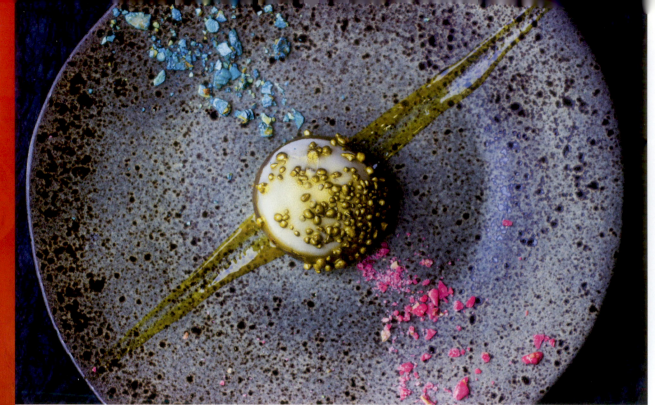

The Walled Gardens Supper Club by Eddie Shepherd, www.veggiechef.co.uk

Later, I learn that both the shape of a glass and the taste of chocolate can alter the perceived flavour of whisky, and that if you eat a peach and a chilli-flavoured jelly bean with a swimmer's nose-clip on, they will taste exactly the same.

The venue is Kitchen Theory, where "modernist" chefs led by Jozef Yousef test wild and wacky food on willing participants. The other man munching jellyfish is Professor Charles Spence, 48, whose quest to demonstrate the scientific effect of not just smell but sight, sound and touch on how we experience what we eat is summed up in his new book, *Gastrophysics*.

This is partly a serious tome - Spence is head of the Crossmodal Research Laboratory at Oxford University - and partly an amusing guide for the layman to a new gustatory world. It may come as no surprise to you that Spence has worked with the gastronomic mad scientists Heston Blumenthal, who supplies a foreword to the book, and Ferran Adria, as well as for food giants such as Unilever and Pepsico. He also

Heavier cutlery can make your guests think you're a better chef.

Anything that takes your attention away from the food, like television, makes people eat 25% more.

won the Ig Nobel Prize (given for scientific research that makes you laugh, then think) for his "sonic crisp" experiment, proving that crisps taste better when they sound, well, crispier.

Gastrophysics is packed with such tasty factual morsels that could be served up at dinner parties. Heavier cutlery can make your guests think you're a better chef, desserts will taste 10% sweeter off white plates than black ones - and the more people like the background music playing, the more they'll enjoy the food and wine.

"Anything that takes your attention away from the food, like television, makes people eat 25% to a third more," Spence adds. "Classical music increases the perceived quality of what you taste and the amount you spend on what you order, be it wine or food." Supermodel Kylie Jenner's belief that the pink wall in her living room acts as an appetite suppressant is, however, "based on some fairly dodgy research". She'd be better off with blue light, apparently.

"We all think we can just taste what is in the glass, but there are thousands of studies now that show we can't, that everything else affects it," says Spence. "I think everyone would benefit from a greater awareness of thinking about the 'everything else'. Eating is the most multisensory thing that you do, three times a day, and among the most enjoyable of life's experiences. There are all these things you can do to enhance that experience so why wouldn't you?"

The answer, of course, is inertia. It is known that the QWERTY computer keyboard is not the most effective layout, but the thought of changing every single keyboard and everyone learning to type again is too daunting to contemplate. Similarly, Spence suggests, it might not make the most sense to eat with cold bits of metal that have been in hundreds of other people's hands and mouths, but the thought of taking our own cutlery to a restaurant is anathema. (People who eat with their hands at least know where they have been.)

As consumers get more attached to experiences than to things, and as Instagram and other social media make the visual presentation of food more important, Spence is convinced change will come. In the book, he says, he "wanted to catch the growing excitement not just from chefs, but product designers, perfume makers, composers" and also win over "some of my colleagues on the science side who too often say, 'well, if it's going in my mouth it can't be scientific, or worthy of serious study'. The opposite is true; some of the hardest things to study are going on in the mouth. And it's important to us all."

Spence has a prop-forward's build and looks like a man who enjoys his food. He grew up in Leeds and is married to Barbara, who teaches international political economy in Oxford. They have no children, and it is Spence who does the cooking. "My wife," he says, "is terrified of the kitchen."

Certainly, the likes of Blumenthal, Adria and the larky duo Bompas and Parr - who have created inhalable gin and tonic, and a $94 spoon with an MP3 player in it that seems silent until it's in your mouth, when it sends soundwaves to your inner ear via your teeth - may seem like they are on the experimental (and expensive) cutting edge.

Desserts will taste 10% sweeter off white plates than black ones

www.veggiechef.co.uk

If people know something has changed they believe it tastes different

But actually, Spence says, 20 years before he and Blumenthal came up with the "sonic dining" dish, The Sound of the Sea, for the chef's Fat Duck restaurant in Bray, England, soundscapes were used to pacify psychiatric patients during mealtimes.

Some food companies have produced showy sensory gimmicks - a device that magnified the sound of Krug champagne bubbles; an audio file that lasted just long enough for a carton of Haagen-Dazs ice cream to soften - but others, Spence says, have been quietly experimenting to lower salt, fat and sugar in products without compromising taste.

They don't tell the public this, because if people know something has changed they believe it tastes different: as Cadbury's discovered when it rounded the corners of its Dairy Milk bars in 2013, and received complaints that it had become sweeter and creamier. (Blobby or circular shapes are associated with sweetness, pointy shapes with bitter or savoury tastes, by the by.)

This brings us to the practical and potentially beneficial applications of Spence's research, beyond the spheres of upmarket gastronomy and expensive marketing gimmicks. "There are three real-world 'good' angles," he says. "Improving hospital food; training people's food behaviour towards eating less, and more insect-based food; and combating obesity."

He says anyone who believes food tastes the same wherever you eat it has clearly never eaten in a hospital. The fact that his own mother has dementia and is in care has made him ponder anew how the eating experience in clinical institutions can be improved (his book cites a study at Salisbury District Hospital that showed elderly and weak patients eat nearly a third more from blue crockery).

If our worldwide hunger for protein refuses to abate, we are going to have to school ourselves to eat more insects ("an excellent source of protein and fat") and he is working with Yousef and Kitchen Theory, of which he is a director, on ways to "make this currently most undesirable food source truly delicious".

And research proves that those who concentrate on their food, who share meals rather than dining solo and who eat from heavier bowls, consume considerably less, and healthier foodstuffs, than those who don't.

If Spence can percolate all these factual morsels to the mainstream, the benefits to all of us would be obvious.

Gastrophysics: The New Science Of Eating by Professor Charles Spence is published by Viking.

Daily Telegraph 31 March 2017
© Telegraph Media Group Limited 2017

WHAT DO YOU THINK?

- **What is the most unusual thing you have eaten?**
- **Would you be willing to try insects?**
- **How important is food in your life?**
- **Do you agree that concentrating on your food and sharing meals makes you eat less?**

Going meat-free

Although they are a small percentage of the population the number of people who avoid animal products is increasing

A poll of 9,933 UK adults aged 15+ for the Vegan Society looked at the eating habits of the general public.

How often, if at all, do you eat any form of meat, fish or shellfish?

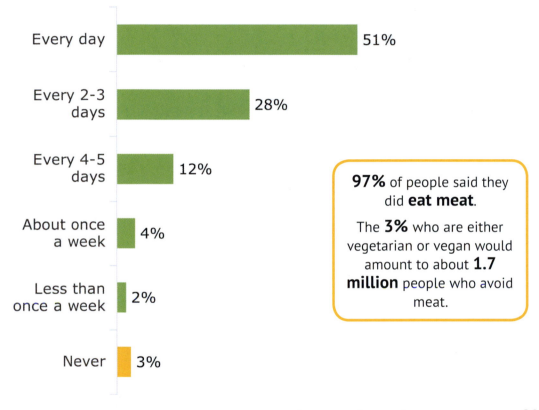

Every day	51%
Every 2-3 days	28%
Every 4-5 days	12%
About once a week	4%
Less than once a week	2%
Never	3%

97% of people said they did **eat meat**.

The **3%** who are either vegetarian or vegan would amount to about **1.7 million** people who avoid meat.

Amongst those who never eat meat, **2%** are **vegetarians** who avoid meat but still consume other animal products such as butter and honey.

1% are **vegans** who never eat meat and also avoid any products that come from animals.

This **1%** would amount to around **half a million** people who follow a vegan diet - a large increase over the 150,000 people identified in the previous survey in 2006.

The increase is likely to continue as the highest proportion of vegans and vegetarians is in the younger age groups.

Percentage who never eat meat

by age group

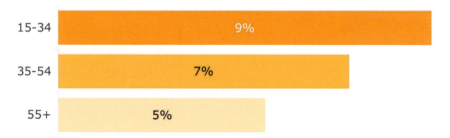

Age group	Percentage
15-34	9%
35-54	7%
55+	5%

QUICK FACTS

- **42%** of all vegans are in the **15-34** age category compared to just 14% who are **over 65.**

- The vast majority of vegans live in **urban or suburban** areas (**88%**) compared with **rural** areas (**12%**).

- **22%** of all vegans in Britain live in **London.**

- **63%** of vegans are **female** and **37%** are **male.**

Source: Vegan Society Poll, 2016,
www.ipsos-mori.com

WHAT DO YOU THINK?

- **What motivates people to avoid meat and other animal products?**

- **How easy is it to live with a restricted choice of foods?**

- **Why does a vegetarian or vegan lifestyle particularly appeal to young people?**

Can you be a part-time vegan?

Veganism is sometimes a lifestyle choice but it should be a lifetime commitment

According to a survey for the Vegan Society, the number of vegans in the UK has increased by more than 300% in a decade. What's more, they expect numbers to continue to increase since the percentages are higher in the 15-34 age group.

The Vegan Society suggests that for many the key reason for this choice is compassion for animals and a desire to have no part in their exploitation. Vegans often refer to 'other animals' or 'other non-human animals' to emphasise the fact that we, too, are members of the animal kingdom. They avoid all products which are derived from animals (including medicines where possible). They argue that no type of farming can really be compassionate, taking into account the welfare of the individual animal. This philosophy extends further, according to the Vegan Society, "Veganism is about so much more than the food on our plate. Veganism means respect for all life. Millions of other animals are kept in captive environments such as fur farms, zoos, safari parks, aviaries, breeding programmes, circuses and other 'entertainment', in private homes and 'collections', and in laboratories."

Photo: Yann Caradec

Serena Williams says she is a 'cheagan' - a vegan who sometimes cheats!

For many, the reported health benefits are what persuaded them to change, at least, their diet. Vegans are credited with having a 33% lower risk of premature death and a reduced likelihood of weight-related illnesses such as heart disease, high blood pressure and diabetes. Ironically, as veganism has become more popular vegan 'junk foods' have been produced, with some of the same flaws in terms of excess salt and sugar, as mainstream manufactured items.

"Veganism means respect for all life."

A further argument for being vegan is that eating only plants results in less pressure on the environment, and is a more sustainable lifestyle. The meat and dairy industry contributes heavily to global warming, deforestation, overuse of scarce water and uprooting of the poorest populations. A plant-based diet requires only one third of the land needed for meat and dairy production.

"My diet hasn't just changed my game, it's changed my life"

Certainly these reasons seem to have rung true with a variety of celebrities and sports stars who credit a vegan diet with giving them more energy and solving health problems. Notable amongst them is tennis star Novak Djokovic, who attributes his health, fitness and success to his changed eating habits, and who has even opened a vegan restaurant. He first changed his diet, and his success rate, when he was advised to go gluten-free in 2010 - and he won Wimbledon the next year. He has spoken about how his previous diet, which included lots of pizza and pasta, was really a product of habit and upbringing. He says of his current regime, plant based with the occasional addition of fish, "My diet hasn't just changed my game, it's changed my life—my wellbeing. And if I feel better, that obviously transfers to my professional life. Eating vegan makes me more aware of my body on the court... more alert. I removed toxins from my body, and with them went all the inflammation and other things that were messing with my energy levels."

Both Venus and Serena Williams, the most successful ever female tennis stars, follow a vegan diet when they are training. Venus adopted this in 2011 after she had suffered from shortness of breath and fatigue as a result of an auto-immune condition. Adopting a vegan, and raw, diet has helped to tackle the inflammation she was suffering from and restore her abilities. Serena took on the same diet in support of her sister but she too has continued to consume mainly beans, nuts and lentils, along with sprouted quinoa and sprouts. The sisters describe themselves, however, as "cheagans", meaning that they will, at times, deviate from plants-only and include animal products in what they eat.

> **" I saw all those cows and pigs and realised I couldn't be a part of it any more."**

Perhaps still more surprising is the number of fighters who choose to follow a vegan lifestyle. Once the received wisdom would have been that to build muscle and maintain stamina you need meat, eggs and dairy products. Numerous successful Mixed Martial Arts contestants, wrestlers and rugby players have adopted a vegan lifestyle. Amongst the most notable is David Haye, who has held boxing world championship titles at both Cruiserweight and Heavyweight. He told the Independent newspaper, "I watched a TV documentary about how animals are farmed, killed and prepared for us to eat... I saw all those cows and pigs and realised I couldn't be a part of it any more. It was horrible. I did some research to make sure I could still obtain enough protein to fight and, once satisfied that I could, I stopped. I'll never go back."

There is no shortage of Hollywood and music stars who are said to be vegans. Jennifer Lopez, Rooney Mara, Jared Leto, Joaquin Phoenix, Casey Affleck and Woody Harrelson have all spoken about the health benefits, as well as the benefits to the planet of their choice to give up all animal products. Beyoncé and JayZ both did a 22 day vegan challenge - earning praise from some but also criticism for not being 'real' vegans.

Where once a vegan lifestyle was seen as eccentric, even outlandish, it is now acceptable and, almost, mainstream. Once someone has been persuaded by the reasons for choosing a plant based diet this seems to lead logically and inevitably to avoiding all animal products, without exception. For these 'true' vegans there is no half-way house, the near-vegans are simply missing the point and are making unethical choices.

For those who have decided that all use of animals for human benefit is cruel, there can be no compromise. While they acknowledge that less exploitation is better than more, they argue that you would never say that racism or sexism is ok if it is only occasional, therefore, equally,

> ## You are either a vegan or you are someone who exploits animals

eating meat or using other animal products cannot be sometimes permissible. For them, cheagans, like the Williams sisters, or those who occasionally eat fish like Novak Djokovic, go against the whole premise of veganism, which is not to use any animal products, ever.

There are other sub-groups too, who are denounced as imposters. Veggans - those who eat eggs - are judging the lives of those chicks to be of less worth than the cows and pigs which they won't eat. Freegans, a name coined from 'free' and 'vegan' are people who buy as little as possible in order to avoid consumerism and minimise their impact on the planet. They often get their food by 'dumpster diving' - retrieving goods from supermarket waste so that they can be eaten rather than sent to landfill. This means they are not contributing financially to the

use of animals, but if they are still choosing to consume animal products, even for free, then for ethical vegans, they fail to pass the test.

A further group 'Flexitarians' are people who mainly eat a vegetarian diet but occasionally eat meat or fish. For vegans this is a nonsense term - it simply means 'most humans', since that describes the diet of the majority of people.

These labels are seen as a way for people to excuse eating or using animal products and are not steps towards veganism. For true vegans you are either a vegan or you are someone who exploits animals, there is no in-between.

While the arguments for veganism might be compelling, it is clearly an ethical choice which can only exist in an advanced society. There remain plenty of places on earth where food choice is a luxury. For the poorest people in the world a decision about whether or not to make use of animals is not a matter of morality but of survival.

It seems also that while abstaining from meat can be a healthy choice nowadays, meat eating was crucial in our evolution. According to recent research, the calories we obtained from meat were essential to the development of the large brain, in proportion to our body size, that makes us the most intelligent of primates. It would have been impossible to obtain sufficient nutrition for our development from a purely plant based diet because of the time-cost of collecting and consuming enough.

In other words, eating meat made us human. Vegans would argue that continuing to eat it makes us inhumane.

Sources: Various, including
www.vegansociety.com
www.livescience.com

WHAT DO YOU THINK?

- **What is the most compelling reason not to eat meat or use animal products?**
- **Do you agree that "You are either a vegan or you are someone who exploits animals"?**
- **Are some of the ways humans use animals, like zoos for example, acceptable?**

Food safety

We trust our senses - and the use-by date - to check that food is fresh

3,118 adults aged 16+ in England, Wales and Northern Ireland were surveyed about their attitudes to food safety.

What methods do you use to tell if particular types of food are safe to eat?

Methods varied depending on the type of food, but how food **smelled** was the most common way to assess whether meat, milk/yoghurt and fish were safe to eat.

- **71%** said that they used this method when checking **milk** or **yoghurt**; **61%** for **meat**; and **57%** for **fish**.

- For **cheese**, the most common method was the way it looked - **63%**.

What people think is the best indicator of food safety

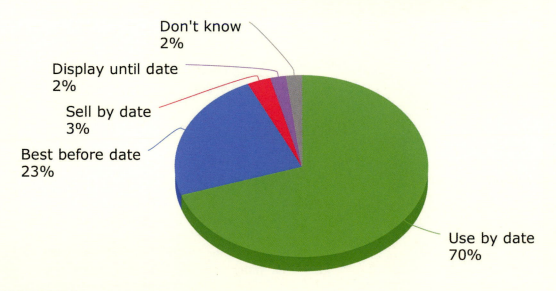

Don't know
2%

Display until date
2%

Sell by date
3%

Best before date
23%

Use by date
70%

QUICK FACTS

- The FSA recommends that the **use by date** is the best indicator of whether food is safe to eat and food should NOT be eaten after this date.

- **Women** were more likely to always check use by dates when shopping - **76%** compared with **64%** of **men** and before cooking or preparing food - **64%** compared with **58%** of **men**.

- **70%** of those surveyed who lived in households with **children aged under 6** always checked use by dates before cooking compared with **60%** of households without young children.

Eating leftovers

When asked how long they would consider eating leftovers from a meal which had been cooked on the Sunday:

- **6%** said they never had leftovers - they always finished the food or threw it away immediately;

- **4%** said the same day;

- **34%** said Monday;

- **34%** said Tuesday;

- **14%** said Wednesday.

- **4%** would eat them on Thursday.

- **3%** would eat them on Friday and up to the following Sunday.

QUICK FACTS

- The FSA recommends storing opened foods in the fridge and using within two days, unless the manufacturer's instructions state otherwise.

Food hygiene

83% of the public now recognise the Food Hygiene Rating Sticker (FHRS)

Local authorities carry out inspections of food businesses to check that they comply with legal requirements and they award food hygiene ratings based on the inspections.

Food businesses are issued with a sticker and the rating is uploaded to *food.gov.uk/ratings* for the public to use.

Businesses in England are encouraged, but not legally required, to display their rating. Displaying a rating has been mandatory in Wales since 2013, and in Northern Ireland since 2016.

Attitudes to eating out

'Eating out" includes eating or buying food from a wide range of establishments.
Almost all respondents - **96%** had eaten out in the **past month,**
43% had eaten out at least **once or twice a week.**

67% had eaten at a restaurant; **55%** had eaten takeaway food from a restaurant
or takeaway outlet; **41%** had eaten in a cafe or coffee shop.

Factors which influence where people decide to eat out

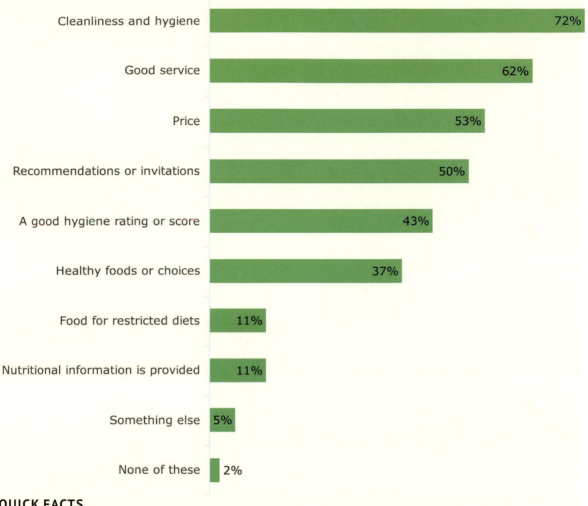

Factor	%
Cleanliness and hygiene	72%
Good service	62%
Price	53%
Recommendations or invitations	50%
A good hygiene rating or score	43%
Healthy foods or choices	37%
Food for restricted diets	11%
Nutritional information is provided	11%
Something else	5%
None of these	2%

QUICK FACTS

- Women were more likely than men to be influenced by the cleanliness and hygiene of the establishment when deciding where to eat out (**75%** of **women**, **69%** of **men**).

- Overall **34%** of women and **26%** of men said this was the **most** important factor in their decision making.

Food & You Survey Combined Report Wave 4 Food Standards Agency © Crown Copyright 2017
www.food.gov.uk

WHAT DO YOU THINK?

- **How do you decide whether food is safe to eat?**

- **Do use by dates just lead to food being wasted?**

- **If you saw a restaurant or a takeaway with a hygiene rating of less than 5, would you still use it?**

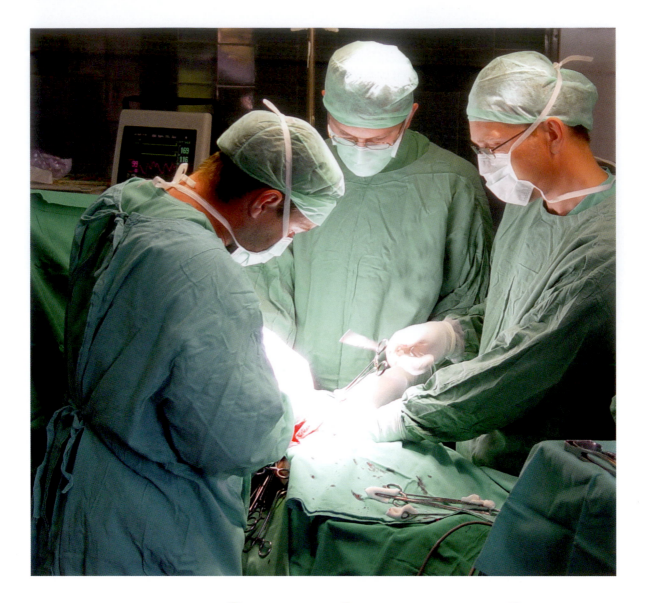

4 in 10 families refuse to donate organs

Every day in the UK about three people who could have benefited from a transplant die because there aren't enough organ donors.

The number of organs donated and transplanted in the UK is very gradually increasing. In 2015/16, 1,364 people became organ donors when they died which allowed 3,519 transplants to take place. But the country still has one of the lowest rates of consent for organ donation in Europe. 4 in 10 families refuse permission for an organ donation after a loved one has died. Families often refuse consent for an organ donation when they don't know the dead person's wishes.

Only 62% of people have agreed to have their organs donated on death. Unfortunately this figure is much lower in Black and Asian communities even though people from these communities have a higher incidence of conditions such as diabetes and certain forms of hepatitis, making them more likely to need a transplant. The consent rate for potential donors from Black, Asian and Minority Ethnic communities is just 34% compared to 66% for white patients.

A key problem is that although almost everyone is willing to accept an organ donation if they need one, far from everyone is willing to donate. Organ donation is relatively rare in the UK, because although more than half a million people die every year, only around 1% do so in circumstances which allow organs to be donated. This means that when a family says no to donation, someone waiting for a transplant may miss out on their only chance for a transplant.

The latest figures show that 4,601 patients' lives were saved or improved by an organ transplant in 2015/16. Every day in the UK about three people who could have benefited from a transplant die because there aren't enough organ donors.

If the UK had the same level of consent as the best countries in the world, (a rate of about 80%) then it is estimated that more than 1,000 extra transplants would take place every year.

Most of the UK has an opt-in system for organ donations. Austria, which has an opt-out system, achieves a consent rating of over 99.9% resulting in far more lives being saved. In an opt-out system your consent is assumed unless you have previously opted out. In December 2015, Wales became the first UK

The UK has one of the lowest rates of consent for organ donation in Europe

country to introduce an opt-out system. By December 2016 only 6% of people in Wales had opted out. In July 2017, Scotland, which already has the highest donation rate in the UK, also proposed adopting an opt-out system.

Organ donations will be more effective in the future because researchers have just discovered a groundbreaking way of reheating frozen organs using nanotechnology. This allows for the safe long term storage of donated organs such as the heart and lungs. At the moment these organs can only be kept for a few hours and there is a desperate rush to find a suitable patient when a donor dies. With this new technique, hospitals will be able to store banks of donated organs at very low temperatures of between -160 and -196 degrees Centigrade and transplant operations can be arranged in advance. It is estimated that this could entirely eliminate the current two year waiting list for a transplant.

Sources: various

WHAT DO YOU THINK?

- Are you prepared to donate your organs to help someone else?

- Why do so many families refuse permission for an organ donation?

- Which way is best to record people's wishes about organ donation: an opt-in or opt-out system?

Medical research

Young people's views on medical research

2,037 young people in England aged 14-18 were questioned about their interest and attitudes to medical research.

Overall
51%
of young people expressed some interest in medical science or medical research;

13%
said that they were very interested.

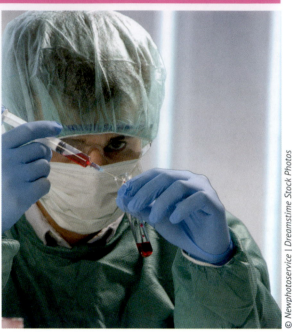

© Newphotoservice | Dreamstime Stock Photos

Are you interested in any of these areas of medical research?

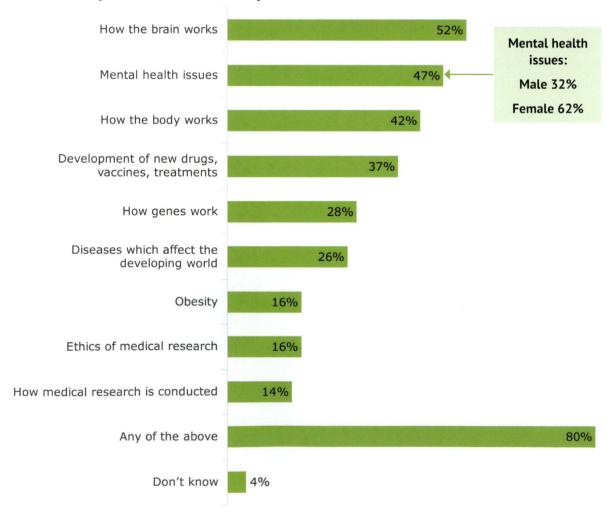

Area	%
How the brain works	52%
Mental health issues	47%
How the body works	42%
Development of new drugs, vaccines, treatments	37%
How genes work	28%
Diseases which affect the developing world	26%
Obesity	16%
Ethics of medical research	16%
How medical research is conducted	14%
Any of the above	80%
Don't know	4%

Mental health issues:

Male 32%

Female 62%

Of all students:

53% of young people had looked for information about an area of medicine; **43%** for medical advice; **17%** for information on medical careers; and **15%** for medical research projects or trials.

Of those who had looked for medical science information:

92% searched online; **24%** talked to a doctor; **22%** talked to a teacher; **29%** talked to other people; **19%** read books; and **8%** attended a lecture or talk.

Gender:

Females were much more likely than males to look up information on medical advice - **51%** compared with **36%** - and medical careers - **23%** compared with **11%**.

Disability within the family:

Students with experience of illness or disability within the family were more likely to seek out information on medical advice - **49%** - compared with students who didn't - **35%**.

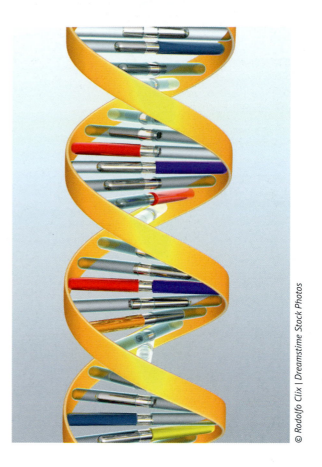

© Rodolfo Clix | Dreamstime Stock Photos

If a doctor asks your permission to use your MEDICAL RECORDS in a medical research study, would you give permission?

● Definitely ● Probably ● Probably not ● Definitely not ● Don't know

| 27% | 46% | 12% | 4% | 11% |

If a doctor asks your permission to use information from your GENES/DNA in a medical research study, would you give permission?

| 22% | 42% | 15% | 7% | 14% |

NB figures do not add up to 100% due to either rounding or questions which allow multiple answers

Source: Wellcome Trust - Science Education Tracker: Young people's awareness and attitudes towards machine learning and Young people's attitudes towards biomedicine, February 2017 https://wellcome.ac.uk

WHAT DO YOU THINK?

- **What parts of medical research interest you most?**
- **How much can you trust medical advice on the internet?**
- **How would you, personally, feel about sharing medical information for research purposes?**

Photo posed by model

Anorexia is not a fad or glamorous

By Frances

When I was 15, my mum noticed my behaviour changing towards food. I thought she was overreacting, being stupid and that there was nothing wrong with me, but she took me to the doctor regardless.

We were told that it was just a teenage phase. In my mind, this confirmed my belief that I was fine.

I didn't know it but I was well in the grips of anorexia by this stage and denial was a huge part of that. I remember my mum was quite switched on and we had lots of arguments.

"When I speak out about my eating disorder, some people patronise me, but I don't need pity - I'm still a human."

I knew I was breaking her heart, but I just couldn't see what she could see.

At school I don't think anyone twigged what was going on. I used to give my lunch away to my friends but I never said why and they didn't seem to wonder why either. This meant I could easily avoid food, when I wasn't around the watchful eyes of my family.

Mum and I would go to the doctors another three times, only to be dismissed. On the fourth visit, my mum said she wasn't leaving until I was treated. I was referred to a specialist and I was given just two weeks to live unless something drastically changed. Even then, hearing that I was going to die, I didn't think I was ill enough for all the fuss.

I lost a lot of my friends, and my social life along with it, during my illness. Anorexia is a very isolating illness that makes you not want to participate in social situations, or anything that may confront your new behaviour. A lot of people also do not know what to say to somebody who's unwell and that can mean losing friends as a result.

I've had relapses since then but I am always able now to recognise when the anorexic voice is stronger than usual and what to do when this is the case.

People tend to trivialise eating disorders, particularly women. You hear the term anorexic thrown around.

I've definitely heard people say they went 'a bit anorexic' because they dieted for a day, or you might hear someone being called anorexic because they are thin.

There isn't the understanding that it's an incredibly serious illness, with the highest mortality rate of any mental health problem.

"I've also been asked for diet tips and questioned in detail about what I used to eat. It feels a bit like it can be glamorised by some people. But I was literally on the verge of death – that's not glamorous."

When I do speak out, I also find people can patronise me. There's often a head tilt and they say they feel sorry for me. I don't need pity, I'm still a human.

Having said all that, I don't shy away from speaking out. Even when people are ignorant, I like that because it gives me a chance to challenge those opinions.

Now I'm working on sharing my experiences to help others. I created an Instagram account and wrote a leaflet called Life As It Is Now. I wanted an alternative to the pro-ana websites and accounts, promoting anorexia, that are so easily accessible these days. I also go into schools and share my story - I find I get lots of questions from young people, particularly boys.

Source: Time to Change, 7 June, 2017
www.time-to-change.org.uk

WHAT DO YOU THINK?

- **Were you surprised that the problem wasn't taken seriously at first?**
- **Why might some people think this illness is 'glamorous'?**
- **How should the people around Frances have reacted?**

'I told my daughter she was selfish for having anorexia'

Marg Oaten

When our daughter Gemma developed anorexia at the age of 10, my husband Dennis and I were completely devastated. She had become painfully thin over time - she existed on just five cornflakes and a small glass of water a day - but we didn't understand what was wrong. She was depressed, isolated and had uncharacteristic low moods.

I will never forget the day we found out she had an eating disorder. We had taken her to see a paediatrician and he said: "If you don't eat you will die – if you don't drink you will die quicker".

Our hearts were broken as we watched on helplessly.

We often had no idea what to say. I would range between anger ("can't you see what you are doing to yourself?"); pure frustration ("for goodness' sake just eat"); and exhaustion ("we're sick to death of this – you are so selfish. What you're doing is affecting everyone.")

Many parents whose children have eating disorders will find themselves repeating these unhelpful comments. Indeed, last week

newsreader Mark Austin spoke about his struggle to cope with his 18-year-old daughter's anorexia.

"What I failed utterly to grasp was that she was seriously mentally ill and could not see a future for herself," he said.

"I told her she was being ridiculous. I told her to get a grip and grow up, to 'just bloody well eat, for Christ's sake'... I even remember saying, 'If you really want to starve yourself to death, just get on with it.' And at least once, exasperated and at a loss, I think I actually meant it."

Like Mark, Dennis and I became world experts in saying the wrong thing, sighing too loud and looking the wrong way. Family life was a war zone and the anorexia had a profound effect on the whole family. We didn't always know to react and I know we made mistakes.

Today, Gemma is a 32-year-old accomplished actress, who has starred in Emmerdale and Holby City. With the right support, we managed to help her recover from her anorexia.

When writing this article, I asked her if she could remember any unhelpful comments we made, and she told me: "To be honest, the biggest one for me was when relatives would say: 'You are destroying this family. Look what you're putting us all through. Mum and Dad are a mess.'

"I remember once someone said this to me when I was in hospital on a drip and I'll never forget it.

"It killed me inside. Rather than encourage me it made me feel even more worthless. It's such a vicious circle, as all your family want is for you to wake up and get well, but all the anorexia wants you to do is disappear. Comments like the above only encourage the demons of an eating disorder."

When Gemma was first diagnosed, Dennis and I had to learn about eating disorders from scratch. We needed to understand that they are not about food at all but that, typically, there is an underlying issue causing the problem.

We learnt that our daughter was being bullied. This had undermined her confidence and she felt the only thing in her life that she could control was her food intake. She began to evaluate herself through her body weight and shape. That was when she began to waste away.

Her personality changed as she became ill and the sadness that was always present in her eyes will be etched into my mind forever. It took her the best part of nine years to recover, but we're so proud of how far she has come.

Her illness also inspired us to set up our charity, SEED Eating Disorder Support Services, which provides support for carers of people with eating disorders. Dennis and I set it up after recognising the lack of literature available and huge gaps in services.

Today, we hold workshops across the country and have helped hundreds of carers. It's not easy being a parent whose child is being attacked by this devastating illness, but with the right support, they can get through it together as a family, and come out stronger - just like we have.

Marg Oaten MBE is the secretary and co-founder of SEED Eating Disorder Support Services

The Daily Telegraph, 7 February 2017
© Telegraph Media Group Limited

What not to say to someone with an eating disorder

- 'For goodness' sake, just eat'
- 'Can't you see what you are doing to yourself'
- 'We're sick to death of this – you are so selfish. What you're doing is affecting everyone'
- 'You're starving yourself'
- 'Why are you doing this to us?'
- 'You're ruining your future'
- 'Stop being ridiculous'
- 'Grow up'
- 'You look really healthy' (they may hear this as "you look bigger")

For more information contact SEED www.seedeatingdisorders.org.uk or the UK's eating disorder charity B-eat www.b-eat.co.uk

What you should say to someone with an eating disorder

- 'I can see you have made an effort to eat what you have been given. Well done'
- 'Look how far you have come – you are slowly getting control back over your life. We are so proud of you'
- 'Well done for going out today/tonight'
- 'Don't worry if you come home early, at least you went'
- 'You should be really proud of yourself'
- 'It's okay to have a rest day'
- 'You're worth more than your eating disorder'
- 'I might not understand but if you need someone to talk to, I'm here'
- 'You look nice. That colour/hat/top really suits you.'

WHAT DO YOU THINK?

- **Do you think that Gemma was selfish?**
- **How should the parents have reacted?**
- **How typical are the parents' reactions?**

Weighty issues

The number of obese adults is increasing

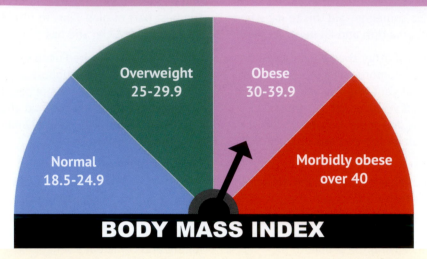

Overweight
25-29.9

Obese
30-39.9

Normal
18.5-24.9

Morbidly obese
over 40

BODY MASS INDEX

Overweight and obesity refer to an excess of body fat and they usually relate to increased weight-for-height.

The most common method of measuring obesity is the **Body Mass Index** (BMI) - this is measured by comparing weight to height.

A combination of weight, height and waist circumference is used to assess health risks from obesity in adults.

A person with a BMI of 30 or above and a waist measurement of more than 102cm for men or 88cm for women is at very high risk of health problems.

Overall, **35%** of **men** and **47%** of **women** had very high waist measurements. This was more common in middle aged and older adults than it was among younger people.

Regional comparisons

England: Obesity in adults increased from 15% in 1993 to 27% in 2015 and the number classed as morbidly obese - where someone is so obese that it is likely to lead to disease or death - has **more than tripled** in that time, reaching 2% of **men** and 4% of **women.**

58% of **women** and **68%** of **men** were overweight or obese.

Wales*: The Obesity rate among women in Wales at 24% is slightly higher than among men - 23%, although more men are **overweight** or **obese** - 63% compared to 56% of women.

Scotland: 67% of people aged 16 or above are **overweight or obese** - of these, 28% are obese.

Women are more likely to be obese - 30% - than men - 29%.

Northern Ireland: In 2015/16, **60%** of people were overweight or obese - 26% were obese and a further **34%** were **overweight.** Men were more likely to be **obese or overweight** - **65%** - than women - **57%**.

*Height and weight measurements are self-reported in the Welsh Health Survey and are therefore not directly comparable with equivalent statistics in Scotland, England and Northern Ireland, where direct measurements are taken.

Obesity among adults in England 2015

Of every 100 people...

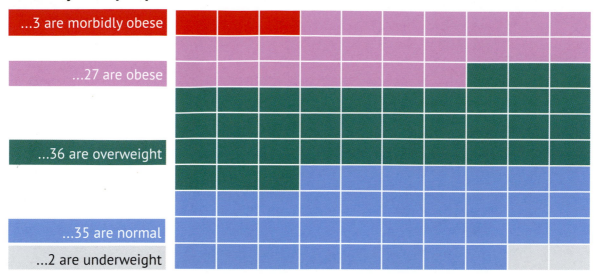

...3 are morbidly obese

...27 are obese

...36 are overweight

...35 are normal

...2 are underweight

Prevalence of overweight and obesity in England by age and gender

Male

● Overweight   ● Obese

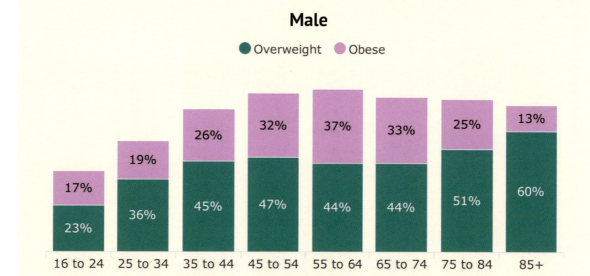

Age group	Obese	Overweight
16 to 24	17%	23%
25 to 34	19%	36%
35 to 44	26%	45%
45 to 54	32%	47%
55 to 64	37%	44%
65 to 74	33%	44%
75 to 84	25%	51%
85+	13%	60%

Age groups

Female

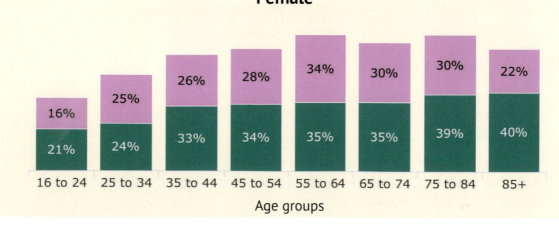

Age group	Obese	Overweight
16 to 24	16%	21%
25 to 34	25%	24%
35 to 44	26%	33%
45 to 54	28%	34%
55 to 64	34%	35%
65 to 74	30%	35%
75 to 84	30%	39%
85+	22%	40%

Age groups

Number of hospital admissions in England where obesity was the primary (main) or secondary reason, by age group

(NB Admissions do not represent the number of inpatients, as a person may have more than one admission within the year)

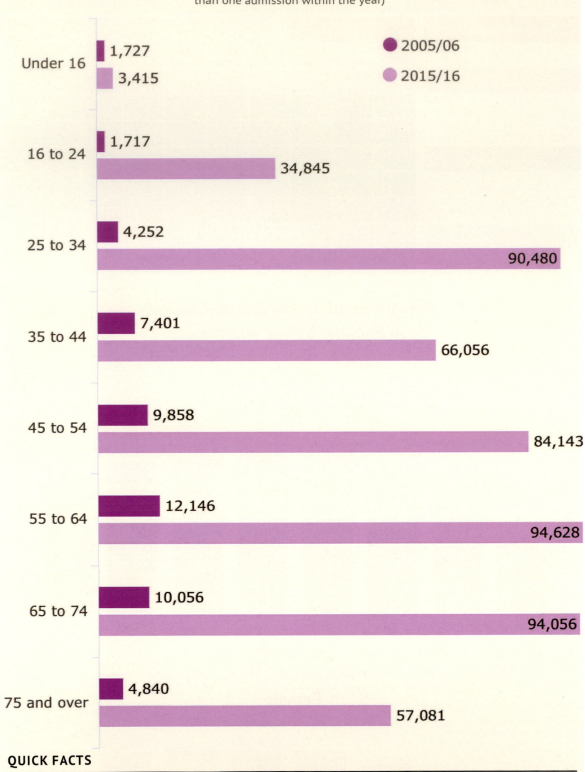

- 2005/06
- 2015/16

Age group	2005/06	2015/16
Under 16	1,727	3,415
16 to 24	1,717	34,845
25 to 34	4,252	90,480
35 to 44	7,401	66,056
45 to 54	9,858	84,143
55 to 64	12,146	94,628
65 to 74	10,056	94,056
75 and over	4,840	57,081

QUICK FACTS

- In 2015/16 there were **nearly 525,000** admissions in NHS hospitals where obesity was recorded as a factor - a **19% increase** on the previous year. **67%** of patients were **female**.

- There were **9,929** hospital admissions where the main diagnosis was obesity. **74%** were **female**. The main reason for admission was for surgery to reduce stomach size to promote weight loss.

Health risks

Obesity reduces life expectancy by an average of **3 to 10 years**, depending on how severe it is.

It's estimated that obesity and being overweight contribute to at least **1 in every 13** deaths in Europe.

Being obese can also increase your risk of developing many potentially **serious health conditions**, including:

- type 2 diabetes – a condition that causes a person's blood sugar level to become too high;

- high blood pressure;

- high cholesterol and atherosclerosis (where fatty deposits narrow your arteries), which can lead to coronary heart disease and stroke;

- asthma;

- metabolic syndrome – a combination of diabetes, high blood pressure and obesity

- several types of cancer, including bowel cancer, breast cancer and womb cancer;

- gastro-oesophageal reflux disease (GORD) – where stomach acid leaks out of the stomach and into the gullet;

- gallstones – small stones, usually made of cholesterol, that form in the gallbladder;

- reduced fertility;

- osteoarthritis – a condition involving pain and stiffness in your joints;

- sleep apnoea – a condition that causes interrupted breathing during sleep which can lead to daytime sleepiness with an increased risk of road traffic accidents, as well as a greater risk of diabetes, high blood pressure and heart disease;

- liver disease and kidney disease;

- pregnancy complications.

Health Survey for England 2015; Statistics on Obesity, Physical Activity and Diet England: 2017 © 2016, Health and Social Care Information Centre
http://digital.nhs.uk/pubs/hse2015
NHS Choices   http://www.nhs.uk/Conditions/Obesity/Pages/Introduction.aspx
House of Commons Library Obesity Statistics January 2017   www.parliament.uk

WHAT DO YOU THINK?

- Were you surprised at the percentage of overweight people in each age group?

- Why do you think there has been such a big increase in hospital admissions over 10 years?

- How would you try to help someone whose weight was causing them problems?

Photo posed by model

TYPE 2 DIABETES

"I WAS ONLY 16

I DIDN'T THINK IT WAS ACTUALLY ABOUT ME"

Before the year 2000 there were no reported cases of type 2 diabetes in children under the age of 18 in the UK. By 2016 there were almost 600 children* with the disease. Hollie was one of them. As an overweight teen, Hollie knew that people would point fingers and say she'd done it to herself. But no one blames Hollie more than she does herself. This is her story, as told to the Children's Food Trust

"All the women on my mum's side of the family are overweight. Growing up, we used to eat lots of home-cooked meals like pies and things. We'd have massive platefuls. I was eating veggies but I was just eating too much food. It was comfortable, that was just how my family was.

"When I started working at a supermarket and I had my own money and staff discount I bought chocolate, sweets and fizzy drinks to have on the way home. I also suffered from depression and eating chocolate and sweets was a big part of that. I'd simply just eat and eat, not caring. I put on even more weight.

"My doctor told me a couple of times that I was at risk of diabetes if I didn't lose weight. But it didn't mean much to me. I thought he was just saying it because he had to. I'd seen the leaflets and stuff on the telly, but I was only 16, I didn't think it was actually about me.

*Diabetes UK State of the Nation 2016

"About a year later I started to feel really poorly. I can't even explain how bad I was feeling. I was so thirsty. My mouth was really dry and I couldn't stop drinking. I was going to the toilet every 10 minutes.

"My mum has diabetes, and so does my aunty and my nan. I knew enough about the symptoms that I started to secretly worry that I might actually have it. But I didn't tell anyone, I hid it. I was scared, not because I thought it was serious, but because people would say it was my fault because I was overweight. I couldn't face being the overweight girl and have diabetes as well.

"Then something weird happened, I lost loads of weight without trying. I was still feeling really awful and eating junk food and drinking sugary drinks, but I lost about three and a half stone really quickly. People were complimenting me and I liked it. I also thought that if I lost weight, then if it was diabetes, it would just go away by itself.

"It was a couple of days after Christmas and I'd been feeling ill for about six months. Mum was shocked to find that all of the drinks she'd bought in for Christmas were gone. I'd drunk 100 cans of diet cola in less than a week. She sat me down and tested my blood sugar level – it was 35 (normal range is 4.0 to 6.0 mmol/L). Mum took me straight to hospital. I still didn't tell her my fears, I didn't want to disappoint her.

"When the nurse took my blood I remember thinking that it looked like red syrup – it came out really slow and sticky.

> I didn't want any of my friends to know. It was only when my closest friend asked what I'd got for Christmas that I said:
> **'I got diabetes for Christmas.'**

"I was terrified when they did an ECG to check whether I'd damaged my heart. I'd only ever thought about the symptoms of diabetes; being thirsty and needing to go to the toilet. I'd never thought diabetes could be damaging my organs. Luckily my heart was fine, but later on when I had an eye test they found that there were early signs of changes in the back of my eyes.

"The thing I remember most is how relieved I was when they said it was type 1 diabetes – I knew that was the one people got through no fault of their own. No one could blame me. So I was devastated when a few months later they diagnosed me with type 2 diabetes. It really was my fault and what was worse, I could have stopped it.

"I didn't want any of my friends to know. I didn't want them looking at me and thinking 'You've done that to yourself.' I already knew it was my fault. It was only when my closest friend asked what I'd got for Christmas that I said: 'I got diabetes for Christmas.'

"I was having to inject myself with insulin before every meal and taking tablets daily. I believed I'd done this to myself and now I was stuck with it. All these terrible things were going to happen like losing my limbs and damaging my heart and eyes, and it was something I could have prevented.

"But the diabetic team told me that I could change it. The dietician got me to keep a food diary and told me that just a few changes could make a big difference.

"I immediately cut out sweets and chocolate. I swapped sugary drinks for water and I thought more about portion sizes and the amount of carbohydrate I was eating. I was amazed that within a year I was able to stop using insulin. It was possible to control diabetes by being careful with my diet and tablets. I started to feel hopeful.

"Today, two years after being diagnosed my blood sugar average is 6.0 mmol/L – that's within the pre-diabetic range. My doctor says that if it reduces even more then I will be able to come off the medication and control it with diet alone. I am working really hard to control diabetes, after that I'll focus on getting my weight even further down.

"If I knew then what I know now I would never have been so casual about my health and my diet. I would have understood how serious diabetes is and I would have done everything in my power to have avoided getting it.

"People my age need to stop and think what they're doing. They don't want to be like me."

Source: Children's Food Trust Blog, 15 February, 2017
www.childrensfoodtrust.org.uk

WHAT DO YOU THINK?

- **Do you understand the reasons why Hollie put on weight?**

- **Should Hollie have confided in her friends?**

- **How does Hollie's warning to people her age make you feel?**

In-game abuse

The extent and nature of bullying in online gaming

2,515 people aged between 12 and 25 were surveyed in-game by Habbo.com for Ditch the Label. Doing the survey in this way ensured that 100% of the sample were people who actively played online games.

It found that **57%** of all online gamers had at some point been subjected to bullying in an online game and **20%** said they had bullied someone in an online game.

Have you ever...

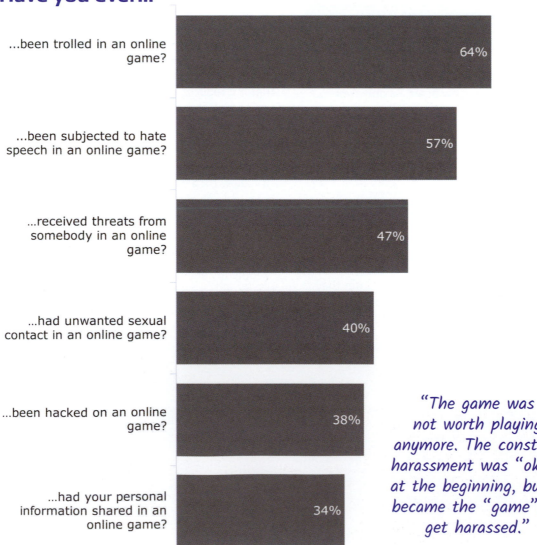

...been trolled in an online game? **64%**

...been subjected to hate speech in an online game? **57%**

...received threats from somebody in an online game? **47%**

...had unwanted sexual contact in an online game? **40%**

...been hacked on an online game? **38%**

...had your personal information shared in an online game? **34%**

"The game was not worth playing anymore. The constant harassment was "okay" at the beginning, but it became the "game", to get harassed."

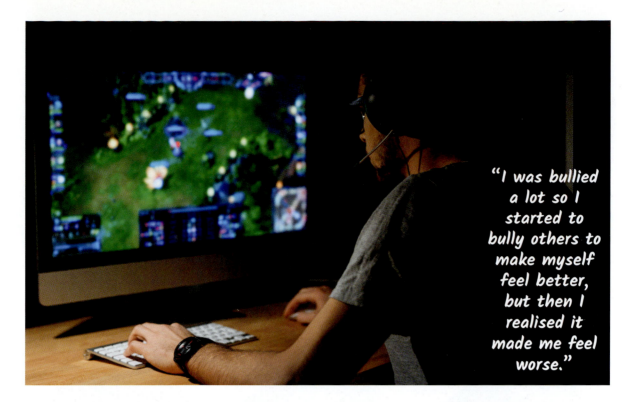

"I was bullied a lot so I started to bully others to make myself feel better, but then I realised it made me feel worse."

Have you ever quit an online game because of bullying?

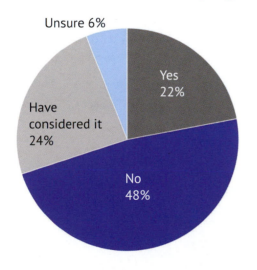

Unsure 6%

Yes 22%

Have considered it 24%

No 48%

Would you enjoy playing games more if bullying and trolling didn't exist?

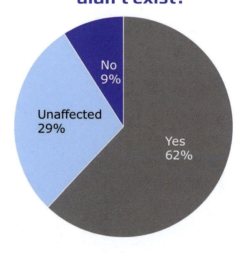

No 9%

Unaffected 29%

Yes 62%

Should bullying within online games be taken more seriously?

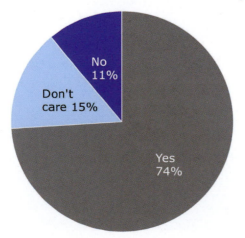

No 11%

Don't care 15%

Yes 74%

Have you ever reported bullying in an online game?

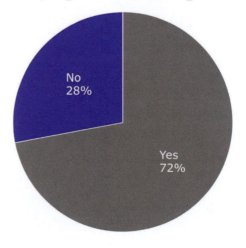

No 28%

Yes 72%

How can bullying be prevented in online games?

53%
extra human moderation

49%
anti-bullying advice & support in-game

48%
rewards for taking a stand against bullying

47%
more reporting & blocking features

42%
harsher punishments for bullying

38%
support for the bullies to help them stop

34%
anti-bullying campaigns in-game

23%
digital citizenship training at school

21%
better automatic moderation

Source: Copyright 2017 Ditch the Label® www.DitchtheLabel.org

WHAT DO YOU THINK?

- What are the attractions of online games?
- Have you ever had to deal with bullying online?
- What action do you think should be taken to stop this?

That noob is rekt!

Video games offer an escape from the everyday world - but not from abuse and bullying.

One of the greatest attractions of playing video games is the opportunity to take a break from the concerns of real life and indulge in something that is playful and in which you don't have to think about serious consequences. From puzzle games like Candy Crush to massively multi-player online games, there is something which will take your mind off routine troubles and give you a taste of excitement and stimulation. Unfortunately even within this artificial world the real world intrudes in the form of abusers and bullies.

Ditch The Label surveyed more than 2,500 players of online games and found that 57% said they had been bullied during a game. This takes the form of trolling, hacking, hate speech, threats, unwanted sexual approaches and even sharing of personal information.

Online play can be very intense and arouse strong emotions. Bullying may well start with one player who gets angry and aggressive. Banter becomes name calling and abusive language both on screen and in voice-chat. Jokes become insults, advice and instructions are replaced by commands and threats. Players are encouraged to report such behaviour but the damage may already be done.

Gaming language and culture

Gaming has its own language - terms which can be used to both include and exclude people. Some of these terms may be within the spirit of the game - it is how frequently they are done and who they are directed at that moves them from gamesmanship into bullying:

Team killing: to end the life of someone (or everyone) who is on your team. In some games it is possible to inflict 'friendly fire' on your allies.

Griefing: similar to team killing - shooting or sabotaging your team-mate - but has a wider meaning of simply doing something that creates 'grief' and prevents another player from enjoying the game, eg making it impossible for them to continue.

Causing aggro: performing (usually) aggressive actions in order to attract attention of Non Player Characters (NPCs) to defeat a player character.

Grinding: repeating an action - often to obtain an item useful within the game, but sometimes just to frustrate another player.

Camping: remaining out of sight somewhere safe within the landscape of the game to avoid damage to yourself and to ambush others. This could be regarded either as cheating or strategic play.

Drop-hacking: when someone deliberately disconnects from the game when they are about to lose.

Rekt: wrecked. When a player is destroyed.

Noob: sometimes n00b, should just refer to someone who is new to the game but it is also a scornful expression for anyone who is less competent or who complains after being beaten.

The problem of abuse is recognised both by players and game designers. BM - bad manners - refers to behaviour which is not exactly cheating but is not fair play. And GLHF - good luck, have fun - which is used before a match, suggests a better spirit and a friendlier ethos.

57%
of players said they had been bullied during a game.

Why do people behave so badly?

Frustration: People get so involved in the game that they find interruptions or errors unbearable.

Character: Either because someone is acting in accordance with their real-life character or against it. Someone who is unused to failure, or who has little personal resilience may want to place the blame for the failure of the task on another player. If that person has not learnt to control their impulses they may then lash out - with aggressive words or actions. Or it may be that a person acts in a way that is completely opposite to their everyday character. Protected by the on-line persona they have created, they can use their avatar to behave in a socially unacceptable way.

Context of the game: The nature of some games encourages - and rewards - aggressive play. A player may then be so caught up in that world that those violent feelings spill over.

Anonymity: Within the game you are quite anonymous. Someone who is tempted to behave badly knows that they are unlikely to be identified or to encounter the actual players they are acting against in real life. They do not have to face the consequences of their rudeness. As in other areas of the internet, anonymity encourages unacceptable behaviour.

Depersonalisation: The victim is remote, someone we are unlikely to see in the real world so unpleasant behaviour is safer.

Sometimes the bully will not even see the victim as a real person at all - he sees an avatar, not so different from the NPCs which are controlled by the computer and which exist only in the world of the game. NPCs don't have feelings, aren't distressed by abuse and are always the same. There is no perception of the real person behind the avatar.

Team: Being part of a team is one of the attractions of multi-player games. Bullying isn't always one on one - if stronger, more successful players turn on a weaker one there is a dilemma about rushing to their defence. In the context of the game there could be an advantage in teaming up against the person targeted, even if they are on your side. It's hard to be the individual that stands out.

Standards of behaviour: Behaviour in the gaming world is different from the real world. What is acceptable is less well defined and more flexible. In that context, bad behaviour shown by one individual can spread widely as there is no hard and fast rule as to what is acceptable, it can appear to be normal to be nasty.

When things go badly wrong

In 2014, Breck Bednar, aged 14, was groomed and murdered by an 18 year old man he encountered while playing online. Within the gaming universe the predator was able to hide behind an alias, create an impressive fantasy life, impose his ideas on an impressionable group, isolate a young man from his family and entice him to meet in real life. The consequences are seldom as tragic as this, but online abuse within games can be disturbing and there is no clear set of actions to counter it. A recent example from a forum for players of 'Overwatch' illustrates the point:

"Tonight I was told to kill myself, multiple times, and was even suggested methods in which I should do it and reasons why...

I know it's said lightly online, but it really hurts. I have posted a report but I needed to vent frustration and maybe make someone think twice before saying it in the future."

Even most of the sympathetic responses suggested that bullying was inevitable - "Internet is toxic, just like water is wet".

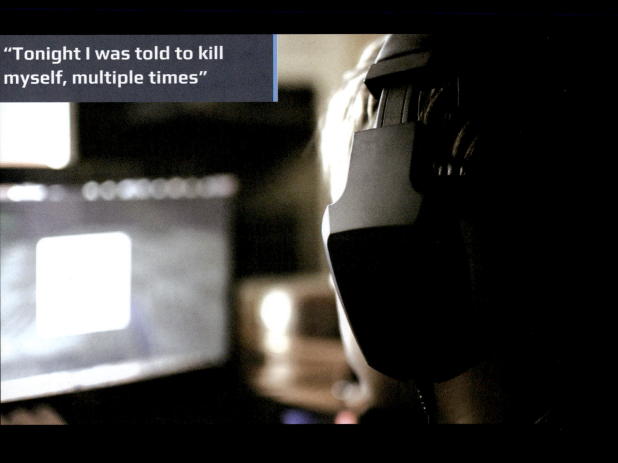

"Tonight I was told to kill myself, multiple times"

Sometimes the bully will not even see the victim as a real person

Sexism

The gaming world can be a hostile place for females. The majority of role-play and multi-player games conform to the 'boys toys' stereotype which perhaps encourages some misogynists to claim gaming as their exclusive territory. The prejudice against females was highlighted by the notorious 'gamergate' scandal in which a female game designer and her supporters were bullied and harassed with death and rape threats so serious that they were forced to leave their homes and go into hiding. There is a familiar vicious circle at work here - the more women are attacked the less likely it is that they will identify themselves as 'gamers'. The fewer women there are in the audience, the less likely it is that games will include scenarios and role models which adult women can relate to and avatars which are not adolescent boys' fantasies.

What can you do about it?

Some games may punish badly behaved players, especially repeat offenders, banning players for team kills, for example. But in the main players do not want heavy handed bans which would affect the game. Game developers could change the social norms within play. If the emphasis was on cooperation and friendliness this could give players a nudge towards good behaviour rather than bad. League of Legends, for example, includes 'The Summoners Code' - six admonitions which include: 'Don't rage, blame or tear people down' and the explanation:

'We've all had tough games where we fell behind, got camped super hard or missed an easy smite, only to get flamed in chat. Avoid making others feel that same way and report the ones who do.'

Can abuse be eradicated from games? Perhaps not. But reporting abusive players and not allowing bullying to become normalised must be a start. Every player is there to have fun, and no player has the right to interfere with that.

Sources: Various

Is social media harming you?

As a young Brit you spend more time than most on the net. What is that doing to you?

Social media has been a growing part of daily life for over a decade. For a young person it is probably an entirely natural and integral part of everyday existence.

But ten years is very little time to measure either the immediate or long-term effects of what is, in fact, a huge change in behaviour from previous generations.

In June 2017 the Educational Policy Institute looked at the evidence about the effect that social media might be having on the wellbeing of children and young people. They found that young people in Britain use the internet more than others of the same age in other developed countries. **Over a third** of UK 15 year olds are online for more than six hours a day at weekends - meaning that they are classified as extreme users. Children in Britain start younger, too, almost a third started their digital life at or before the age of six.

We know that the internet has many positive impacts and many ways of making life better. Young people value the emotional support and practical advice that is readily, and discreetly, available. It can help shy youngsters become more socially active and there is some evidence that online suicide prevention is effective and those at risk can be identified and supported through social media. But because the internet is constantly changing - mobile devices make interaction more rapid and frequent, you can share more easily with others and keep things private from parents - it difficult is for research to keep pace and to analyse what might be happening to your behaviour, your brain and your mental health.

Age at which young people started using the internet

● UK ● OECD average

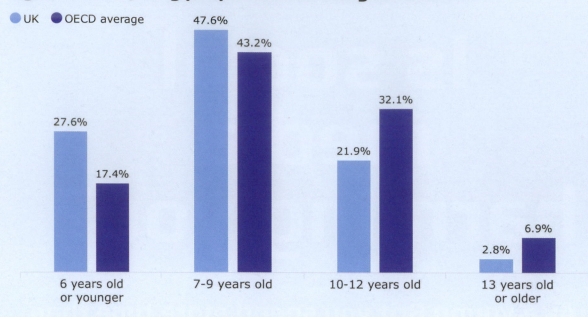

6 years old or younger: UK 27.6%, OECD average 17.4%
7-9 years old: UK 47.6%, OECD average 43.2%
10-12 years old: UK 21.9%, OECD average 32.1%
13 years old or older: UK 2.8%, OECD average 6.9%

Internet use on a typical WEEKEND day

● UK ● OECD average

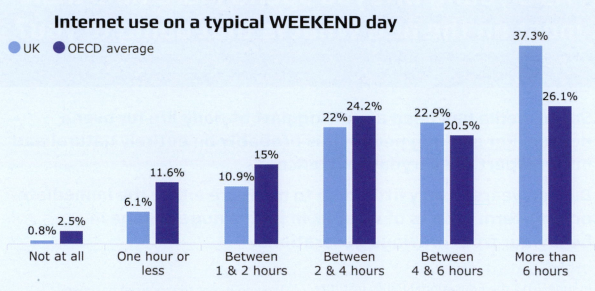

Not at all: UK 0.8%, OECD average 2.5%
One hour or less: UK 6.1%, OECD average 11.6%
Between 1 & 2 hours: UK 10.9%, OECD average 15%
Between 2 & 4 hours: UK 22%, OECD average 24.2%
Between 4 & 6 hours: UK 22.9%, OECD average 20.5%
More than 6 hours: UK 37.3%, OECD average 26.1%

Internet use outside of school on a typical WEEKDAY

● UK ● OECD average

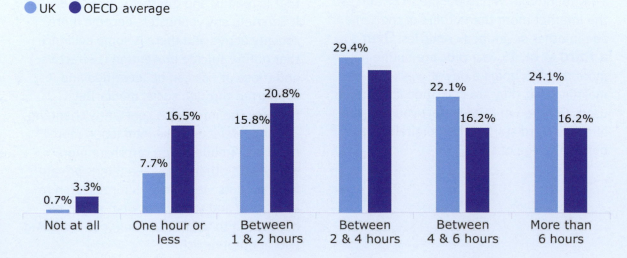

Not at all: UK 0.7%, OECD average 3.3%
One hour or less: UK 7.7%, OECD average 16.5%
Between 1 & 2 hours: UK 15.8%, OECD average 20.8%
Between 2 & 4 hours: UK 29.4%
Between 4 & 6 hours: UK 22.1%, OECD average 16.2%
More than 6 hours: UK 24.1%, OECD average 16.2%

How much time is too much?

Different age groups disagree about how much time is 'too much' to spend online. However, there is evidence that people can feel a compulsion to be connected. In an Ofcom survey, **59%** of UK 16-24 year olds felt they spent too much time online, a quarter said they felt nervous or anxious when they were offline through fear of missing out - the FOMO phenomenon. **37%** said they had neglected work of some sort to remain online. Teenagers said they'd missed sleep - **72%** - or neglected studies - **60%** - and, inevitably, had been told off by their parents - **78%** - for spending too much time on the internet.

Oversharing

It is becoming easier and easier to share our lives wherever we are and whatever we are doing. The internet breaks down old barriers between what is private and what is public. Something as trivial as sharing pictures of meals, for example, was literally unthinkable before smartphones and constant connectivity.

On the internet people behave differently - actions which you would be unlikely to consider, and words which you might normally think but not say in real life, seem acceptable. You routinely share personal information with strangers, act and speak in a more intense way.

Smartphones have increased the risk of sharing too much, especially if you are a bit vulnerable - in an emotional state, or having over-indulged. The consequences of sharing or having others share something you would have preferred to keep private can be very damaging. Surprisingly, despite the impression given by the media, sharing naked selfies does not seem to be very widespread. In an NSPCC survey in 2016 only **2.9%** of youngsters said they had ever taken such a picture and **55%** of those had shared it.

Something as trivial as sharing pictures of meals, for example, was literally unthinkable before smartphones and constant connectivity.

Cyberbullying

Often the bullies and the victims of cyberbullying are the same people in the real world. However, cyberbullying has some special aspects which make it particularly harmful. You can be sheltered from physical bullying at home and in school but online abuse is unlimited in the times and places it can occur. A single incident of abuse can be forwarded and multiplied, and the abuse can be intense and hurtful in its content. Interestingly, extreme internet users are likely to be the victims of bullying behaviour in real life.

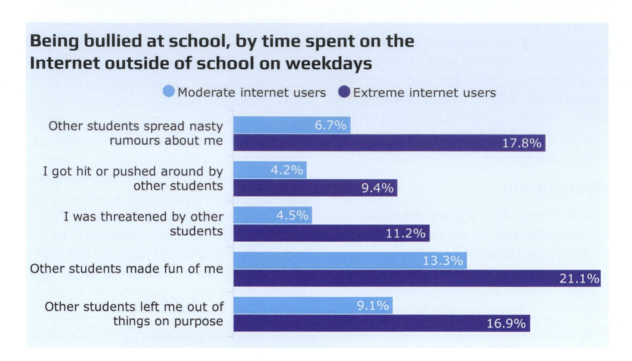

Being bullied at school, by time spent on the Internet outside of school on weekdays

- Moderate internet users
- Extreme internet users

Other students spread nasty rumours about me — 6.7% / 17.8%

I got hit or pushed around by other students — 4.2% / 9.4%

I was threatened by other students — 4.5% / 11.2%

Other students made fun of me — 13.3% / 21.1%

Other students left me out of things on purpose — 9.1% / 16.9%

Body Image

Young people, who may feel self-conscious about their bodies, constantly encounter idealised images online. You may have online friends who big up their lifestyles and enhance their pictures to try to make people envious. Research suggests that this can, in fact, make people anxious and promote feelings of inferiority.

Harmful information

While the web gives you access to useful information it can also encourage unhealthy behaviours. There are sites and groups which promote eating disorders, discuss self-harm and even advocate suicide, giving detailed information on methods. These harmful behaviours are being presented as legitimate lifestyle choices. There is a possibility that someone looking for help with a problem might instead start to see dangerous actions as a normal and reasonable response.

Risks

34% of young internet users in the UK reported that they had experienced something identified as a 'risk' online - such as bullying, sexual content or harmful content. Most were able to shrug it off, only **15%** suggested that they had been bothered by it (though girls and older teenagers were more likely to be upset). Bullying was the most upsetting behaviour.

According to the NSPCC only **22%** of children who experienced a problem would speak to someone about it - and that someone was often a friend rather than an adult. When they were asked if they knew how to block a user or change their privacy settings it was clear that older children had more skills than younger ones. It seems that using the internet helps you to develop the skills you need but young children need to be taught how to navigate it safely.

A smartphone addiction brings with it anxiety about getting an immediate response and approval for what they post online

Concerns remain about time spent on the internet and about new threats and dangers. Livestreaming, for example, can mean that your actions could be instantly circulated to a wide audience, with or without your consent, or that you could come across distressing, even traumatising, live material - such as the (very few) incidences of livestreamed assaults or suicide attempts.

At the same time as there has been a rise in the use of social media, there has been an apparent rise in mental health problems amongst young people, particularly young women. The two trends may be unrelated, currently there is not enough evidence to prove that one causes the other. The figures do tend to point to a link between social media use and mental health problems. **12%** of children who spend no time on social media have symptoms of mental ill health but this rises to **27%** for those who are online for three hours or more per day. There has been research which links excessive internet use with depression, poor sleep and emotional problems as well as effects on concentration and calmness. For some people a smartphone addiction brings with it anxiety about getting an immediate response and approval for what they post online. Time spent online is also associated with poor academic results.

The figures may tell us that cyberspace is a disturbing place to spend any length of time. Or it may be that people who are already experiencing difficulties with their mental health are using the internet as a way to cope. There is no conclusive answer and research will continue to lag behind the fast pace of developments.

Sources: Social media and children's mental health: a review of the Evidence 2017 - Education Policy Institute & others
https://epi.org.uk

WHAT DO YOU THINK?

- Based on the definitions, would you class yourself as a moderate or extreme internet user?
- Do you believe that use of the internet damages some people?
- What research should be done to see how these changes are affecting people?

Internet vs TV time

People still spend more time with television than with the internet — but that's changing fast

Average daily TV and internet consumption per person worldwide in minutes

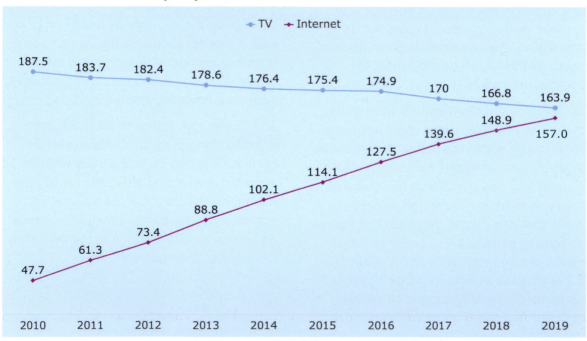

2017-2019 are estimates
Source: Zenith www.zenithmedia.com

WHAT DO YOU THINK?

- **Does this chart seem to fit your experience?**
- **What factors are behind this change in behaviour?**
- **Do you think TV watching will become a thing of the past?**

IT'S TIME TO UPDATE YOUR
PASSWORD

James Titcomb, Telegraph technology news editor

Think of a password that is impossible for you to forget but equally impossible for anybody else to guess. Too farfetched? Not at all. As it turns out, you were born with one: your body.

From the make-up of our fingerprints to the colour patterns of our eyes, our dental records, and even the structure of our veins, our biological identities are unique to us – and technology that can tell who we are by scanning a thumb or iris is no longer the preserve of science fiction.

Biometric technology is not new, but it is now becoming an increasingly common part of our lives. Your mobile phone can now be unlocked by reading your fingerprints, banks are using voice-recognition technology as a precaution and our passports contain identification chips that remove the hassle of queuing at airports.

But this is only the beginning. Imagine walking into a pub and putting your finger into a vein scanner. Instantly, the terminal knows what your favourite drink is, orders it and then takes payment from your credit card.

Such gadgetry may sound years away but "FingoPay" technology is already being trialled by Sthaler, a British company. Vein authentication – just one example – is more secure than any PIN: the chances of two people having the same vein structure is 3.4 billion-to-one.

Reliable biometric technology has the potential to go a considerable way towards eradicating fraud. It may be easy to obtain someone's password or driving licence but incredibly difficult to steal their iris or fingerprint (although, it should be said, not impossible).

All new technologies, though, have upsides and downsides. As we live more and more of our lives online, the risks of hackers infiltrating our lives grows. Just last year billions of accounts were compromised and the need for greater security becomes more imperative. We need to be careful what we wish for.

Yes, the benefits of technology are dazzling, but the potential drawbacks – if unmet – are alarming. A world in which CCTV cameras can instantly recognise people using facial recognition technology or by analysing their walking gait may be as disturbing as it is reassuring. It's a brave new world. And we must be too.

WHAT DO YOU THINK?

- Are you already used to biometric identification?
- Are there any drawbacks to this sort of technology?
- How do you feel about CCTV cameras being able to recognise you?

Should the police in Britain carry guns?

Almost every other country in the world routinely arms their police. Why is Britain different?

After a spate of terrorist attacks in Europe, there was a deadly attack in London in March 2017 in which an unarmed policeman was murdered. A terrorist driving a lorry mowed down passers-by on Westminster Bridge killing 4 people, then killed PC Keith Palmer who was guarding the Houses of Parliament. The terrorist was then shot dead. Should PC Palmer have been armed? Why aren't all British police armed?

Almost every other country in the world routinely arms their police. Why is Britain different? Aren't armed police better able to tackle any situation in a world that is increasingly unpredictable and where terrorists are more ruthless than ever?

The fact that British police aren't usually armed is the most distinctive characteristic of British police. Only a handful of other countries, all small, have police who are normally unarmed: Norway, Iceland, New Zealand and Ireland.

Yet the sad truth is that in countries where the police are armed, such as France, Turkey and Germany, there have still been murderous terrorist attacks which the police have been unable to prevent.

Unarmed policing is part of a British tradition. It encourages greater trust in the police and places an emphasis on policing by consent. Unarmed police can be seen much more as part of the community. They are more approachable.

If all our police carried arms, the atmosphere on our streets would inevitably be different. Seeing guns naturally puts people on edge. It could also lead to some criminals deciding that they too should be armed. Armed police in other countries are often known for a more confrontational and aggressive style of policing.

In fact, despite some fairly rare, but highly publicised, cases there is no evidence that Britain needs to arm its police. In England and Wales in the 12 months to March 2016, police fired guns on just seven occasions and this was the greatest number of times since 2009.

Unarmed police can be seen as part of the community.

But don't guns give the best protection to police themselves? In fact, police deaths are rare in the UK. 27 have been killed since the year 2000, 10 of whom have died since 2010. In the USA, on average, 151 police officers are killed every year for a population that is just 5 times bigger than the UK's.

When police are routinely armed, there is obviously a much greater chance of the police shooting and killing people. 1,092 people were killed by US police in 2016 including a disproportionately high number of native Americans and black people. In the USA these killings have undermined confidence in the police and driven a wedge between the police and minority communities.

Inevitably with armed police there is always the danger of the wrong person being shot and killed as in the notorious case of Jean Charles de Menezes, the Brazilian man shot dead by police on the London Underground in 2005 after being wrongly identified as a terrorist (soon after the July 2005 London bombings).

Arming the police would require massive extra expenditure in terms of buying firearms and training programmes for officers. This would divert resources and attention from all the other key areas of policing.

The police in the UK already have access to specialist armed officers on the rare occasions when they are required as well as access to tasers since 2000.

Crime in Britain, as in most western countries, is generally declining. Where crime is rising, for example many more children and young people are carrying knives, would arming the police help to tackle this problem?

Sources: Various

Armed Crime - the facts

- **Britain has one of the lowest rates of murders using a firearm in the world.**

- **There were 19 deaths resulting from offences involving firearms in the year ending March 2015.**

- **Firearms were only used in 0.2% of all recorded crimes (year ending March 2015).**

- **The number of crimes involving guns has fallen by 67% since 2004.**

Police training in Indiana, USA.
Photo: John Crosby

WHAT DO YOU THINK?

- How would you feel if all the police on our streets were armed?

- Would Britain be safer with an armed police force?

- What are the main arguments for and against arming the police?

Firearms officers - the facts

Since the recent terror attacks in London and Manchester, questions have been raised about whether all officers should be routinely armed

The term AFO - authorised firearms officer - can be used to refer specifically to an armed officer trained at the basic level as well as to any officer who is authorised to use firearms in general.

Armed officers, 31 March 2009 to 31 March 2017, England and Wales

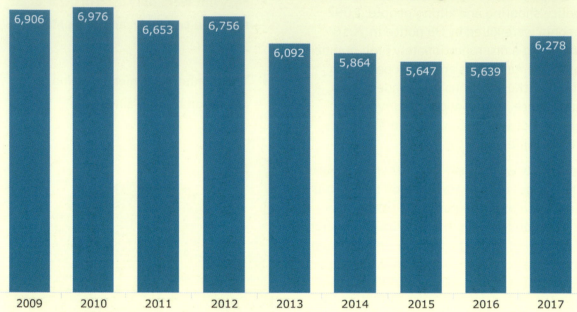

2009	2010	2011	2012	2013	2014	2015	2016	2017
6,906	6,976	6,653	6,756	6,092	5,864	5,647	5,639	6,278

QUICK FACTS

- The number of AFOs at 31st March 2017 was up by **11.3%** on 2016, and was the first increase in the number of armed officers since 31st March 2012.

- Between 31st March 2009 and 31st March 2016, there had been an overall decrease of **1,267** armed officers **-18%**.

- **5%** of all police officers were AFOs.

- There were a total of **15,705 operations** for which the issue of firearms was authorised.

- There were **10 incidents** in which police discharged firearms.

- The National Police Chief's Council said there will be **1,500 extra officers** in total by the end of 2018 across the 43 Home Office forces – some of which will be highly specialised in responding to ongoing terrorist incidents.

"We have the ability to move more quickly to resolve situations. Previously the approach was to locate, contain and neutralise. Now it is to locate and confront. Our tactics are more aggressive."

Deputy Chief Constable Simon Chesterman
National Police Chief's Council Lead for Armed Policing

"I don't think the public want to live in a place where we are all armed to the teeth."

Cressida Dick
Metropolitan Police Chief

Source: Police use of firearms statistics, England and Wales, Home Office © Crown copyright 2017 www.gov.uk
National Police Chiefs' Council www.npcc.police.uk

Why are we seeing a rise in acid attacks?

They aren't new

Right from the time of the industrial revolution there were reports of attacks with a noxious substance. Vitriol - sulphuric acid - was used in textile bleaching and other processes and was therefore readily available. Often the attacker was motivated by jealousy or having been rejected by a lover. Acid attacks were common enough to have acquired a specific name: vitriolage.

They aren't only happening in Britain

We are, unfortunately, used to hearing about incidents of women in the developing world being assaulted with acid because they have turned down a proposal of marriage or transgressed in some, often very minor, way against their village elders. However, in the UK attacks have also targeted men, in fact they are twice as likely to be victims as women.

Why acid?

In contrast to other 'weapons' it is easy to access. There are already strict laws to restrict guns and to sentence people who carry knives. If you attack someone with a knife the charge is likely to be murder or attempted murder. If you attack someone with acid you would be charged with Grievous Bodily Harm.

Corrosive substances are an essential part of many domestic cleaning materials and liquids and gels used to remove paint or rust. These are readily available in hardware and general stores; there are no restrictions on buying them.

Acid is easily concealed - simply transfer it to a different container and it will appear completely innocent. In any case it is not an offence to have it in your possession - unless it can be proved that you intend to cause harm with it. It is easy to use - from a distance - and leaves no traces of the attacker, and a small amount can cause a great deal of irreversible damage.

Why now?

That depends on the reason behind the attacks. There has been a reported increase in hate crimes since the Brexit campaign and vote. The attack on Resham Khan and her cousin who had acid thrown on them in their car has been labelled a hate crime. It was obsessive jealousy that caused Mary Koyne to throw acid at a former friend, an act for which she has recently been sentenced to 12 years in jail.

Theft seems to have been the motive in a series of attacks on moped riders. Ammonia has been used in car jackings. An acid attack in a London nightclub which left twenty or more people needing treatment was linked to an argument over drugs. There's a difference here from other types of theft. When threatened with a gun or a knife the victim has a choice - give up your goods or else get hurt. In an acid attack the assault comes first, the victim is disabled, and disfigured to enable the theft.

There is also speculation that the sheer horror of the crime is an attraction for some young gang members - a way to instantly build a reputation. From a safe distance, even anonymously, the attacker makes a calculated assault.

These attacks have a devastating effect on the victim's life, their physical and mental wellbeing and the future they had expected. The intention is generally not to kill, it is to ruin and to mark. To ruin, specifically, the face of the victim, to mark them out so everyone looks at them but they can hardly bear to look at themselves. People attacked in this way suffer years of medical intervention but are often denied a full recovery.

The community also suffers in these attacks. Everyone who knows the victim, and possibly the aggressor, will feel some level of fear. Wider society is disturbed by the frequency, ease and barbarity of the crime. And fear has an effect on security. According to the Metropolitan Police, since 2014 about 74% of investigations into acid attacks have been wound down because of problems identifying perpetrators, or because victims have been unwilling to press charges.

Number of acid attacks, UK
including London

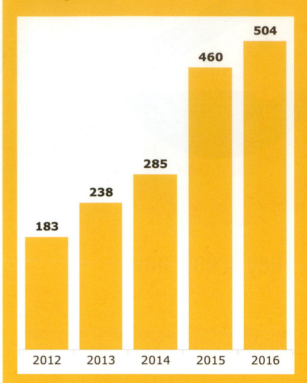

Year	Number
2012	183
2013	238
2014	285
2015	460
2016	504

Figures from police forces across the UK suggest that the number of assaults involving corrosive substances has risen by **30% in two years.**

408 acid or "corrosive substance" attacks were recorded between November 2016 to April 2017, according to the National Police Chiefs' Council.

Bleach, ammonia and acid were the most commonly used substances.

20% of known offenders were **under 18** years old.

Number of acid attacks, London

The Metropolitan police registered **458** offences involving noxious or corrosive liquids or the throwing of corrosive fluids with intent to do grievous bodily harm in 2016, compared to just **116** in 2014.

From January 2014 to April 2017 the police force recorded **949** attacks that fell into this category.

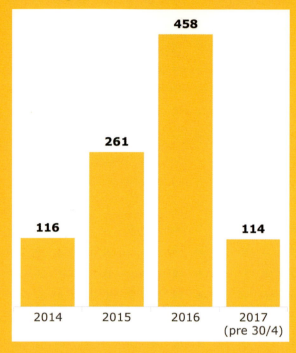

	116	261	458	114
	2014	2015	2016	2017 (pre 30/4)

Of the **833** attacks carried out between January 2015 and April 2016, nearly **50%** were in just 3 London boroughs.

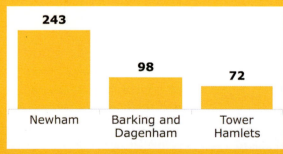

243	98	72
Newham	Barking and Dagenham	Tower Hamlets

In July 2017, the Metropolitan Police started to fit response vehicles with acid attack kits.

They include protective gear and a 5 litre bottle of water, which officers can use to help treat victims immediately following an attack.

Photo: Flickr/EDDIE used under Creative Commons Licence

What is the law at the moment?

There is no specific law dealing with acid attacks.

Possession of acid or other corrosive substances with intent to do harm can be treated as possession of an offensive weapon under the Prevention of Crime Act, which carries a maximum penalty of four years in jail.

Someone charged with GBH for an acid attack can receive a life sentence in certain circumstances.

What can be done?

There are calls to restrict the sales of corrosive chemicals, either by registering all sales or by age restrictions. Jaf Shah, of Acid Survivors Trust International wants the government to make it compulsory when purchasing corrosive chemicals to pay by card that is traceable to an individual and to make acid available only under licence. Such substances could also be included on the list of items which shopkeepers must inform the police about if they are bought by someone suspicious.

Sentencing guidelines can be reviewed so that people accused of carrying acid with the intent to harm receive the maximum penalty. Assistant Chief Constable Rachel Kearton, suggests "To have an acid in a different bottle to the one it was purchased in can be an offence"

Victims fight back

Katie Piper has refused to be defined by the scars she was left with after an acid attack arranged by an ex-boyfriend nine years ago. Her charitable foundation helps other victims and her high media profile has inspired victims with hope. In this open letter, she responds to the horrific series of attacks across London in one night.

Attacks with various corrosive substances appear to be on the rise in some parts of the UK and I'm sharing my experiences below in the hope that it may help to shape the future and prevent further attacks on others. I am writing in an open access medical journal to reach out to experts, as well as the general public and lawmakers.

In March 2008, when I was 24 years old, a man I had been dating arranged for an accomplice to throw sulphuric acid in my face. This attack left me partially blinded, with severe, permanent scarring to my face, chest, neck, arm and hands.

I couldn't recognise myself when I woke up from a coma and I wanted to commit suicide. I also swallowed some of the acid in the attack, damaging my throat, and I still require ongoing surgery on my throat to help me swallow and prevent scars closing it entirely; I suffered dangerous complications from one of these surgeries and my life was at risk once again.

Since the attack I have undergone over 250 operations to improve my physical functioning, including operations to help me breathe through my nose, as well as hours of psychological therapy to help me to deal with the trauma of the attack and to accept my 'new face'. I will continue to need operations and therapy for life.

For acid attack survivors, the aftermath is a life sentence.

Soon after I left hospital, I set up a charity to help adults with burns from any cause, with the goal of setting up a residential burn rehabilitation centre in the UK.

Through my charity work, and via social media, I have met or spoken to many others who have been attacked with corrosive substances and whose lives have been shattered by the trauma of the attack, their permanent change in appearance and the loss of their identity; some have also lost vision and physical function.

Through my charity's support and rehabilitation work I see that it is not only the individuals, but also their families and friends, who are affected. Lives can be destroyed in moments.

Survivors of such attacks often have to live with the immediate fear that their attackers may still be at large, and in the longer term—even if the attackers are caught and sentenced—may be released to potentially live alongside them after serving a minimum term.

I meet many inspiring individuals who have worked hard to rebuild their lives after an attack; however, it can be hard to stay motivated when the justice system does not always reflect the severity of these crimes.

At present, it is all too easy for someone to buy a corrosive substance and throw it, sometimes from a distance, at another person. It is vital that we do everything we can to halt these types of attack.

The current legislation does not always recognise the severity of the offence and, therefore, the sentencing does not reflect the severity of the crime in some cases.

Tougher sentencing would surely act as a deterrent to further attacks. The issue of penalties for carrying corrosive substances needs to be addressed and restrictions on the sale of corrosive substances need to be looked at seriously and methodically through a scientific and well-resourced approach that leads to swift action.

This situation cannot be allowed to continue or escalate and this is my plea to prevent more lives being destroyed. My sincere thanks to those who are already proactively looking at these difficult, but important, issues and working towards solutions.

https://katiepiperfoundation.org.uk/

Resham Khan was the victim of an acid attack on her 21st birthday. She has used the publicity surrounding her case to start a petition for reforms:

I cannot sit back whilst others remain indoors in fear of this happening to them. This problem needs to be eliminated. I refuse to allow the country I grew up in to simply get used to corrosive substance attacks. The fear is real. The crime is real. And I propose that action be taken now:

1. The Metropolitan Police play a vital role in shaping the approach individuals take towards atrocious acts. ... By declaring a **zero-tolerance** stance, this will deter criminals and send out a clear message to the citizens of this country – that they are safe and protected. There is no place in any society for corrosive substance attacks, so let's have those that protect us remind the country.

2. From the easy, cheap instore sale of these substances in its many forms, to the ease of online sales to anyone with debit card details, we ask **retailers to act more responsibly** in regards to corrosive substances...we hope retailers contribute to helping to create a safer society.

3. Although attacks don't last for long, all the victims of corrosive substance attacks are left with a life time of physical and psychological pain and scarring. Whilst in hospital I have learnt that it is not just the burn or the scar, it's everything else; preparing to face the world again feeling like a different person, all the time spent in fear of and in pain due to procedures, spending hours questioning how and if the world will accept you, and wondering why any

human being would do this to another human being. The person who attacked me didn't want to just take away my face, he wanted to burn all aspects of my life. For this, I ask that the UK government introduce **stricter punishment** for those who choose to scorch innocent people.

4. In regards to corrosive substances themselves, knowing the correct way to approach the problem has proved challenging. We ask for the **possession** of corrosive substances without good reason to become a **punishable offense** and that legislation on the possession of an offensive weapon be updated to include certain concentrations of corrosive substances, and that advice and guidance is provided to prosecutors so that it is effectively recognised that this is a serious offence.

5. Additionally, we propose the UK government impose **licensing regulations** for the buying of corrosive substances.

Source: resham.online

WHAT DO YOU THINK?

- **What actions should be taken to prevent such attacks?**
- **Would harsher punishments be a deterrent?**
- **What help should be offered to the victims?**

Victims of crime

People's experience of crime

The Crime Survey for England and Wales is a face-to-face survey of 35,000 adults and 3,000 children in England and Wales about a selected range of offences which happened in the 12 months prior to the interview.

It includes incidents which were not reported to the police and focuses on personal experiences.

It includes a broad range of victim-based crimes but there are some crimes which are high harm but relatively rare, such as homicide and sexual offences, which are not included.

Excluding fraud and computer misuse offences, adults aged 16 and over experienced about **5.9 million** incidents of crime in the year ending March 2017.

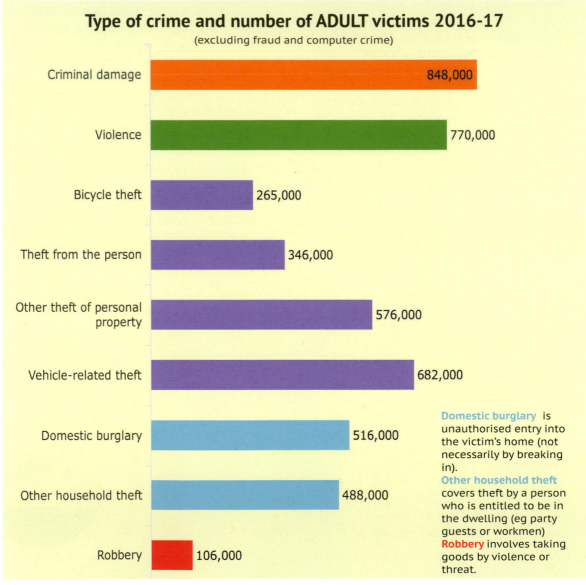

Type of crime and number of ADULT victims 2016-17

(excluding fraud and computer crime)

Type of crime	Number of victims
Criminal damage	848,000
Violence	770,000
Bicycle theft	265,000
Theft from the person	346,000
Other theft of personal property	576,000
Vehicle-related theft	682,000
Domestic burglary	516,000
Other household theft	488,000
Robbery	106,000

Domestic burglary is unauthorised entry into the victim's home (not necessarily by breaking in).
Other household theft covers theft by a person who is entitled to be in the dwelling (eg party guests or workmen)
Robbery involves taking goods by violence or threat.

QUICK FACTS ON CRIME RATES

- Although the figures may seem large the crime rate has been steadily decreasing.

- **2.7 %** of people experienced any **violence**.

- **4.2%** of owners suffered any **theft** related to a vehicle.

- **4.8%** of people mentioned **criminal damage.**

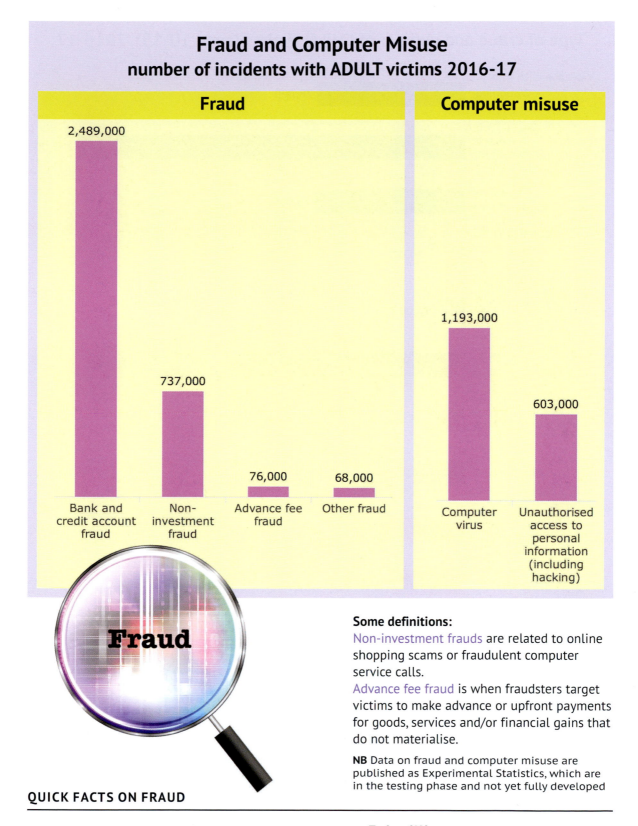

Fraud and Computer Misuse
number of incidents with ADULT victims 2016-17

Fraud

2,489,000

737,000

76,000

68,000

Bank and credit account fraud

Non-investment fraud

Advance fee fraud

Other fraud

Computer misuse

1,193,000

603,000

Computer virus

Unauthorised access to personal information (including hacking)

Fraud

Some definitions:

Non-investment frauds are related to online shopping scams or fraudulent computer service calls.

Advance fee fraud is when fraudsters target victims to make advance or upfront payments for goods, services and/or financial gains that do not materialise.

NB Data on fraud and computer misuse are published as Experimental Statistics, which are in the testing phase and not yet fully developed

QUICK FACTS ON FRAUD

- Adults aged 16 and over experienced an estimated **3.4 million** incidents of fraud up to the end of March 2017 - **57%** being cyber-related.

- **74%** of all fraud was related to bank and credit accounts.

- In addition, there were an estimated **1.8 million** computer misuse incidents. **66%** were computer virus-related and **34%** were related to unauthorised access to personal information (including hacking).

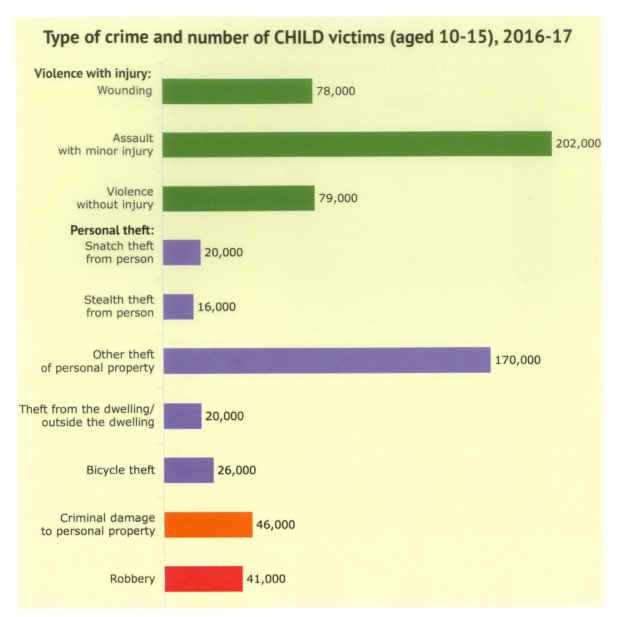

Type of crime and number of CHILD victims (aged 10-15), 2016-17

Violence with injury:
Wounding — 78,000

Assault with minor injury — 202,000

Violence without injury — 79,000

Personal theft:
Snatch theft from person — 20,000

Stealth theft from person — 16,000

Other theft of personal property — 170,000

Theft from the dwelling/ outside the dwelling — 20,000

Bicycle theft — 26,000

Criminal damage to personal property — 46,000

Robbery — 41,000

QUICK FACTS

- A total of **697,000** crimes were experienced by children.
- **52%** of them were **violent crime** - with the majority being low level violence.
- **36%** were **thefts** of personal property.
- **7%** involved **criminal damage** to personal property.
- **6%** were classified as **robbery** - which means theft using force or fear.
- Around **11%** of children aged **10 to 15** were victims of at least 1 crime.

Source: Crime in England and Wales: year ending March 2017 © Crown Copyright www.ons.gov.uk

WHAT DO YOU THINK?

- Are you surprised at the number and type of crimes that children reported?
- Why would a higher proportion of children than adults report that they had experienced violence?
- Not all crimes are reported to the police. Why not?

BEYOND THE BLADE:
THE TRUTH ABOUT KNIFE CRIME IN BRITAIN

Teenage knife crime is a tabloid obsession, blamed on feral youth running riot in our cities. But the reality is much more complex – and we cannot save lives if we do not understand it

by Gary Younge

On Monday 23 January, shortly after 3pm, the regular din of children turning out of the Capital Academy secondary school in north-west London was interrupted by a sudden hush. "All the kids were running around like usual," said one neighbour. "But then it just went quiet. I got up to draw the curtains and saw kids running away, screaming."

Quamari Barnes, a 15-year-old student, had been stabbed several times. He fell just yards from the school gate. A woman cradled him in her arms as paramedics rushed to the scene before whisking Quamari away to hospital.

By most accounts, Quamari danced to the beat of his own drum. As a precocious child, he held court in conversations with adults from an early age; by his teens, he could cook a full Sunday roast on his own. When he was younger, he had no problem being the only boy in his dance class; as a teenager, while his friends were into grime and rap, he went old-school – Bob Marley, Dennis Brown and Aswad.

After the attack, his family had been confident that Quamari would pull through. He had been talking to his mother in the ambulance, and the school sent out an email alerting parents to the tragedy, which said that he was expected to survive. But he didn't make it. One tribute from a fellow pupil, left at the school gate along with flowers, balloons, candles and a Jamaican flag, said: "I can see you laughing at my art and craft skills. It was only yesterday you told me how proud you were that I chose drama. You made me think I was beautiful and confident ... You stood up for me when no one else did."

A 15-year-old boy, who cannot be named for legal reasons, has been charged with Quamari's murder.

One day later, at the Old Bailey, another 15-year-old boy was sentenced to 13 years in prison for fatally stabbing Folajimi Orebiyi, 17, in the neck and the back near Portobello Road in west London last July. Fola, as he was known, ran into a group of boys – one of whom had been involved in a longstanding feud with one of Fola's friends. Invited to a spot off the main road to settle the dispute, Fola assumed he was heading for a fist fight. But the presence of a knife "took this incident to a whole different league of trouble", the prosecutor told the jury. "It turned out that this wasn't so much a fight as an ambush. Within seconds, Fola was singled out and stabbed to death."

Fola's mother, Yinka Bankole, described her son as "a vibrant and intelligent young man" who planned to go to university to study maths and accounting. "I was in labour for 23 hours with him, yet it took less than four minutes to stab him to death," she said. "What are the government doing about this knife crime that seems to have taken over the streets of London? How many more of our children have to die before the government act?"

It's a good question. Sadly, despite the nation's episodic fixation with the issue, it is unlikely to receive a satisfactory answer.

A week before Quamari was killed and Fola's killer was sentenced, the government's quarterly crime-statistics

> **The presence of a knife took this incident to a whole different league of trouble**

bulletin reported that **knife crime** in England and Wales had **increased 11%** on the previous year, while National Health Service data showed a **13% rise** in **hospital admissions** for knife wounds. The report concludes that this increase reflects both an improvement in record-keeping and "an actual rise in knife crime". "The warning lights are flashing," said the previous Metropolitan police commissioner, Sir Bernard Hogan-Howe.

A Metropolitan police report released last month indicated that between 2014 and 2016 the number of **children carrying knives** in London schools **rose** by almost **50%**, while the number of **knife offences** in London schools rose by **26%**. The Liberal Democrat leader, Tim Farron, called it a "wake-up call".

Scotland appears to have bucked this trend. In 2014/15, recorded crimes of **handling an offensive weapon** (which includes knives) **fell to their lowest** in 31 years, while the number of young people under the age of 19 **convicted** of carrying an offensive weapon **fell 82%** between 2006/7 and 2014/15.

In October, the Sentencing Council published draft guidelines for stiffer sentences for people carrying knives. Chief Constable Alf Hitchcock, who leads the National Police Chiefs Council taskforce on knife crime, told the London Evening Standard in early March that the "peak age" for carrying knives is "getting younger", and is currently between 13 and 17. "You've got a group of people probably being influenced by their siblings, by their peer group, and carrying, which is not a good trend," he said.

In Manchester, parents of a 14-year-old were ordered to pay £1,000 to a boy their son stabbed several times outside school.

During a month-long **amnesty** in Surrey, police **collected 237 knives**, which will be used, along with knives collected by police across the country, in a 27ft sculpture called Knife Angel, which may yet adorn the empty fourth plinth in Trafalgar Square.

The answer to Fola's mother's question – "How many more of our children have to die before the government act?" – is both damning and complex. Many more children will die from knife-related violence; indeed, four more have been stabbed to death since she posed it. But it is not because the government and related agencies are not acting. Pretty much every week, somewhere in the country, there is some kind of initiative to tackle "knife crime'" – an amnesty, a new charity in the name of the fallen, an appeal from police, a mayoral statement.

The trouble is that these efforts seem to have little effect. That might be because efforts to make a positive intervention are dwarfed by all the things the government is doing that are making the situation worse. These deaths occur at a moment when the country has made a conscious decision to defund and under-resource its young. When you slash youth services, underfund child mental health services and make swingeing cuts to education and policing, there will be an effect. The most vulnerable will suffer. Austerity didn't invent knife crime, but it is certainly contributing to the conditions in which it can thrive.

The Guardian, 28 March 2017
© Guardian News & Media 2017

This is a shortened version of a longer article, part of a Guardian project to gather data on knife crime. You can follow the project here:
www.theguardian.com/uk-news/2017/mar/28/beyond-the-blade-the-truth-about-knife-in-britain

Many more children will die from knife-related violence.

WHAT DO YOU THINK?

- What do you know about knife crime in Britain?

- This article is part of a series. What other reasons do you think could be put forward to explain the rise of knife crime?

- What would you suggest could be done to improve the situation?

BEYOND THE BLADE:

KNIFE CRIME AND THE NEWS

Sometimes a stabbing is big news and sometimes it is ignored - it often depends on the type of victim

by Gary Younge

Quamari Barnes, the 15 year old stabbed outside his London school in January 2017, was the fifth young person to be killed by a knife this year. The third, Leonne Weeks, 16, died a week earlier. Her body was found on a muddy piece of wasteland in Dinnington, South Yorkshire. Dinnington is a short drive from Rotherham, Sheffield and Worksop, and a series of irregular buses connect this former mining town with the wider world, but it has no train station of its own.

The pit used to look after everyone, says James McIver, 77, a former assistant pit supervisor, including "the sick, the lame and the lazy". When it shut in 1992, everybody suffered. With more than half the children in the town now living in poverty, Dinnington serves as a commuter base for the surrounding towns.

A trainee beautician, Leonne posted dozens of selfies on her Facebook page, mostly with friends, and all with the same lip-smacking pout. Her body was found between two fly-tipping grounds in the centre of town. An abundance of floral tributes, balloons and hand-drawn pictures of Leonne were surrounded by broken refrigerators, remnants of old televisions and discarded soft furnishings.

Leonne's death attracted considerable attention: in the print editions of national newspapers, 27 stories appeared about her killing. Quamari's death was on the front page of the London Evening Standard, but there were only three stories in national

newspapers. Coverage of the knife deaths of children and teens in the national press varies widely. There were 68 stories in national newspapers about Katie Rough, a seven-year-old girl who was stabbed in York this January; at the other end of the spectrum, one fatality has not been reported at all.

"The media's response to the murder of young people is inconsistent," says Patrick Green, the manager of the Ben Kinsella Trust in London, which is named after a 16-year-old boy who was stabbed to death in Islington in 2008 after a night out celebrating the end of his GCSEs. "Some of these tragic deaths get little or no coverage. These stories are often lost because it's a busy news day or because they consider the young person to be an unworthy victim. The media are more likely to report on the murder when a bright, educated young person from a privileged background is killed, and we all think: 'How did this happen to them?' But we don't hear about or ask the same questions about the murders of young people from more vulnerable backgrounds."

Ben Kinsella, for example, was the brother of Brooke Kinsella, who played Kelly Taylor in EastEnders, which made his death high-profile. The attack was also caught on CCTV, which kept it in the public eye. "Media interest in knife crime goes in cycles," explains Green. "We go through phases when suddenly they'll be all over it, and I'll get lots of calls from media outlets asking me to comment on a recent murder, and it is front-page news. And

Christian Adams, Daily Telegraph, 14 July 2008 © Telegraph Group Ltd 2008

just when I think we are making headway, getting the message out there that this is a big and growing problem, there will be another couple of murders and I'll hear nothing or see nothing in the papers or TV. Absolutely nothing – or if I do, the victim won't get more than a couple of lines."

Over time, these inconsistencies have become glaring. Crimes committed with knives are nothing new – Shakespeare's plays are full of them. "Knife crime" as a phenomenon, however, is relatively recent. A survey of the national press and the London Evening Standard in 2000 revealed just one mention of the term; three years later, it was up to 24. Coverage

Some of these tragic deaths get little or no coverage.

peaked in 2008 – with 2,602 mentions that year – before trending precipitously downwards. What is significant about these statistics is that they bear only the vaguest correlation to the frequency of knife crime – which peaked in 2011, by which time the media had begun to lose interest. Last year, even as the number of such crimes rose, the number of mentions of them fell.

The media did not invent "knife crime" either. But, with considerable help from the politicians, it has certainly shaped – or rather distorted – our understanding of it.

The Guardian, 28 March 2017
© Guardian News & Media 2017

This is a shortened version of a longer article, part of a Guardian project to gather data on knife crime. You can follow the project here: www.theguardian.com/uk-news/2017/mar/28/beyond-the-blade-the-truth-about-knife-in-britain

WHAT DO YOU THINK?

- Where does your information about knife crime come from?

- This article is part of a series. What other reasons do you think could be put forward to explain the rise of knife crime?

- What makes a story newsworthy?

Found it? Kept it? Then you are a thief!

If you found a £20 note on the floor would you keep it, or hand it in? And if you did keep it, would you expect to be charged with theft? It turns out that it is a crime to keep money - or anything else - that someone else has lost.

The old saying "Finders keepers, losers weepers" turned out to be very bad advice for a 23-year-old woman in Stoke-on-Trent.

Nicole Bailey was in her local One Stop convenience store when she picked up a £20 note from the floor and kept it.

The note had been dropped by another customer a short time before, when he had withdrawn some cash. He noticed that he had lost the money and came back to ask staff about it but it could not be found.

CCTV

When staff checked the CCTV they recognised Nicole, who used the shop regularly. She was seen picking up the note only seconds after it had been dropped.

Police were called in and the young woman was interviewed. At first she denied that she had taken the money, but she admitted it when she was shown the CCTV footage.

In court

She was charged with theft and, when her case came up at the Magistrate's Court, she pleaded guilty. She was given a six month conditional discharge (which means that if she stays out of trouble for six months she doesn't receive a punishment) and ordered to pay £175 in court costs and other charges.

In her defence, her lawyer argued that she had been naive, she didn't know who the money belonged to, and like most people did not realise that you cannot just keep something you have found. He also argued that to prosecute her was excessive - a police caution would have been more appropriate.

What is theft?

The legal definition of theft is "A person is guilty of theft if he dishonestly appropriates property belonging to another with the intention of permanently depriving the other of it."

Lottery winnings

In 2009 a woman who found a lottery ticket on the floor of her local supermarket and cashed it in for the £30,000 prize was given a suspended sentence when the owner of the ticket was able to prove to the organisers that it was hers.

However, the couple who found it had already spent £15,000 on paying off debts, buying new carpets and buying treats for their children. When the case went to court they were found guilty of theft and dishonesty and each of them received an 11 month suspended sentence.

This was little consolation for the rightful owner of the ticket. Although she received the remaining £15,000, the lottery organisers did not accept any responsibility for paying the wrong people, they had paid out according to their rules. They also warned people to take care to hold on to their tickets.

The rightful owner of the ticket had to bring a private prosecution in which the court ordered the couple to pay back the £15,000 plus £111 interest.

A lucky find - or not?

A builder who was renovating a flat found nearly £18,000 in neatly packaged £20 notes hidden under a kitchen unit. The flat had been damaged in a fire six months earlier and had been empty ever since. He handed it in to police and, when no one claimed it, he expected that he would be entitled to the money.

But the police decided, and the courts agreed with them, that a large amount of money, all the same type of note, neatly packaged, hidden and unclaimed, must be the proceeds of crime and therefore it was confiscated under the Proceeds of Crime Act which prevents criminals from benefiting from their illegal gains. The builder was commended for his honesty.

Sources: Various

WHAT DO YOU THINK?

- Would you have kept the £20 note?

- Would it make a difference if you saw who had dropped it? Or if that person was obviously poor? Or obviously rich?

- In the case of the lottery ticket, who was right?

- "Honesty is the best policy" is another old saying. Does that apply in the case of the builder?

The betrayed girls

'The men who groomed the Rochdale sex abuse victims are still at large'

Eleanor Steafel interviews Maggie Oliver, the police officer who helped expose the child sexual abuse scandal.

In the early hours of Tuesday 16th May, Maggie Oliver was woken by a frantic phone call.

Earlier that night, the nation had watched in horror as the harrowing experiences of the victims of the Rochdale abuse scandal were laid bare in the BBC drama, *Three Girls.*

For the young women whose stories it told, watching their ordeal play out on screen was at once painful and cathartic.

But, sat at home, Amber (as she was known in the programme; all the girls' identities are protected by a court order), was becoming increasingly distressed by threats pouring in on social media, from people wishing to 'out' her as one of the three.

"She rang me, hysterical, at 2 o'clock in the morning," Oliver says. "I told her: 'Look, ring the police because you're two hours away [from me].' But on their systems there is no record anywhere of her having been a victim of all these men."

This, despite the fact that Oliver had interviewed her on video a number of times herself in 2011, in her former role as

detective constable for Greater Manchester Police.

The failing is characteristic, she believes, of a force which turned a blind eye for years, as girls as young as 13 were groomed for sex by gangs of Asian men; plied with alcohol and presents, before being repeatedly raped under threats of violence.

Oliver was so appalled by what she describes as GMP's "gross criminal neglect" of vulnerable young victims that she quit the force so she could speak out in public - believing that she could be of more help to the girls as whistleblower than detective.

We meet at her home in south Manchester, ahead of the BBC's follow-up documentary, *The Betrayed Girls,* in which Oliver appears alongside four previously unheard Rochdale victims - whose chilling accounts of their abuse are almost too raw to watch - and claims GMP were aware of sexual grooming going on far beyond the Lancashire town, as early as 2003.

Oliver doesn't look remotely like a police officer. More glamorous granny than hard

The trust
these girls
had placed
in her
had been
betrayed
again.

Photo posed by model

nosed detective (she is immaculately coiffed and balks at revealing her age when I tentatively enquire) - it's hard to believe she was key in exposing one of the biggest scandals in this country's history.

"Everybody says that," she laughs, as she makes me a cup of tea in her sunny little flat; the happy faces of her four grown-up children and three young grandchildren shining from photographs on every surface. "But I always used to say I'm a person first and then I'm a police officer. I think it made me so much better at the job."

Oliver was a key adviser on both Monday's documentary and *Three Girls*, in which she was played by Lesley Sharp, and which was the most watched drama on BBC iPlayer last month. The public reaction to the programme has gone some way to restoring her faith in humanity, after years as a "lone

voice" in the police. But her dedication came at a high personal cost.

She was first asked to investigate claims of sexual abuse in 2003, while her husband Norman was suffering with terminal cancer. A 15-year-old girl called Victoria Agoglia had died of a drug overdose, leaving behind a letter confessing to having being abused by so many older men she couldn't even remember how many she had slept with.

"At that point, it was just about looking into whether or not there was anything there, it wasn't being described as on-street grooming," says Oliver, who went on to convince the assistant chief constable to fund a full investigation, named Operation Augusta, which identified dozens of young victims and suspects in Hulme and Rusholme, in inner city Manchester.

But while on a leave of absence in 2005, to care for her husband in his final months, the investigation was, in her words, "buried" without one suspect being arrested. "For every one of those victims that I knew were being abused in 2003, that was allowed to evolve over a period of almost 10 years, before we got to the trial."

An investigation that began in Rochdale in 2008 was dropped the following year, with the girls labelled unreliable witnesses, and Amber accused of being complicit in the grooming, despite having been abused herself from the age of 14. Oliver wasn't approached again until 2011, when the investigation was resumed as Operation Span. She refused to become involved until she received cast-iron guarantees that the girls would be supported if they spoke out.

GMP had decided they needed Amber's testimony to be able to go to trial, and Oliver was tasked with regaining her trust, and that of her sister (known as Ruby in the programme), whom she discovered had become pregnant by one of her abusers and had an abortion.

phoning [Amber and Ruby's] family, because it was so important that I didn't let them down. It was about the bigger picture, it wasn't just about their abuse. We had a list of 47 girls."

And then suddenly, history repeated itself: Amber was dropped as a witness; Oliver believes because her evidence opened up so many lines of enquiry, "there was no way they could have a quick hit. This job would have escalated. It was huge and still is huge."

Oliver was devastated that the trust these girls had placed in her had been betrayed again - but her protests went unheard.

Ringleader Shabir Ahmed and another eight men were eventually jailed in 2012. But seven have already been released, after less then five years in jail, having been convicted of trafficking and sexual activity with a child, rather than rape, which would have carried a longer sentence.

> **"I put my heart and soul into this because I believed this was our opportunity to deal with this kind of crime."**

"Over a period of five months, Amber gave six or seven interviews, went to ID parades, identified offenders, told me about the most horrendous abuse, about being threatened at gunpoint by the offenders.

"The powers that be were begging me to get her to trust me. And she did, and she named 30 men that had raped her over a period of months," says Oliver, "I put my heart and soul into this because I believed this was our opportunity to deal with this kind of crime. I didn't really know the scale of the abuse but I knew that what was happening in Rochdale was what I'd seen before."

So crucial was Oliver to the investigation, that when her granddaughter Macie died suddenly, just shy of her third birthday, in January 2011, she was asked not to take time off work: "I had a week off while we arranged the funeral," she tells me, her voice cracking slightly. "But in that week I was still

Many more, who Amber identified in 2011, are "still out there now", says Oliver. Her priority is not to get every single one behind bars - she knows better than to expect this might happen - but to see two major changes in the way the police deals with these kinds of crimes.

The first is proper accountability for senior officers. "To this day, even though this has been a national scandal, with however many thousands of victims that have been abused and failed, not one senior officer has been held accountable. They've all walked away and left a country strewn with vulnerable children who have been abused, and they don't have a backward glance.

"I firmly believe that unless they can be held personally accountable for failing to take action when they have the evidence in front of them, and the children prepared to talk about what's happened to them, I don't think things will change."

> ## "They're just ordinary girls that had a rough deal, and they've all got things to offer."

The second is the attitude towards girls like Amber and Ruby, dismissed as an "under class". "If you're a victim of a rape it doesn't matter if you're from a palace or a council estate - you are a victim and you deserve to be protected by the public services.

"They are invisible victims and they expect nothing. But when they do come forward they are written off."

It is five years since Oliver gave up the job she loved - warning her children that she was prepared to go to prison, if that was what it took to expose the truth - and dedicated her life to helping these girls, who are now like family to her.

"I've helped the ones that I could help but I can't help everybody.

"My kids have met some of them now. They're just ordinary girls that had a rough deal, and they've all got things to offer.

"They're good little mums now, they're just getting on with life. A lot of them are very grown up for their years."

Doesn't she ever wish she could just shut the world away? "If a girl starts to rely on me, how can I walk away from them?" she says. "These girls, I will always be there for them."

Daily Telegraph 2 July 2017
© Telegraph Media Group Limited 2017

Europe's recipe for crisis and chaos in the Mediterranean

Photo: Irish Defence Forces

Rescued migrants are brought to southern Italian ports.

As a doctor on a ship rescuing migrants, I've seen the deadly results of EU policies

Dr Craig Spencer working for Médecins Sans Frontières (Doctors Without Borders) in international waters north of Libya

As the number of people attempting the perilous passage across the Mediterranean Sea continues to rise, Italy and the European Union recently approved new measures to "stem the migratory flow."

Sadly, what they are proposing — additional support for the Libyan Coast Guard and a "code of conduct" for NGOs — will only cause more to drown at Europe's doorstep.

Pouring millions of euros into training the Libyan Coast Guard — an organisation whose legitimacy and reliability are as fractious as the country itself — has been a central part of the EU's plan to slow migration.

But from my experience working as a physician on a search-and-rescue vessel operated by the NGO Doctors Without Borders (MSF), it is obvious this approach has failed. If Italy and the EU continue to expect positive results from a losing formula it will be responsible for putting more lives at risk.

The Libyan Coast Guard has been accused of multiple maritime law and human rights violations by search-and-rescue organisations. In May, our vessel witnessed the Libyan Coast Guard dangerously disrupt a rescue operation and put the lives of migrants and rescue teams at risk. Dozens of people jumped off a boat after armed members of the coast guard boarded it and intimidated its passengers, reportedly demanding money, mobile phones and personal belongings. Mass panic ensued as they shot into the air and people desperately tried to swim toward our ship.

The Libyan Coast Guard turned a standard rescue into crisis and chaos.

The Libyan Coast Guard turned a standard rescue into crisis and chaos.

Continued insistence on training and financial support also overlooks the fact that even if the Libyan Coast Guard were to carry out successful rescue operations at sea — an unlikely prospect in the short term — it would only return migrants to inhumane detention centres in Libya.

In my clinic on board our search-and-rescue vessel, patients routinely describe these centres as "prisons" where detainees are starved, raped or forced to call family members while they are tortured in an attempt to solicit ransom.

I treat the physical and psychological wounds inflicted in these centres, and my patients frequently tell me, "I'd rather die at sea than be brought back to Libya."

Photo: Irish Defence Forces

Essential Articles & Facts

> My patients frequently tell me, "I'd rather die at sea than be brought back to Libya."

As troubling as this part of the EU's plan is, a code of conduct for NGOs involved in Mediterranean rescue operations is even more hypocritical and alarming.

The EU's proposal implies NGOs have been operating without one. But organisations like ours maintain strict adherence to long-established humanitarian principles — humanity, neutrality, independence and impartiality — as well as all internationally mandated search and rescue and maritime laws.

As Italy and the EU are certainly aware, the Maritime Rescue Coordination Centre (MRCC) in Rome coordinates all search and rescue activities in the Mediterranean. In compliance with international maritime law, every vessel — including all NGO vessels involved in rescue operations — receive and follow orders from the MRCC about where rescues can safely occur, how to coordinate rescues in that area and in which ports rescued persons can disembark.

MRCC has handled this massive undertaking miraculously well, despite the surge in arrivals on Italian shores. In the absence of concrete examples in which NGO vessels have flouted the authority of the MRCC, international maritime law or long-established humanitarian principles, the insistence on a code of conduct is an empty diversion that undermines the contribution of NGOs.

Pouring additional resources into Libya will not make people safer at sea, nor will it improve the inhumane conditions in the Libyan detention centres, where rescued persons will be returned.

Similarly, pointing fingers at NGOs that have taken on a larger proportion of the rescues assigned by MRCC while the EU continues to pull back its commitment will only make it harder for NGOs to operate and save lives in the Mediterranean.

Europe needs to come up with real solutions. We need a strong commitment to improving conditions in departure countries, expanding dedicated search-and-rescue operations in the Mediterranean, and providing dignified, safe and legal passage.

Without these essential ingredients, any proposal will fail to address why people have no choice but to attempt the dangerous passage from Libya to Europe in search of safety and a better existence.

www.politico.eu 25 July 2017

Craig Spencer is a medical doctor and public health professional working onboard a search-and-rescue vessel in the Mediterranean for MSF Médecins Sans Frontières/Doctors Without Borders. He is also the director of global health in emergency medicine at New York-Presbyterian/Columbia University Medical Centre in New York City.

> Organisations like MSF maintain strict adherence to long-established humanitarian principles — humanity, neutrality, independence and impartiality

WHAT DO YOU THINK?

- Are most people aware of the courage and determination of the people aboard the rescue ships? If not, why not?
- How desperate must people be to try to cross the Mediterranean Sea in tiny boats?
- Why is Dr Craig Spencer so critical of the European Union's new measures?

The Mediterranean crossing

Refugees and migrants continue to take their chances aboard unseaworthy boats and dinghies in a desperate bid to reach Europe

Most refugees and migrants entered the EU through three primary routes:

- from North Africa to Italy;
- from Turkey to Greece, Bulgaria, and Cyprus; and
- from North Africa to Spain.

362,376 people arrived via these routes in 2016 (a **64%** decrease on 2015). The majority of those attempting this dangerous crossing are fleeing war, violence and persecution.

Arrivals by sea via the Mediterranean 2016

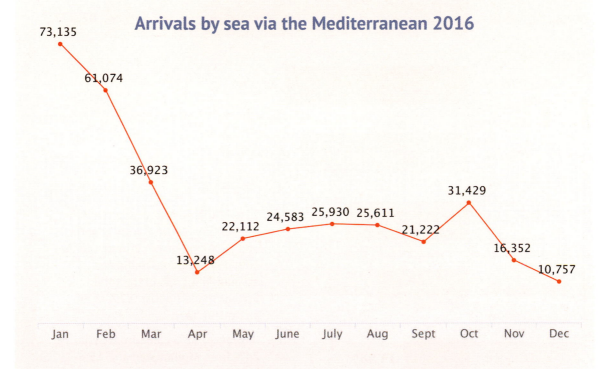

Jan	Feb	Mar	Apr	May	June	July	Aug	Sept	Oct	Nov	Dec
73,135	61,074	36,923	13,248	22,112	24,583	25,930	25,611	21,222	31,429	16,352	10,757

Every year there is a tragic loss of human lives.
There were 5,096 deaths in the Mediterranean in 2016, the highest number on record, amounting to one in 40 of all those crossing.

© UNHCR/Achilleas Zavallis

A young girl is carried by her father after her family arrived on the shores of Lesbos island, having crossed the sea in an inflatable boat

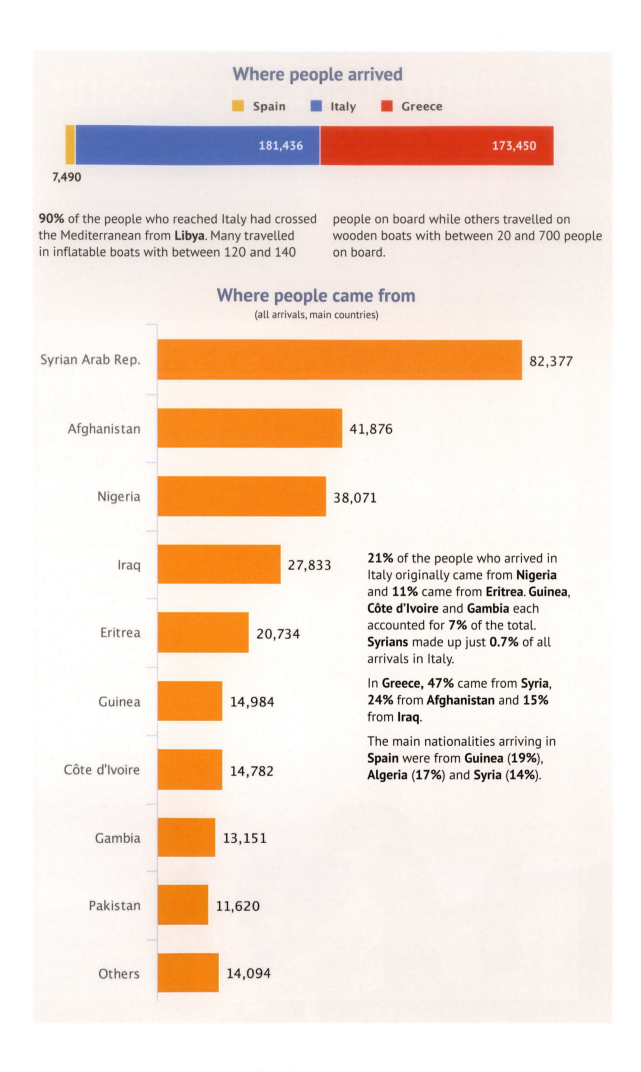

Where people arrived

Spain · Italy · Greece

7,490 · 181,436 · 173,450

90% of the people who reached Italy had crossed the Mediterranean from **Libya**. Many travelled in inflatable boats with between 120 and 140 people on board while others travelled on wooden boats with between 20 and 700 people on board.

Where people came from
(all arrivals, main countries)

Syrian Arab Rep.	82,377
Afghanistan	41,876
Nigeria	38,071
Iraq	27,833
Eritrea	20,734
Guinea	14,984
Côte d'Ivoire	14,782
Gambia	13,151
Pakistan	11,620
Others	14,094

21% of the people who arrived in Italy originally came from **Nigeria** and **11%** came from **Eritrea**. Guinea, **Côte d'Ivoire** and **Gambia** each accounted for **7%** of the total. **Syrians** made up just **0.7%** of all arrivals in Italy.

In **Greece, 47%** came from **Syria**, **24%** from **Afghanistan** and **15%** from **Iraq**.

The main nationalities arriving in **Spain** were from **Guinea (19%)**, **Algeria (17%)** and **Syria (14%)**.

© UNHCR/Ivor Prickett

A boat full of Syrian men, women and children arrives in Greece after a rough crossing from Turkey

Who arrived

| ■ Children | ■ Women | ■ Men |

| 26% | 17% | 57% |

"We wanted to go to Italy. We were on a boat.
After a while the boat began to take in water and soon after it sank.
There was a boy who survived, and I held onto him for many hours.
He saved me. But my father and mother both died.
I did not see them again."

Will, aged 8, an unaccompanied boy from Nigeria, is now in detention in Libya.

QUICK FACTS

- Of the **181,436** arrivals in Italy in 2016 via the Central Mediterranean Route, **28,223,** or nearly **16%,** were children.

- **90%** of children who crossed the Mediterranean were **unaccompanied**.

- A total of **25,846** children made the crossing, which is double the previous year.

- **700** children died crossing the sea between Libya and Italy.

On every step of their dangerous journey, from Sub-Saharan Africa to Libya, including 1,000 kilometres across the Libyan desert and 500 kilometres across the Mediterranean Sea, refugees and migrants are easy prey.

Children are the most vulnerable to all forms of violence, abuse and exploitation, including human trafficking. Unaccompanied children are especially vulnerable.

A deadly journey

The Central Mediterranean Route - from Libya to Italy - is not only a risky route taken by desperate people, but also a billion-dollar business route controlled by criminal networks.

On reaching Libya, many migrants are detained - there are illegal prisons run by criminals who claim money from the government to buy food water and clothing for the refugees (which they do not provide) and at the same time control the trafficking of these people across the Mediterranean.

> *"They arrested us and brought us into the Zawia prison. No food. No water. They beat us every day. No doctor, no medicine."*
>
> *Kamis, a 9-year-old Nigerian girl in detention in Libya.*

Photo: Unicef/Romenzi

A migrant gestures from behind the bars of a cell at a detention centre in Libya, January 2017.

Sources: United Nations High Commission for Refugees www.unhcr.org/uk
A Deadly Journey for Children, www.unicef.org.uk

WHAT DO YOU THINK?

- If you travelled 1,500 kilometres from your home, where would you arrive?

- Why are there so many children amongst the refugees?

- Is enough being done to help desperate people?

- Where would intervention be most effective?

Compassion or crime?

A father asks you to rescue his child - but to do it you have to break the law. What do you do?

It may be easy to generalise about what governments should do in the 'refugee crisis', but what happens when it becomes personal? What if there was something that you - only you - could do to help?

You are about to leave for home after witnessing the horrors of a refugee camp. A desperate man begs you for a hiding place in your car, not for him but for his four-year-old daughter. You know that, left in the camp, her life would be bleak and her prospects nil. If she can get to England she has relatives to help her and the chance of a future. But you would be smuggling in an illegal immigrant, albeit a small, innocent child. What would you do?

You would be smuggling in an illegal immigrant - a small, innocent child

Rob Lawrie committed his "crime of compassion" when he was volunteering at the infamous Jungle refugee camp in Calais. In what he describes as an irrational moment, he agreed to hide four year old Bahar Ahmadi, an Afghan refugee, in a compartment above the driver's seat of his van.

When he was caught and charged, his case gathered publicity worldwide, and with it both criticism and praise. It has brought him thousands of supporters online and the possibility of a film being made about him. It could have brought him a jail sentence, but instead of throwing the book at him for people-smuggling, the French court gave him a suspended sentence and a fine for

Rob Lawrie playing with Bahar Ahmadi at the Calais refugee camp
Photo: YouTube

Photo: YouTube

"We cannot save everybody, but we can all save somebody"

Rob Lawrie speaking in the Sky News YouTube video: Child Refugees | What Would You Do?

having a endangered a child - as she was not wearing a seat belt. It was a sentence which was greeted with loud applause. Lawrie's own response was: "The French justice system has sent out a message today. Compassion was in the dock, and compassion won."

On the freezing October night in 2015 when he made his 'irrational and stupid decision', Bahar had been fast asleep on Lawrie's knee and her father, Reza, was pleading desperately, not for the first time, to get his daughter out of the camp. Overcome with emotion, Lawrie agreed to hide Bahar in his van and take her to relatives who lived only a few miles from his home in Guisely, Yorkshire. When he was stopped at the border controls, ironically, it was the presence of two Eritreans who had secretly stowed away in his van that alerted the sniffer dogs. When he was arrested, Lawrie had to tell the police about Bahar who was sleeping peacefully in her hiding place.

"Compassion was in the dock, and compassion won."

Although he was spared prison, the 49-year-old former soldier has lost a great deal in his determination to aid refugees. His marriage broke up over his smuggling attempt and he has spent all his savings as well as selling the carpet cleaning machines that earned him his living. He was so worried about the prospect of being jailed that he attempted suicide. He admitted that he had regrets but they were offset by the publicity he had gained, "Look at the light it has shone on the human side of the refugee crisis," he says.

At the end of his trial in January 2016, Lawrie returned to Leeds, while Bahar and her father went back to the Jungle refugee camp in Calais. In October that year, the French authorities demolished the camp and dispersed the occupants, including Bahar and her father, to asylum centres around France, although there were reports of people, including children, sleeping rough in the ruins of the camp because they could not be accommodated.

"Look at the light it has shone on the human side of the refugee crisis"

Lawrie continues to campaign for refugees, especially children who have 'lost out in the birth lottery'.

Asked whether he would ever try the same thing again he replied "I'd never do that again, no," Then: "Well, you know, would I get a child to safety if I could get away with it? Yeah, I would."

He is not the only person to have been moved from being a bystander to being an activist. Swedish journalist Fredrik Onnevall was faced with a direct request from a 15-year-old boy when he was reporting on the refugee crisis in Greece. "Take me with you" Abed* said.

Onnevall knew that, if he refused, the boy would attempt to get to Sweden anyway,

*Not his real name

by leaping onto a speeding lorry. Abed had a cousin in Sweden and, if he could get to him, the teenager would have the chance of a better life, of any life. The journalist felt that if he did not act the knowledge that he had betrayed and abandoned the youngster would be with him forever.

"I knew the price of not helping him."

Onnevall, his cameraman and an interpreter together managed to get Abed to Sweden. All three were arrested for people smuggling.

In February 2017 the court convicted them. Their lawyers had argued they should be acquitted since they acted only out of concern for the boy and out of compassion. However the court ruled that someone could not be acquitted on those grounds, gave them suspended sentences and ordered them to complete 75 hours community service each. There will be an appeal against the sentences.

Asked if he would do the same again, Onnevall's reply was similar to Rob Lawrie's: "It is a difficult question. With Abed I would draw the same conclusion, I knew the price of not helping him. Do I regret it? Not for a second."

Sources: Various

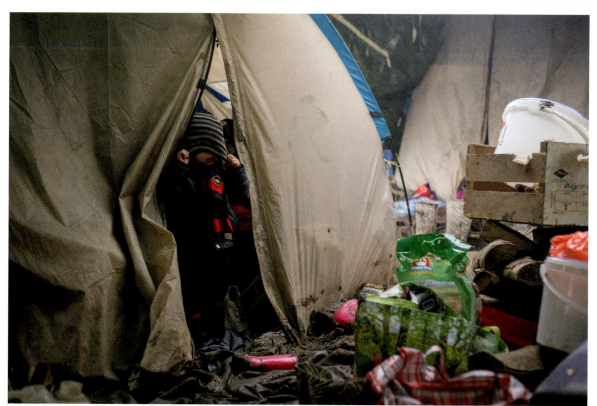

© UNHCR/Federico Scoppa

WHAT DO YOU THINK?

- Were these people right or wrong to do what they did?

- How would you answer someone who said "Only you can help me?"

- What causes would you personally support? And what would you be prepared to do to support them?

- Are there any laws that you think are wrong? What could you do about them?

The charity rebuilding the lives of refugee children in Britain

Ahsanullah Ahsas suffered horrors on the way to the UK, but help from the Children's Society has transformed his existence

David Conn

It would be comforting to be able to say of Ahsanullah Ahsas, a young man from Afghanistan who loves volleyball, clothes and the warmth of friendship, that he is now a regular teenager again, after fleeing his country's horrors when his father was killed by the Taliban. But the world has been catastrophically cruel to him and recovery is not so simple – his struggles and worries continue even in this country, even in Leeds, to where the Home Office "dispersed" him from Dover when he arrived here at the end of his terrible journey.

> He remembers cold terror in the back of a lorry

As he relates some of his traumas, Ahsanullah is hunched, quiet, at times heartbreakingly raw. He had to run from home because, as the eldest of three sons, he had received death threats; his mother paid an "agent" in Kabul to transport him to England, where she believed he could be safe.

On the suffocatingly hot car journey across Iran, he and three others were crammed underneath the back seats, and could barely breathe. He was arrested, imprisoned and beaten by police in Europe; he tramped miles through woods in the rain; finally he remembers cold terror in the back of a lorry from Calais, before he jumped out and found himself in Kent, alone, with no possessions.

He believes it was Dover, and he turned himself in at a police station. Several times, he recounts with awed wonder how decent the English police officers were; that rather than beat him, one reached out and affectionately ruffled his hair. "I didn't expect that from a police officer, to rub my head, like a friendly person," Ahsanullah says. "In other countries I had been beaten, put in prison, punished, for no crime. But here, the police were very nice."

There are moments when he does break into a smile, and looks like a young lad who knows what happiness is. He smiles when he remembers school, friends, the good teachers and playing volleyball back home in Afghanistan before the terror – and here in Leeds, when he

talks of what the Children's Society has done for him to turn his life around.

The Children's Society gives concentrated, practical support to vulnerable, severely traumatised young people who arrive in Britain unaccompanied.

Din Nazim, the Children's Society advocacy worker, himself a refugee from Afghanistan who marshals a remarkable range of professional skills and languages, is part of a small team in Leeds, which last year provided one-to-one help to 62 young people, and reached almost 700 more at drop-in centres and other services. Mostly they are, like Ahsanullah, boys alone, who have fled conflicts or civil turmoil in Afghanistan, Syria, Eritrea, Sudan and elsewhere.

Nazim first found Ahsanullah in Urban House in Wakefield, an "initial accommodation centre" to which asylum seekers are sent before being dispersed across Yorkshire. Ahsanullah says he was 16 when he fled his home last summer, but he has been officially assessed here as 18, and so an adult needing no young person's support. He was allocated a house shared with other adults, and an asylum seeker's £36 per week welfare, which paid for bare subsistence.

When Nazim went to see him at the house, he found Ahsanullah in a dreadful state. "He was just sitting with his head down; he wasn't doing anything. He was just crying, all the time," Nazim remembers. "He was very, very upset."

Nazim went to work. He saw Ahsanullah every day to help address his trauma and start rebuilding his confidence. Nazim secured a referral from the Refugee Council for a solicitor to help with Ahsanullah's asylum claim and age assessment challenge, and helped him enrol at college to learn English.

Ahsanullah says he was 16 when he fled his home

The teenager is now at Leeds city college three days a week, where he works at his English and has made friends with other young people. He attends a youth group, First Floor, an orientation and harm prevention programme which is fun too, run with the West Yorkshire Playhouse theatre, and – here Ahsanullah smiles brightly – he has made friends there as well.

An important part of the Children's Society's work is partnering refugees with young volunteers who act as mentors; Ahsanullah talks of his as if he was a guardian angel: Isidoros Lapsatis, from Greece, who was a student at Leeds Beckett university. "He was very nice," Ahsanullah says. "He came to my house, took me round Leeds, he showed me where to buy cheap food and clothes, showed me the pound shops, took me to the museum, showed me the stadium – he showed me everything."

Ahsanullah volunteered to talk about his experiences, and the help he has had, because Nazim's and the Children's Society's support has transformed his existence here. But then, asked if he would like to add anything, he returns immediately to the lurking horror at the forefront of his mind. He cannot turn the lights out at night and sleep, he says, because he has flashbacks to seeing his father killed.

Nazim looks downcast. Funding of mental health services for refugees has been slashed, he says. The Children's Society says £50,000 a year could fund a full-time counsellor. The charity appeal money will pay for more project workers like Nazim and a drop-in service staffed by volunteers. They hope to start a new service in Kent, with one-to-one support and a local volunteer service, to help young people's orientation in their first days after arrival.

"I was so lucky to meet Din," Ahsanullah says, "so lucky to be in the youth group. I am learning English and want to speak it very well. I am very, very worried about my asylum claim and where I could be sent if it fails, and Din has helped with that too. The Children's Society has turned around my life. I want that to happen for all young people who come to this country."

> ## Funding of mental health services for refugees has been slashed

The Guardian, 23 December 2016
© Guardian News & Media 2016
www.childrenssociety.org.uk

Picture posed by model

WHAT DO YOU THINK?

- If you had to leave your home, where would you go?

- Do you know how much money you would need to cover your living expenses for a week?

- If you were living in a foreign country, what would you miss most about your home?

Artificial intelligence

The ability of machines to imitate human behaviour has developed over time and will continue to grow.

In an online YouGov survey of 2,019 GB adults:

36% believed that the development of Artificial Intelligence (AI) posed a threat to the long term survival of humanity.

60% thought that the rise of AI would lead to fewer jobs by 2026 with **27%** predicting that it would decrease the number of jobs 'a lot'.

Preferred roles:

49% thought intelligent machines could carry out household tasks, eg cooking and cleaning - for older or disabled people;

48% thought they could fly unmanned search and rescue aircraft;

45% thought they could fly unmanned military aircraft;

70% thought they could be act as monitors for crops.

Trust: The public didn't trust intelligent machines to take on roles where lives could be in danger.

53% distrusted robots to carry out surgical procedures;

49% distrusted them to drive public buses;

62% distrusted them to fly commercial aircraft.

Gender:

- Only **17%** of **women** felt optimistic about the development of AI compared to **28%** of **men**.

- **13%** of **men** believed they could be friends with a robot compared to **6%** of **women**.

Age:

- Those aged **18-24** were most open minded about a future that included AI - **28%** envisaged that robots could be future co-workers and **10%** thought that they could regard them as family members.

- **55%** of this age groups also thought that intelligent machines could take up the role of servants in a household.

Source: YouGov survey for British Science Association
www.britishscienceassociation.org

WHAT DO YOU THINK?

- **When robots replace humans at work is that bad because of increased unemployment or good because they take over boring jobs?**

- **If we use robots more in caring roles, will we lose touch with other humans?**

- **Do robots threaten us in ways other than taking jobs?**

How much should we fear the rise of Artificial Intelligence?

From the games program AlphaGo to the movie 2001, we are often warned of the threats posed by computers. But there is a way to live alongside technology

Tom Chatfield

Machines, four. Humanity, one. That was the result of the match between Google's AlphaGo and human champion Lee Sedol at the fiendishly complex game of Go, and it came with a disconcerting question: what next? Where will the machines claim their next victory: putting you out of a job; solving the mysteries of science; bettering human abilities in the bedroom?

AlphaGo's success was down to artificial intelligence (AI): the computer program taught itself how to improve its game by playing millions of matches against itself. But the trouble with using games such as chess and Go as measures of technological progress is that they are competitions. There's a winner and there's a loser – and this month's biggest tech news story had a clear victor.

This is a common narrative of human-machine interactions: a creation is pitted against its creators, aspiring ultimately to supplant them. Science fiction is full of robots-usurping-humans stories, sometimes entwined with a second strand of anxiety: seduction.

Machines are either out to eliminate us (Skynet from Terminator 2, Hal in 2001: A Space Odyssey), or to hoodwink us into a state of surrender (the simulated world of The Matrix, the pampered couch potatoes of WALL-E). On occasion, they do both. These are just stories, but they're powerful and revealing – and easier to grasp than what's actually going on.

According to a YouGov survey for the British Science Association of more than 2,000 people, public attitudes towards AI vary greatly depending on its application. Fully 70% of respondents are happy for intelligent machines to carry out jobs such as crop monitoring – but this falls to 49%

Artificial intelligence is OK at a distance

once you start asking about household tasks, and to a miserly 23% when talking about medical operations in hospitals. The very lowest level of trust comes when you ask about sex work, with just 17% trusting robots equipped with AI in this field – although this may be a proxy for not trusting human nature very much in this situation either.

The results closely map the degree of intimacy involved. Artificial intelligence is OK at a distance. Up close and personal, however, the lack of a human face counts more and more. All of which both makes intuitive sense, yet leaves a pressing question unaddressed: just what does it mean for a machine to carry out a task in the first place?

We are not in competition with information technology, we are adapting our world into something machines can comprehend

Here the image of a robot stepping into the shoes of a human worker couldn't be more wrong. When it comes to technology's most significant applications, we are neither usurped or seduced – because the systems involved are nothing like us in either their function or faculties. As a species, we are not in competition with information technology at all: we are, rather, busily adapting the fabric of our world into something machines can comprehend.

Consider what it means to teach an autonomous robot to do something as simple as mowing grass. First, you take a long wire and lay it carefully around the borders of your lawn. Then you can set your mower loose. It doesn't know or care what a lawn is, or what mowing means: it will simply criss-cross the area bound by the wire until it has covered all the ground. You have successfully adapted an environment – your lawn – into something a machine understands.

I've borrowed this example from the philosopher of technology, Luciano Floridi, who in his book The Fourth Revolution explores the degree to which we have radically adapted most of the environments we work and live within so that machines

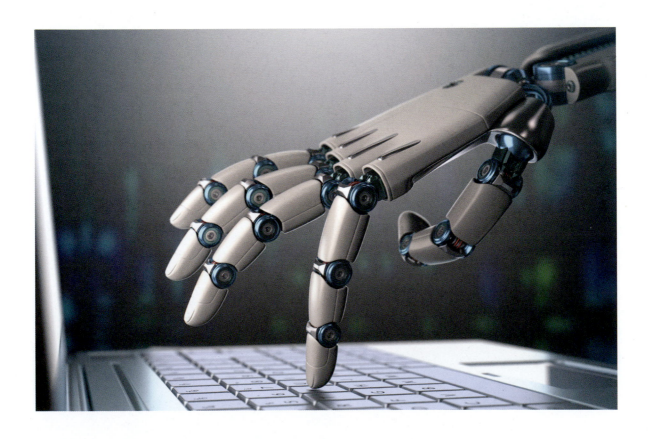

are able to grasp them. We have, he notes, "been enveloping the world around [information technologies] for decades without fully realising it" – wrapping everything we do in layers of data so dense that they can no longer be comprehended outside of machine memory, speed and pattern-recognising power.

I say comprehended, but AlphaGo no more understands the game of Go than a robot mower understands the concept of a lawn. What it understands is zeroes and ones, and the patterns that can be drawn from their prodigiously smart crunching. We translate, the machine iterates and performs. Increasingly, machines translate for other machines, carrying on their data exchanges without our intervention.

> ## The flexible partner will eventually adapt their entire life around the inflexible partner's insistences.

When the arena is something as pure as a board game, where the rules are entirely known and always exactly the same, the results are remarkable. When the arena is something as messy, unrepeatable and ill-defined as actuality, the business of adaptation and translation is a great deal more difficult.

Let us imagine, Floridi suggests, two people in a relationship. One is extremely stubborn, inflexible and unwilling to change. The other is the opposite: adaptable, empathetic, flexible. It doesn't take a genius to see how things will develop. When one person is willing to compromise and the other isn't, more and more tasks end up being done the way the uncompromising partner insists. The flexible partner will eventually adapt their entire life around the inflexible partner's insistences.

When it comes to human-machine interactions, even the smartest AI is orders of magnitude more inflexible than the most intransigent human. We either do things the way the system understands, or we don't get to do things at all. Hence one of

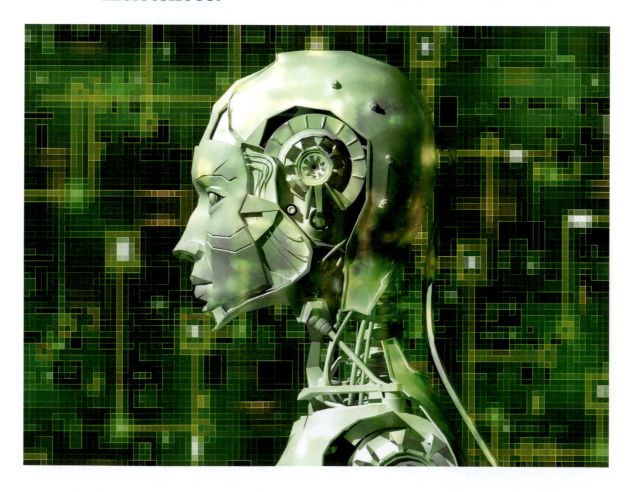

If "Computer says no," it doesn't matter what a million people might want

the most useful phrases to enter popular culture in the past 15 years, "computer says no". It comes from a sketch in the comedy series Little Britain, and will provoke groans of recognition from anyone ever flummoxed by a system that doesn't recognise their wishes as an option.

"Computer says no," mumbles a morose employee in response to a perfectly reasonable request, assaulting her keyboard with a single digit. It doesn't matter what a million people might want – if the option isn't on the menu, it might as well not exist.

In social science, this is sometimes known as minority rule. Just 5% of a population can, for instance, remove a particular choice from everyone else through inflexibility. If I'm cooking for 100 people and I know five of them are lactose intolerant, I will cook something that suits everyone; if there are a couple of vegans coming and I don't have the capacity to make multiple dishes, I'll rule out even more kinds of food.

In an era where machines are implicated in more and more of our most intimate decisions, the minority whose rules apply are those designing machines in the first place. Even the smartest AI will relentlessly follow its code once set in motion – and this means that, if we are meaningfully to debate the adaptation of a human world into a machine-mediated one, this must take place at the design stage.

By the time it gets to "computer says no", it's too late. The technology is in place, its momentum gathering. We need to negotiate our assent and refusals earlier, collectively.

And for this negotiation to work, we must ask what it means to translate not only productivity and profit but also other values into a system's aims and permissions: justice, opportunity, freedom, compassion. "Humanity says no" isn't a phrase for our age, yet. But it may need to become one.

The Guardian, 18 March 2016
© Guardian News and Media

WHAT DO YOU THINK?

- **What are the most recent ways in which we have adapted our behaviour to suit technology?**

- **Do you agree that machines will make inflexible decisions?**

- **Who should be in charge of deciding how machines work for us?**

Intelligent machines

How much do young people trust technology?

2,044 young people in England aged 14-18 were questioned about their awareness and trust in technology.

Machine learning: When machines or computers are able to adapt, learn and make recommendations or decisions on their own without a human giving them ongoing instructions. It is a form of artificial intelligence that we use every day: in internet search engines, email filters to sort out spam, websites to make personalised recommendations, banking software to detect unusual transactions, and lots of apps on our phones such as voice recognition.

Awareness of machine learning applications

Have you seen or heard anything about...?

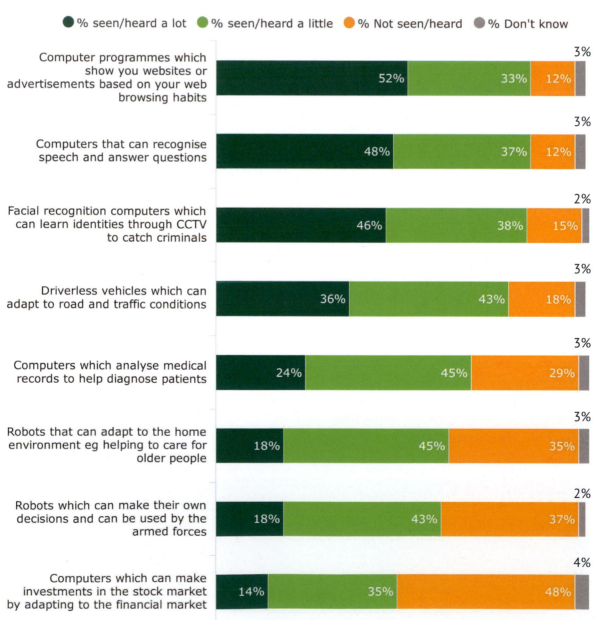

● % seen/heard a lot ● % seen/heard a little ● % Not seen/heard ● % Don't know

Application	seen/heard a lot	seen/heard a little	Not seen/heard	Don't know
Computer programmes which show you websites or advertisements based on your web browsing habits	52%	33%	12%	3%
Computers that can recognise speech and answer questions	48%	37%	12%	3%
Facial recognition computers which can learn identities through CCTV to catch criminals	46%	38%	15%	2%
Driverless vehicles which can adapt to road and traffic conditions	36%	43%	18%	3%
Computers which analyse medical records to help diagnose patients	24%	45%	29%	3%
Robots that can adapt to the home environment eg helping to care for older people	18%	45%	35%	3%
Robots which can make their own decisions and can be used by the armed forces	18%	43%	37%	2%
Computers which can make investments in the stock market by adapting to the financial market	14%	35%	48%	4%

NB figures do not add up to 100% due to either rounding or questions which allow multiple answers

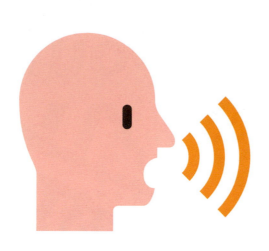

Level of trust

Would you trust a machine or computer to...?

● Yes ● No ● Don't know

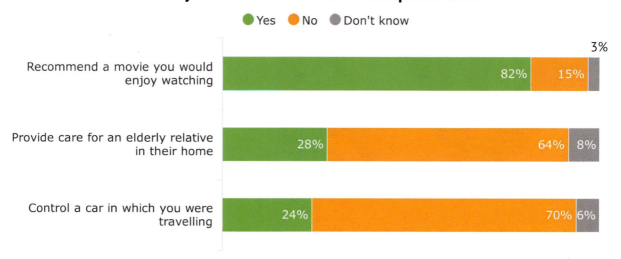

Recommend a movie you would enjoy watching — 82% | 15% | 3%

Provide care for an elderly relative in their home — 28% | 64% | 8%

Control a car in which you were travelling — 24% | 70% | 6%

Level of trust by gender

● % male ● % female

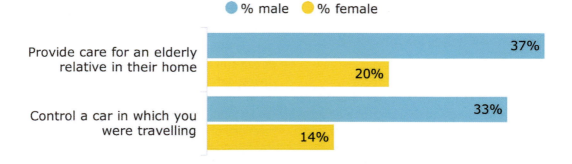

Provide care for an elderly relative in their home — 37% / 20%

Control a car in which you were travelling — 33% / 14%

Source: Wellcome Trust - Science Education Tracker: Young people's awareness and attitudes towards machine learning and Young people's attitudes towards biomedicine, February 2017 https://wellcome.ac.uk

WHAT DO YOU THINK?

- What is the most useful aspect of machines being able to learn?

- Do we place too much trust in machines?

- Can you account for the fact that young men trust machines more than young women do?

Evidence of Doubt

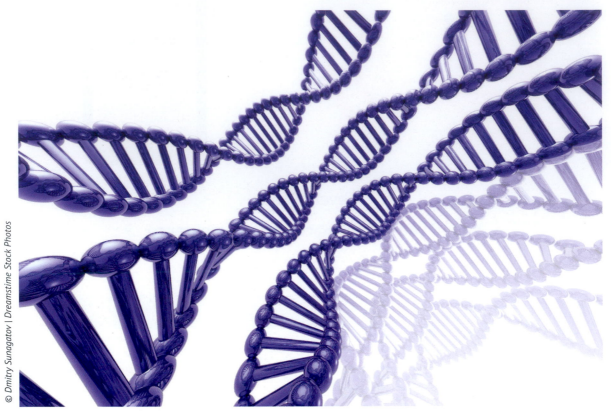

© Dmitry Sunagatov | Dreamstime Stock Photos

How the science of DNA profiling can help or hinder

DNA at a crime scene - the final proof?

We are probably all familiar with the scene in a film or TV crime series where the white-suited specialists check every centimetre for the elusive biological trace which will lead to a conviction and the whole case is solved as result of some clever deductions based on a sample of DNA.

It's certainly true that our DNA is unique - or at least 0.1% of it is, but it is also true that we cannot help spreading and sharing this evidence of our presence wherever we go. And that is both an opportunity and a problem for forensic scientists.

Scientific advances such as PCR (polymerase chain reaction) have made it possible to analyse smaller and smaller residues by generating multiple copies, so a tiny amount of DNA is converted to a large amount that can be used for different types of profiling. Ironically, the very advances in sensitivity of detection may make DNA profiling less useful than before. Small amounts of DNA can be spread onto people and places from talking, sneezing, shedding skin cells or touching surfaces.

Narrowing down the options

While the presence of DNA doesn't automatically tell us when or how it arrived at the crime scene, it can still be a tremendously useful tool in investigations. A really good sample, from blood, saliva or semen, can be analysed for markers or short tandem repeats (STRs) - these are small sections of DNA made up of short sequences that are repeated. The number of times this sequence is repeated (and hence the length of the section), tends to differ from individual to individual. Usually 16 of these, plus a sex marker, will be examined.

Why 16? If a forensic scientist looked at only one marker then there would be a chance, sometimes as high as one in 20, of this matching more than one individual. A DNA profile based

A DNA profile based on 16 markers only has a one in 100 million billion chance of matching more than one individual

on 16 markers only has a one in 100 million billion chance of matching more than one individual. If a full DNA match is made it gives proof of identity, but we should remember that proof of guilt requires other corroborating evidence.

A relatively new technology called forensic DNA phenotyping uses DNA to make predictions about someone's appearance. It is a useful way of narrowing down a pool of suspects if there is no match in a national DNA database.

It is only currently possible to predict eye and hair colour from a DNA sample — although none of these tests are 100% accurate. Skin colour is likely to be the next appearance trait that forensic scientists will be able to predict from DNA. It can't, however, tell us about every physical feature - especially those traits that are also influenced by environment such as weight, height, fitness or skin condition.

Why aren't we all on a DNA Database?

The UK National DNA Database contains samples taken from crime scenes (usually only serious crimes) and from police suspects, though samples from people not charged or not found guilty are deleted. It holds about 5 million profiles from individuals, 80% of them male. When a new sample is added there is an automatic search for matches and it can be used for matching potential relatives as well as complete matches.

It has sometimes been argued that DNA is so useful in solving of crimes that the database should record the DNA of everyone in the country, whether or not they have ever been a suspect in a criminal case. There are strong arguments against this as an invasion of privacy and even a presumption of guilt. Compulsory DNA testing could reveal delicate, confidential information about health and ancestry to whoever is running the test.

Everyday DNA

There are even arguments for extending DNA testing to much more mundane uses. In Hong Kong an attempt was made to shame litterbugs by putting up reconstructions of their faces, taken from DNA retrieved from discarded chewing gum or cigarette butts, all over the

city. But since physical build and facial structure cannot be predicted, the reconstructions could not identify culprits with any certainty.

In 2016 a London borough ran a pilot scheme to identify which owners were not cleaning up after their dogs by establishing a dog DNA database. A year later they reported a 50% drop in the amount of dog mess in three parklands and said they had also used the technology to produce 'e-fit' images of offending pooches, with breed, coat pattern, and even facial characteristics.

Hong Kong tried to stop litterbugs with DNA and in London they've used it to reduce dog fouling

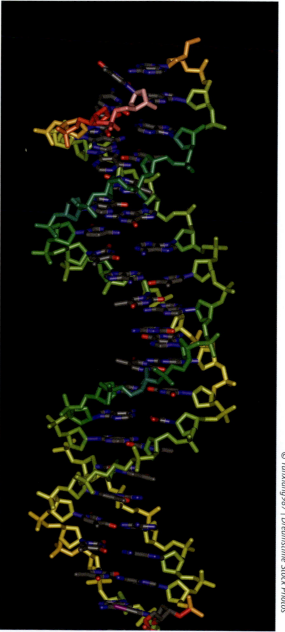

© Yunxiang987 | Dreamstime Stock Photos

The UK's DNA database holds about 5 million profiles – 80% of them are male.

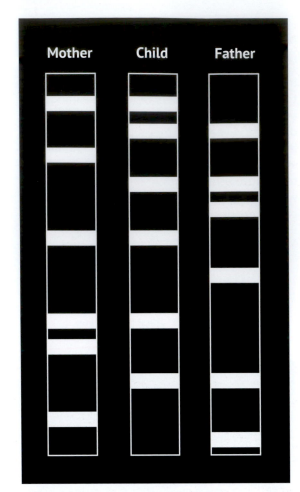

Mother   Child   Father

Each band on a child's DNA fingerprint should match a band on one of its parents

Paternity testing - the proof is in the profile

Paternity testing is an example of a field where we can be certain of the results of a DNA test.

STRs can be used in paternity testing since 95% of human DNA is made up of these non-coding repeats. STRs have a unique pattern in every person except identical twins. These different fragment lengths of STRs can be separated to produce a genetic fingerprint.

Since we inherit half of our genetic material from our mother and half from our father, each band on a DNA fingerprint should have a corresponding band in the parents' DNA fingerprint. This can be used to establish, with certainty, whether someone is the genetic father of a child.

Scientific certainty versus human error

No scientific advance can counter the effects of human error. Mistakes can happen at a crime scene or the lab, through failure to collect samples or contamination, through mislabelling or misinterpretation. In a courtroom misjudgements can occur through too much reliance on DNA or a failure to understand statistical probability. Extending the use of DNA might have benefits but also has considerable ethical risks.

Case study

The killing of Meredith Kercher - Background DNA and confirmation bias

When British student Meredith Kercher was stabbed to death in Perugia Italy, suspicion fell on her American flatmate Amanda Knox. The prosecution claimed that a knife found at the flat of Amanda Knox's boyfriend was the murder weapon. It had small traces of Meredith Kercher's DNA on the blade but no blood. The prosecution argued that this was because the blood had been cleaned off - this is confirmation bias, moulding or ignoring evidence to fit a previously decided idea.

There were other ways that the DNA could have been deposited on the blade - it could have been transferred there by her flatmate. The methods of storing evidence were also suspected of being likely to have allowed cross contamination. Amanda Knox and her boyfriend were acquitted of murder.

Source: Adapted from Making Sense of Forensic Genetics, and other sources, senseaboutscience.org

WHAT DO YOU THINK?

- **Should everyone's DNA be recorded somewhere, just in case it is needed?**

- **Who should have access to the DNA information?**

- **Do you agree with the use of DNA testing for relatively trivial purposes like littering?**

Science education

What motivates young people towards a career in science?

The very first Science Education Tracker (SET) surveyed 4,081 young people aged 14-18 in 2016 to assess young people's views of their experiences of science in England.

How interesting do you/did you find science lessons at school?

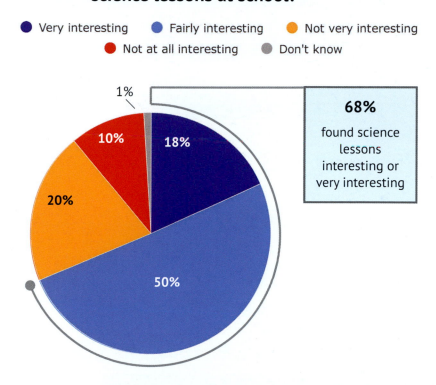

- Very interesting
- Fairly interesting
- Not very interesting
- Not at all interesting
- Don't know

1%

18%

10%

20%

50%

68% found science lessons interesting or very interesting

Which of these have you done in the last 12 months outside of school?

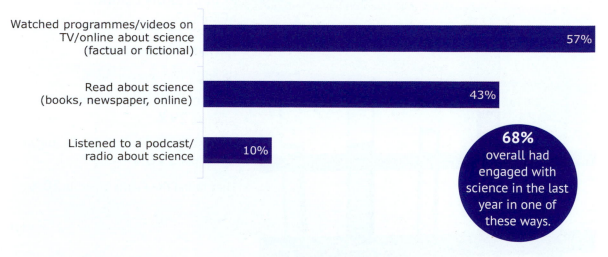

Watched programmes/videos on TV/online about science (factual or fictional) — 57%

Read about science (books, newspaper, online) — 43%

Listened to a podcast/ radio about science — 10%

68% overall had engaged with science in the last year in one of these ways.

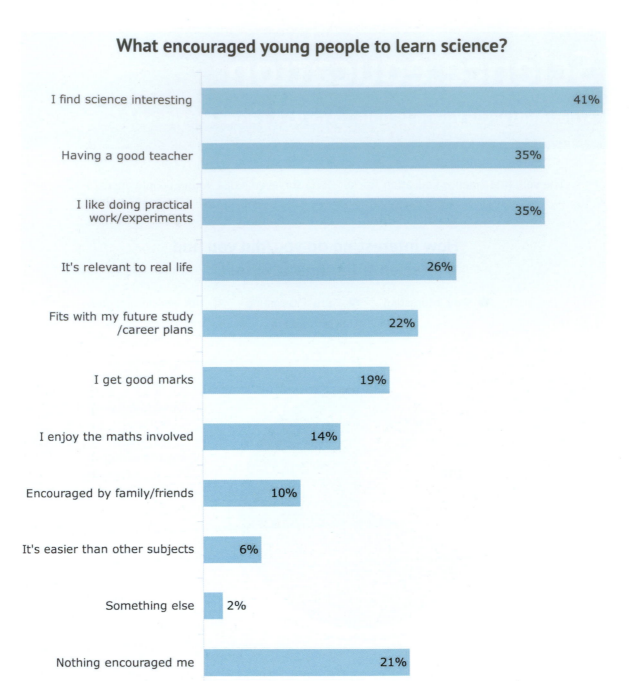

What encouraged young people to learn science?

Reason	Percentage
I find science interesting	41%
Having a good teacher	35%
I like doing practical work/experiments	35%
It's relevant to real life	26%
Fits with my future study /career plans	22%
I get good marks	19%
I enjoy the maths involved	14%
Encouraged by family/friends	10%
It's easier than other subjects	6%
Something else	2%
Nothing encouraged me	21%

WHAT DISCOURAGES YOUNG PEOPLE FROM LEARNING SCIENCE?

The top reasons were:

Having a bad teacher **33%**

It was more difficult than other subjects **29%**

It didn't fit in with their future study/ career plans **26%**

They found the maths difficult **20%**

Careers

43% of young people were interested in a science-related career.

Why are you interested in a career involving science, computer science, engineering or maths?

(Base: young people interested in a science career 1,792)

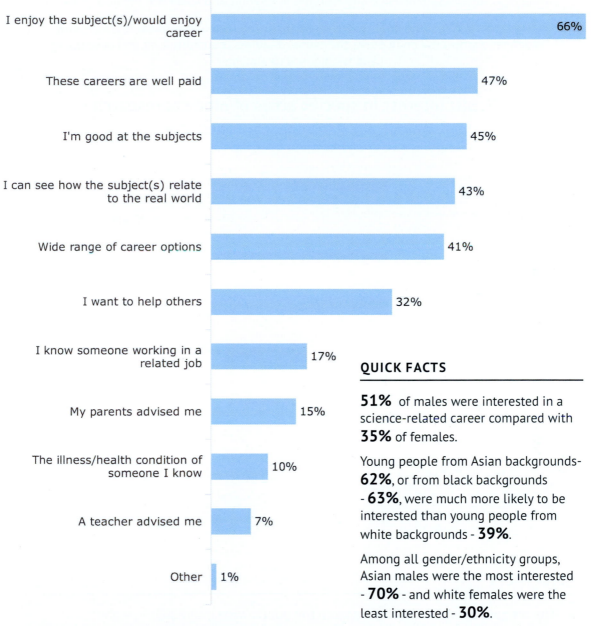

I enjoy the subject(s)/would enjoy career	66%
These careers are well paid	47%
I'm good at the subjects	45%
I can see how the subject(s) relate to the real world	43%
Wide range of career options	41%
I want to help others	32%
I know someone working in a related job	17%
My parents advised me	15%
The illness/health condition of someone I know	10%
A teacher advised me	7%
Other	1%

QUICK FACTS

51% of males were interested in a science-related career compared with **35%** of females.

Young people from Asian backgrounds- **62%**, or from black backgrounds - **63%**, were much more likely to be interested than young people from white backgrounds - **39%**.

Among all gender/ethnicity groups, Asian males were the most interested - **70%** - and white females were the least interested - **30%**.

Source: Wellcome Trust - Young people's views on science education, Science Education Tracker Research Report, February 2017
https://wellcome.ac.uk

WHAT DO YOU THINK?

- **How would you encourage more young people to take an interest in science?**

- **How important is it to have some understanding of science in your everyday life?**

- **Could, or should, anything be done to shift the gender and ethnic imbalance?**

Public views on science

Science is such a big part of our lives that we should all take an interest

The Wellcome Trust surveyed 1,524 UK adults aged 18+ to measure the public's awareness, interests, knowledge and attitudes in relation to science and medical research.

It found that **77%** of the public were very or fairly interested in medical research which is defined as: how the body works, the causes of illnesses and diseases, and developing and testing new treatments.

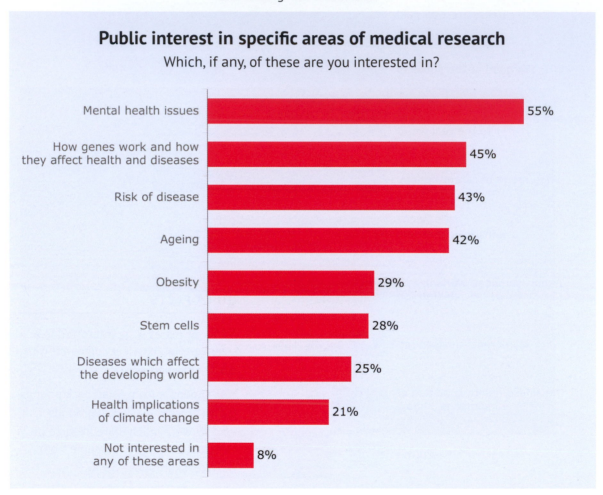

Public interest in specific areas of medical research

Which, if any, of these are you interested in?

- Mental health issues — 55%
- How genes work and how they affect health and diseases — 45%
- Risk of disease — 43%
- Ageing — 42%
- Obesity — 29%
- Stem cells — 28%
- Diseases which affect the developing world — 25%
- Health implications of climate change — 21%
- Not interested in any of these areas — 8%

QUICK FACTS

- The broader areas of medical research the public were interested in were: the development of new drugs, vaccines and treatments - **61%**; how the body works - **46%**; and how the brain works - **45%**.

- **Gender:** Women were more likely than men to say they were very or fairly interested in medical research - **80%**, compared with **74%**.

- **Age: 83%** of those aged 50 and over, compared with **68%** of those aged 18 to 34 expressed an interest in medical research.

- The most common way the public actively search for information about medical research is on the internet - **90%**, followed by talking to another person **40%**, and visiting a hospital or doctor's surgery **31%**.

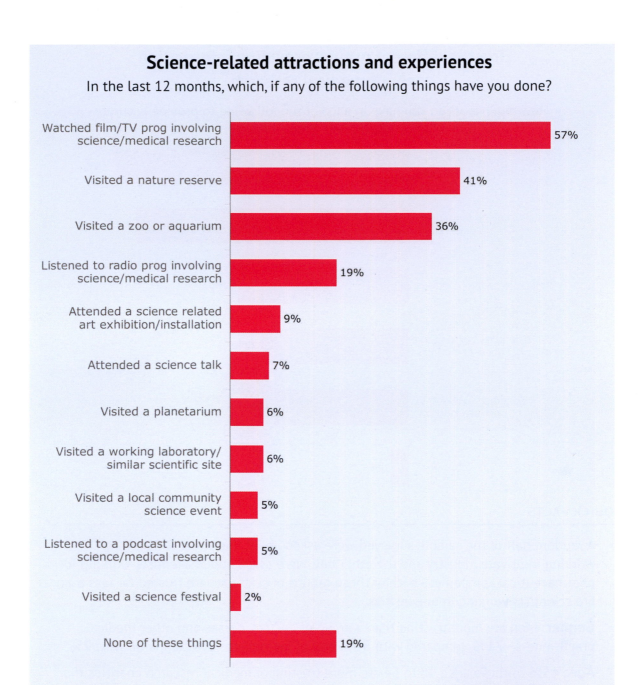

Science-related attractions and experiences

In the last 12 months, which, if any of the following things have you done?

Watched film/TV prog involving science/medical research	57%
Visited a nature reserve	41%
Visited a zoo or aquarium	36%
Listened to radio prog involving science/medical research	19%
Attended a science related art exhibition/installation	9%
Attended a science talk	7%
Visited a planetarium	6%
Visited a working laboratory/similar scientific site	6%
Visited a local community science event	5%
Listened to a podcast involving science/medical research	5%
Visited a science festival	2%
None of these things	19%

QUICK FACTS

- **20%** of the public had visited a science museum or science centre in the last 12 months, and **71%** said that they had visited a science museum or science centre at some point in their life.

- By contrast, **33%** of the public had visited a history museum in the last 12 months, and **30%** had visited an art gallery.

Trust in different groups providing information about medical research

How much trust do you have in each of the following to provide accurate and reliable information about medical research?

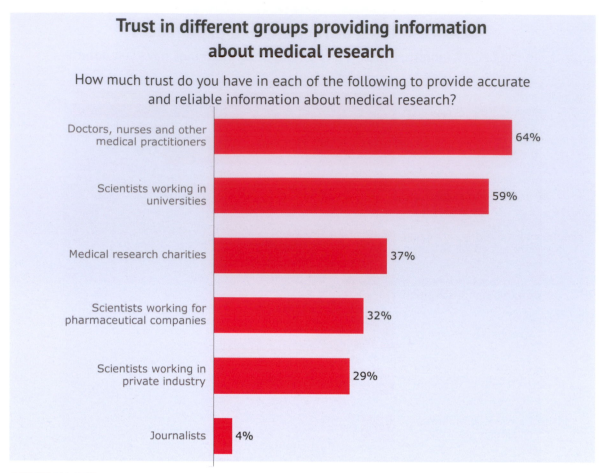

- Doctors, nurses and other medical practitioners — **64%**
- Scientists working in universities — **59%**
- Medical research charities — **37%**
- Scientists working for pharmaceutical companies — **32%**
- Scientists working in private industry — **29%**
- Journalists — **4%**

QUICK FACTS

- A random half of the sample surveyed were asked about their trust of scientists working in private industry and the other half were asked about scientists working for pharmaceutical companies - both of these groups of scientists are trusted far less than are scientists working in universities.

- **Gender:** Men are more trusting than women of doctors, nurses and other medical practitioners - **71%**, compared with **58%** and of journalists - **5%** compared with **2%**.

- **Age: 45%** of those aged 18 to 34 are more trusting of medical research charities than those aged 65 and over - **28%**. They are also more trusting of scientists working in private industry - **36%** compared to **19%**.

Why do people trust certain professions?

The most commonly mentioned reason was that the professionals are knowledgeable, or are experts.

12% said they trusted doctors, nurses and medical practitioners because they had "no choice but to trust them".

The most common reason for **distrusting** journalists to provide accurate and reliable information was a belief that they would exaggerate information relating to medical research - **49%**.

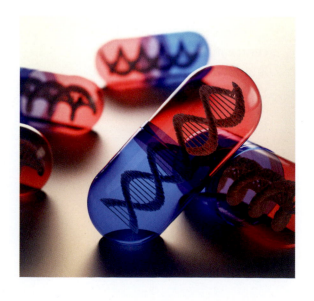

Quality of life

94% of the public believed that medical research would definitely, or probably, lead to an improvement in the quality of life for people in the UK in the next 20 years.

Public participation in medical research

24% of the public said that either they, or a family member, had taken part in a medical research project. **12%** of this 24% said that they themselves had taken part in a medical research project such as testing a new drug or treatment; providing samples of blood or tissue; completing a survey or questionnaire; monitoring health or behaviour; and allowing access to medical records.

77% said they were **willing** to share their medical records for the purposes of medical research as long as the detail was anonymous.

A similar proportion - **75%** - said they were willing to share information from their genes for medical research purposes, again on an anonymous basis.

The main concern among those who were **unwilling** to share their anonymous medical records or genetic information for the purposes of medical research related to confidentiality and privacy.

Other concerns included:

- a lack of trust;

- concerns with the research and what it was;

- not being interested or wanting to take part; and, especially for sharing genetic information:

- not knowing enough about this type of research.

Source: Wellcome Trust Monitor, Wave 3 - Tracking public views on science and biomedical research © 2016, Wellcome Trust; Ipsos Mori (2016) http://dx.doi.org/10.6084/m9.figshare.3145744   www.wellcome.ac.uk/monitor

WHAT DO YOU THINK?

- **What areas of scientific research interest you most?**

- **What are the advantages and risks of using the internet as a source of scientific information?**

- **What accounts for different levels of trust?**

- **How much medical information would you share in the interests of science?**

Active lives

An insight into the physical activity of the nation

The Chief Medical Officer recommends that adults should be physically **ACTIVE** for at least 150 minutes over several days a week and in bouts of 10 minutes or more.
The activity should be of at least **moderate intensity** which means your heart rate is raised and you feel a little out of breath.

198,911 adults aged 16+ in England were asked about how active they were.

Levels of activity:

INACTIVE Less than 30 mins a week	**FAIRLY ACTIVE** 30-149 mins a week	**ACTIVE** 150+ mins a week
25.6%	13.7%	60.7%

Which gender is most active?
(Figures do not add up to 100% due to rounding)

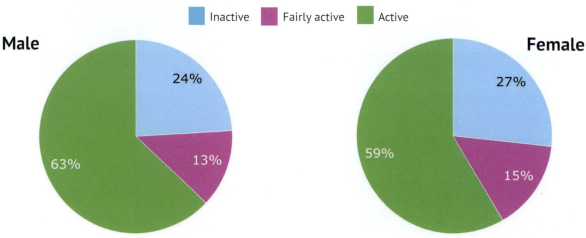

Inactive   Fairly active   Active

Male

24%
13%
63%

Female

27%
15%
59%

Which age groups were most active?

% who are active

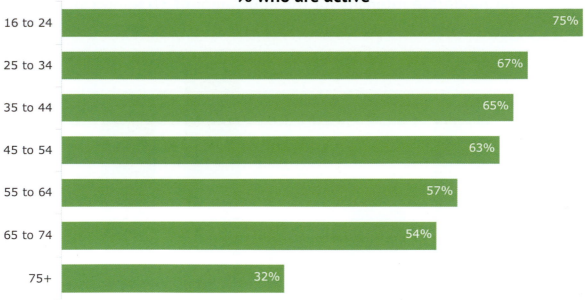

Age group	%
16 to 24	75%
25 to 34	67%
35 to 44	65%
45 to 54	63%
55 to 64	57%
65 to 74	54%
75+	32%

Activity by level of disability

There are differences between those with or without a disability:

- only **36%** of those with **three or more impairments** are **active** compared with
- **45%** of those with **two impairments**;
- **51%** of those with **one impairment**; and
- **65%** of those **without a disability**.

© Seema_illustrator | Dreamstime Stock Photos

People who are most active by their type of occupation

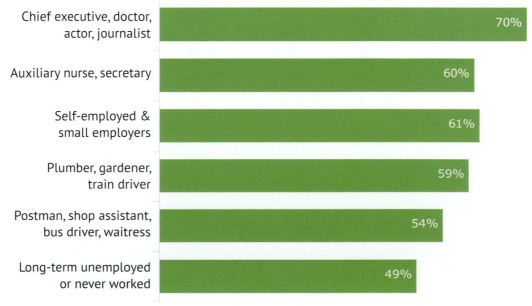

Occupation	%
Chief executive, doctor, actor, journalist	70%
Auxiliary nurse, secretary	60%
Self-employed & small employers	61%
Plumber, gardener, train driver	59%
Postman, shop assistant, bus driver, waitress	54%
Long-term unemployed or never worked	49%

Types of sport and physical activity
(at moderate intensity for the equivalent of 30 minutes)
taken part in at least twice in the last 28 days

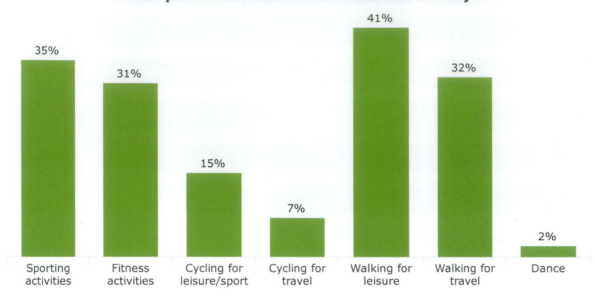

NB Where an individual had taken part at least twice in the last 28 days in more than one of the activities above, they were included in the results for each. They were not double counted in the overall results.

Percentage of males and females
taking part in each activity

● % Male ○ % Female

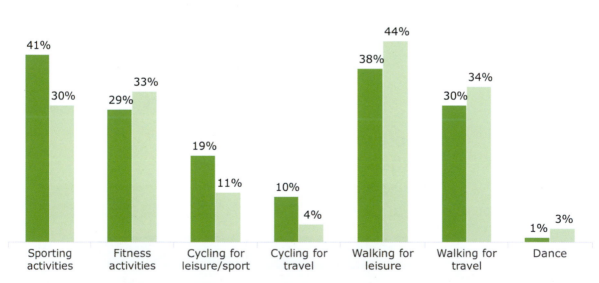

Active Lives Survey 2015-16 Year 1 Report, Sport England www.sportengland.org

WHAT DO YOU THINK?

- **What are the benefits of being active?**

- **How would you encourage people to be more active?**

- **In what ways would your job affect how active you might be?**

Benefits of exercise

Physical activity and mental health

Research by the Sport and Recreation Alliance looked at the role of sport and physical activity in mental health. It interviewed 2,006 adults and found that:

32% of people who are currently inactive would take up physical activity if they knew more about the mental health benefits.

55% said they took part in regular activity because it improved their mental wellbeing.

They were asked:
How does exercise make you feel better?

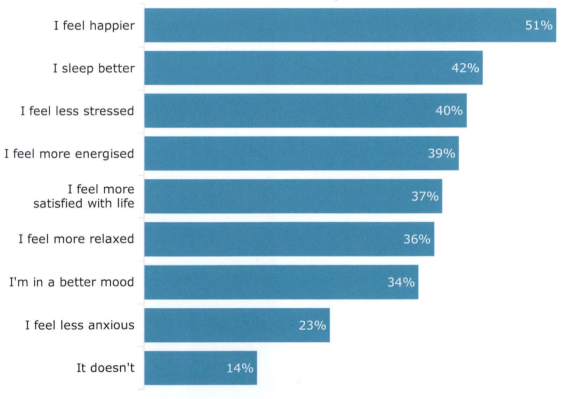

I feel happier	51%
I sleep better	42%
I feel less stressed	40%
I feel more energised	39%
I feel more satisfied with life	37%
I feel more relaxed	36%
I'm in a better mood	34%
I feel less anxious	23%
It doesn't	14%

Source: Sport and Recreation Alliance   www.sportandrecreation.org.uk

WHAT DO YOU THINK?

- **What do you feel is the best effect of being active?**
- **Why doesn't physical activity help some people?**
- **Are some sports more beneficial than others?**

Head injuries to footballers

Football stars: we'll never forget them - if only THEY could remember

Scientists have found that repeated headers throughout a professional football career may be linked to long-term brain damage leading to dementia later in life.

Their research follows anecdotal reports that players who mainly headed balls for a living in the 1950s and 1960s – traditionally the central defenders and strikers – may be more prone to developing dementia. To perfect their heading, footballers would practise repeatedly. The balls at that time were made out of rubber with a leather casing which absorbed water from the rain adding to the weight and the impact.

When we examined their brains we saw the sorts of changes that are seen in ex-boxers

Researchers from University College London, (UCL) and Cardiff examined at autopsy the brains of six players: five had been professional footballers and one was a committed amateur. They had played football for an average of 26 years with old, heavy footballs. All six went on to develop dementia in their 60s. In four cases scientists found signs of brain injury – chronic traumatic encephalopathy (CTE) which has been linked to memory loss, depression and dementia.

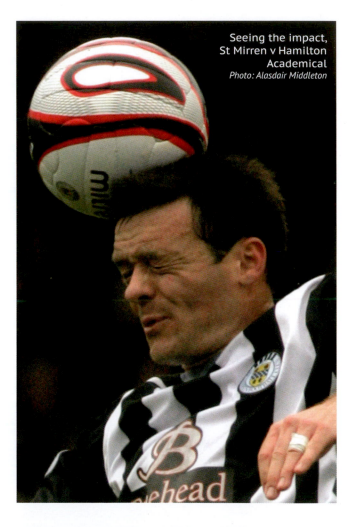

Seeing the impact, St Mirren v Hamilton Academical
Photo: Alasdair Middleton

Professor Huw Morris of UCL explained, "When we examined their brains at autopsy we saw the sorts of changes that are seen in ex-boxers, the changes that are often associated with repeated brain injury which are known as CTE."

"So for the first time in a series of players we have shown that there is evidence that head injury has occurred earlier in their life which presumably has some impact on them developing dementia."

Each brain also showed signs of Alzheimer's disease and some had blood vessel changes that can also lead to dementia.

Researchers speculate that it was a combination of factors that contributed to dementia in these players. But they acknowledge their research cannot once and for all prove a link between heading footballs for a living and dementia, and are calling for larger studies to look at footballers' long-term brain health.

Dr David Reynolds, on behalf of the charity Alzheimer's Research UK, said: "The causes of dementia are complex and it is likely that the condition is caused by a combination of age, lifestyle and genetic factors."

"Further research is needed to shed light on how lifestyle factors such as playing sport may alter dementia risk, and how this sits in the context of the well-established benefits of being physically active."

Previous cases involving boxers and American footballers have pointed to a relationship between repetitive blows and long-lasting, progressive brain damage.

Families of players such as Jeff Astle and Nobby Stiles believe that football authorities fear a wave of compensation cases and are therefore dragging their heels about accepting the connection. The Stiles family have expressed no wish for financial gain from any research into links between heading and dementia but do want the decline of former players to trigger action which might help future generations.

Ian St John, one of the legends of Liverpool's Bill Shankly era, says. "All the big names among players from the 1950s and 1960s are suffering from memory lapse or dementia in varying degrees. They need compensation to pay carers, people to help and assist them in their everyday lives; for hospitals and treatment. They ought to be compensated to get the best help they can for their condition, and be able to lead a dignified life in the years they've got left, but it's not happening.'

'All the big names among players from the 1950s and 1960s are suffering from memory lapse or dementia in varying degrees.'

Ian St John

Case studies

Jeff Astle

Played 361 games for Notts County and West Bromwich Albion, plus 5 games for England, scoring 174 goals. He died in 2002 aged 59 from a degenerative brain disease that had first become apparent 5 years earlier. He had been an exceptional header of the ball, and the coroner found that the repeated minor traumas had been the cause of death. In 2014 it was claimed by a neurosurgeon that Astle may well have died as a result of CTE - the first time a British footballer was said to have died as a result of heading a football.

Dawn Astle, his daughter, said "At the coroner's inquest, football tried to sweep his death under a carpet. They didn't want to know, they didn't want to think that football could be a killer and sadly it is. It can be." The *Justice for Jeff* campaign was launched, calling for an independent inquiry into a possible link between degenerative brain disease and heading footballs.

Frank Kopel

The former Dundee United and Manchester United defender, was diagnosed with vascular dementia in 2008, and died in 2014 aged 65. His wife Amanda is convinced that his dementia was a result of heading footballs. She is campaigning for Frank's Law, the introduction of free personal care for dementia patients under the age of 65. Frank Kopel needed it but was too young to receive state support.

1966 World Cup winners

Martin Peters, Ray Wilson and Nobby Stiles have all been diagnosed with dementia. Jack Charlton suffers from memory problems.

Stan Bowles

A legend at QPR, where he spent 7 successful years, Bowles continued to play even after his retirement from professional football. He now suffers from Alzheimer's.

Young people

If Injuries to the head can have terrible consequences later in life for even our fittest and most dedicated sports people, what about when childrenplay football?

Since 2015 heading footballs by children aged under 10 has been banned in the USA. British neuroscientist Dr Michael Grey, from the University of Birmingham says 'If it was my children I would not have them heading the ball at low ages … What is clear is we need more research across the board and one thing is certain, there's no shortage of money in football to fund it.'

In December 2016 the Professional Footballers Association called for the authorities to consider a similar ban in the UK.

Sources: various

In March 2017 the Football Association finally committed funds to finance a major, independent study into whether footballers are more likely than the average person to suffer from degenerative brain injury.

WHAT DO YOU THINK?

- Do you think that there is a link between heading footballs and brain injury?
- Who should be responsible for paying for the care of footballers suffering from dementia?
- Should children be stopped from heading footballs?

Risk of injury

Traditionally 'dangerous' sports don't result in more injuries than 'safer' sports

Sports the public BELIEVE to be the most dangerous

(Most to least dangerous)

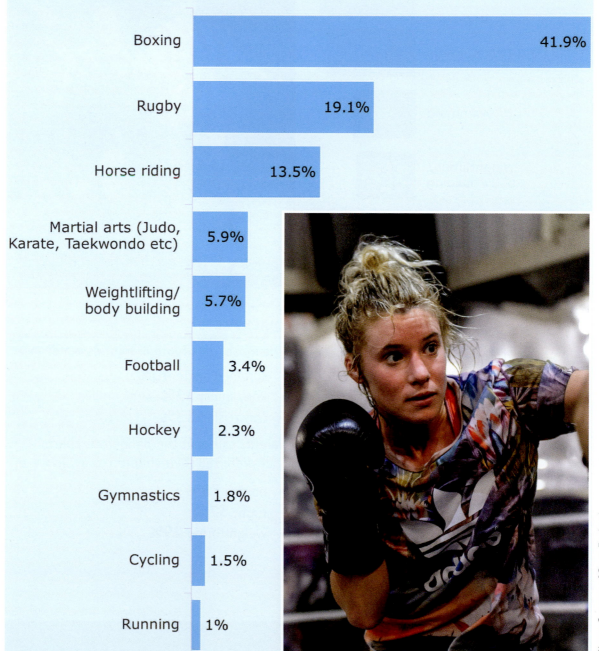

Sport	%
Boxing	41.9%
Rugby	19.1%
Horse riding	13.5%
Martial arts (Judo, Karate, Taekwondo etc)	5.9%
Weightlifting/ body building	5.7%
Football	3.4%
Hockey	2.3%
Gymnastics	1.8%
Cycling	1.5%
Running	1%

Photo: Courtesy of Sport England

Despite the popular belief that rugby is one of the most brutal UK sports, the study showed that people are **four times more likely** to suffer an injury playing football.

Percentage of participants injured whilst playing sport

(most to least likely)

Sport	Percentage
Football	18.9%
Running	9.4%
Rugby	4.9%
Cycling (track, road)	4.5%
Swimming	3.2%
Weightlifting/body building	3%
Tennis	2.8%
Martial arts (Judo, Karate, Taekwondo etc)	2.8%
Horse riding	2.6%
Badminton	2.3%

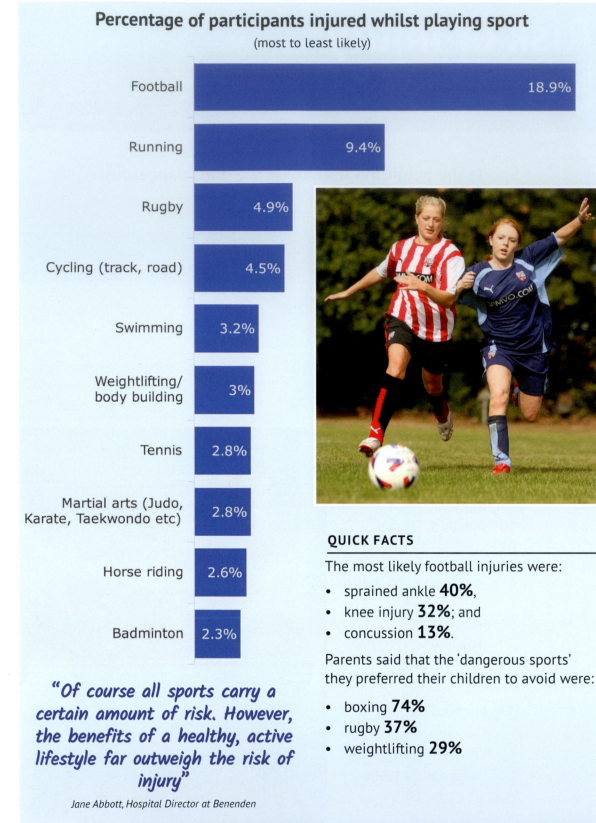

Photo: Courtesy of Sport England

"Of course all sports carry a certain amount of risk. However, the benefits of a healthy, active lifestyle far outweigh the risk of injury"

Jane Abbott, Hospital Director at Benenden

QUICK FACTS

The most likely football injuries were:

- sprained ankle **40%**,
- knee injury **32%**; and
- concussion **13%**.

Parents said that the 'dangerous sports' they preferred their children to avoid were:

- boxing **74%**
- rugby **37%**
- weightlifting **29%**

Source: Benenden   www.benenden.co.uk

WHAT DO YOU THINK?

- Are some activities worth the risk?
- Do you agree that a healthy lifestyle outweighs the risk of occasional injury?
- When people injure themselves doing a sport should they pay for their treatment?

Batman Begins

Meet Haseeb Hameed, English cricket's rising star

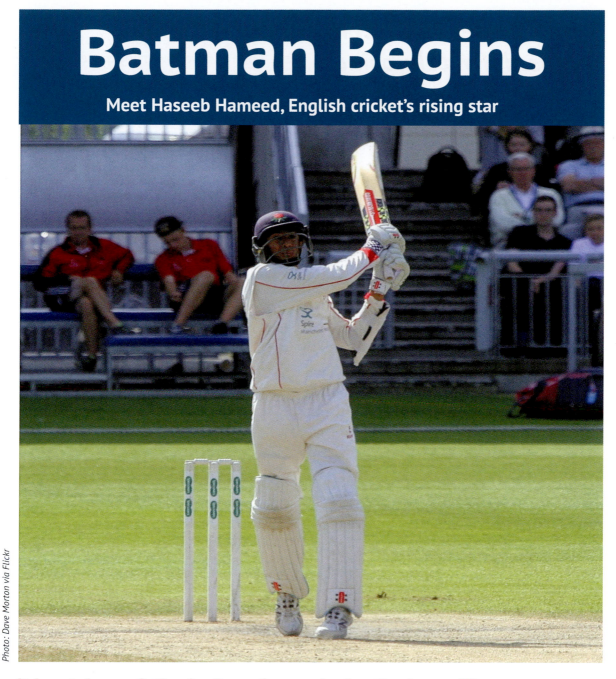

Photo: Dave Morton via Flickr

It has taken a father's obsession and a brother's sacrifice to create the brightest cricketing prospect England has seen in years.

Tim Lewis

In a fledgling career as a cricketer, 20-year-old Hameed – "Has" to his friends – has earned a reputation for toughness. Last November against India, in his third Test match for England, a ball snapped a bone in his little finger. England were getting thumped and Hameed could, and probably should, have retreated to the sick bay. But he came out for the second innings and batted with bravery and no little skill to score 59 not out, with only two paracetamol tablets to numb the pain. A "very special knock" said his captain Alastair Cook. Virat Kohli, the supreme stylist in cricket right now, was impressed, too. "You can sense it, this guy is intelligent," the India captain commented. "He's a great prospect for England and he's definitely going to be a star in all forms."

This is high praise and there are signs that we could be seeing the emergence of a very

"You can sense it, this guy is definitely going to be a star in all forms"

special talent. Aged eight, a tiny Hameed tried out for Lancashire under-11s; they decided he was too small, but he forced his way into the team the next year. At 13, Worcestershire tried to lure him to play for them, offering a boarding scholarship to the illustrious Malvern College – effectively worth £100,000 – as an incentive. Lancashire made a counter-offer, including a place at the fee-paying Bolton School, and Hameed stayed.

He had started playing against adults when he was 12 in the gnarly Bolton League and he became known locally as "Baby Boycott" – after the legendary England opening bat, Sir Geoffrey. Opposing bowlers did not go easy on the diminutive Hameed, certainly not after he flayed them around the park. Last winter he became England's youngest-ever opening batsman and, in short order, the first teenager to score two half-centuries for England in Test cricket.

Not bad for a kid who was trained by his dad on a concrete playground behind their house, and who still lives at home with his parents in a modest semi in Bolton. We meet at Farnworth Social Circle, Hameed's first proper cricket club. It's out of season, so we are let into the pavilion by the chair of Bolton Cricket League, John Hutchinson. As we wait for Hameed, Hutchinson talks about how he scored a century on his debut for the second XI – a precocious achievement for a child playing with seasoned grown-ups. When Hameed arrives bang on time, in a decidedly unfootballery Vauxhall Corsa, I ask him if he recalls the match. Sports people often have a savant's recall for their past performances and Hameed is no different. "Actually, my first match for the second team was at Tonge," he replies. "We bowled first and I got four wickets with my leggies [leg breaks] and then I got 83 not out chasing it, I think. I got my first 100 here, I don't know how many games later."

It is the day after his 20th birthday – big night? "Nah," laughs Hameed, rubbing his elephantine little finger, still swollen from the surgery. "Just a nice meal at home with the family." The highlight was his kit sponsor sending him a miniature set of gloves and pads for his four-year-old cricket-mad nephew. "He came out to India this winter and since then he's been pestering everyone just to throw balls at him," says Hameed. "And it's funny because every time he wants to play, my mum and dad get memories of me wanting to do the same thing." Hameed stops, ponders. "But it was weird, turning 20," he goes on. "It sounds so… old."

Hameed's father, Ismail, and mother, Najma, moved to England in 1969 from the Indian village of Umraj in Gujarat. "We've never spoken about why they came here," says Hameed, "but it's a very small village, so I imagine it was to earn a decent living." They settled in Bolton and Ismail became a driving instructor. The couple had five children: three boys, two girls.

Personally I don't want to put my success down to talent. I'm a believer in work

Ismail was a fanatical cricketer, an opening bat and spin bowler, who played semi-professionally for Huddersfield Cricket Club. According to family lore, after one match, Iqbal Qasim – an international player for Pakistan – sought out Ismail in the car park and told him to go back to India and play cricket seriously. Hameed sighs affectionately, like he has heard the story many hundreds of times: "Apparently he said, 'If you don't play Test cricket for India, I'll shave my 'tache off!'"

Photo: Dave Morton via Flickr

It didn't happen for Ismail, but he began to wonder if his sons could make it as professional cricketers. The elder boys, Safwaan and Nuaman, both showed promise, but started to play seriously only as teenagers, comparatively late. That left Haseeb, who was born a decade later. When he [Haseeb] was seven or eight, Ismail had an operation that meant that he could no longer work as a driving instructor. The family restructured: Safwaan [the eldest son] went to work in a call centre for NatWest and became the main breadwinner, while Ismail became more involved in Haseeb's cricket development.

This was clearly not an easy time for the Hameeds, and Haseeb is well aware of the sacrifices that his family made. "Obviously Dad stopped working, Mum has never worked, so my brother had to start working and unfortunately that meant having to put a stop on his dreams of playing professional cricket," he says. "And Dad became not a full-time cricket coach as such, but he dedicated all his time towards me."

Safwaan, who is 31 now, puts it simply: "Being the eldest son, I had to provide, you've got to pay mortgages and stuff like that, don't you?" he says. "And we all knew that Has was a special talent. He was naturally so gifted; people would just watch him and be in awe of how good he was for his age. My dad's always had a dream of one of his sons playing for England and for Has to finally achieve that is a great satisfaction for all of us really."

Practice mostly took place on the playground behind their house, off the busy Halliwell Road. Ismail was particularly strict on technique. His heroes were not the showy, flamboyant batsmen, but the ornery, belligerent ones: men like Boycott, India's Sunil Gavaskar and the Australian Ian Chappell. With Haseeb, he set out to create a cricketer with bulletproof methods; a player who was equally proficient against fearsome fast bowling and tricksy spinners.

"The process of learning the basics of the game happened quite early for me," says Hameed. "Sometimes you just play the game and whack the ball as far as you can and you enjoy the game – and that was still the case for me, I was still loving it, but I was also learning the important aspects of the game with it. So it was always me trying to pursue a career in cricket from a very young age."

I want to be a role model for the next generation of people

In the summers Hameed, who is a Muslim, would play cricket, sprint off to mosque and then back to finish the game. "Personally I don't want to put my success down to talent," he goes on. "I don't really think of it that way. I'm a believer in work."

At home, the family tried to ensure there weren't too many distractions, that he didn't waste days playing computer games. To this day Hameed tends to be playing cricket, thinking about it or watching Manchester United. "Any normal child from the age of 13 or 14 would be hanging round with mates, playing football and all the rest of it," says Safwaan. "But Has has just kept himself focused on cricket. And that's what has got him to where he is now."

The emergence of a new hero for English cricket is rather timely. It has been a wobbly few months for the national team. They lost five out of the seven Test matches they played this winter in Bangladesh and India, and finished the year fifth out of 10 in the world rankings. Alastair Cook, the country's longest-serving Test captain, stepped down in February, admitting he didn't have the energy to take the team forward. Meanwhile, the formidable South Africans await this summer, with the supreme test of an Ashes tour in Australia looming in November.

Hameed, who has only played three matches for England, is wary of getting ahead of himself, but you can feel his eyes scanning the horizon. "In terms of watching the game, my first real memory is the 2005 series against Australia," he says, citing the thrilling matches where Andrew Flintoff et al regained the Ashes after 16 years. "I was eight years old then, so that's the one that inspired me the most."

The novelty of British-born Asians representing England is long gone, but Hameed still hopes he can be an example to others. According to official stats, almost 40% of recreational players in the UK are of Asian heritage, but only recently has that been reflected in the England test team. "I want to be a role model for the next generation of people," he says. "To represent it well."

He's proud, too, to be a positive story coming out of Bolton, a town that is rated among the most deprived in England. "I remember when Amir Khan went to the Olympics at a young age and won silver," he says. "You had someone representing Bolton on a world stage and so, of course, it inspired me. When he was coming out in his ring entrance and they said, 'the Pride of Bolton Amir Khan', it kind of stuck with me."

So, I ask, how does standing around in the cold posing for the Observer compare to batting in a Test match with a broken finger? Hameed gives the question serious thought: "This is harder," he decides.

The Observer, 19 March 2017
© Guardian News and Media 2017

WHAT DO YOU THINK?

- **What problems can arise when someone achieves success and fame early in their career?**

- **Talent or work? Which one is more important?**

- **Do you think young sports stars will regret the sacrifices they made?**

Lance Armstrong in the yellow jersey of the Tour de France leader on the final stage on the Champs Elysees, 2004

Lance Armstrong's drug of choice 'doesn't work', scientists claim

By Henry Bodkin

When in 2012 disgraced cyclist Lance Armstrong finally confessed to the most "sophisticated, professionalised and successful" doping programme the world had ever seen, he became sport's ultimate bogeyman.

His admission that for years he took a suite of supposedly performance-enhancing drugs, most prominently erythropoietin (EPO), saw him stripped of his seven Tour de France titles and Olympic medals, his career and reputation in tatters.

So it may be with a certain queasiness that he learns today about the results of ground-breaking new research which suggests his prolonged campaign of abuse was pointless - because EPO confers no advantage at all.

In the first study of its kind, scientists challenged a group of 48 cyclists to tackle a series of challenges, including the infamous Mont Ventoux ascent, which often forms part of the Tour.

Half had been given eight weekly injections of EPO, a drug that promotes red blood cell production with the aim of increasing delivery of oxygen to the muscles, while the other half took a dummy.

But after the gruelling 21.5km climb - which was preceded by a 110km cycle for good measure - the average results of the two groups showed no difference whatsoever.

The scientists behind the trial, which is published in the Lancet, say athletes are "naive" about the benefits of illicit substances such as EPO, but that myths about their effectiveness go unchallenged in the murky world of doping.

"It's just tragic to lose your career for something that doesn't work, to lose seven yellow jerseys for a drug that has no effect," said Jules Heuberger, who led the research at the Centre for Human Drug Research in The Netherlands.

Due to anti-doping rules, it would have been impossible to conduct the study among professional athletes, so the researchers selected the fittest and most experienced amateur riders they could find.

While those who had been injected with EPO did show higher average concentrations of haemoglobin, the oxygen-carrying molecule of red blood cells, this did not translate to better efficiency, heart rate or other respiratory indicators.

Adam Cohen, who was first author on the study, said the simple act of illegally taking drugs like EPO may have given cheats like Armstrong an advantage as a psychological placebo.

"An important level of performance at this high intensity is the mental aspect," he said.

It's just tragic to lose your career for something that doesn't work

Jules Heuberger, The Centre for Human Drug Research in The Netherlands

The Dutch team hope today's study will serve as a wake-up call to both professional and amateur athletes who are tempted to cheat that there is "little to no evidence" justifying the use of many banned drugs.

As well as EPO, Armstrong admitted to using testosterone, human growth hormone and the steroid cortisode during his seven back-to-back Tour victories from 1999 to 2005.

But Mr Cohen said: "Quite possibly all the stuff he was taking was useless.

"Even less is known about many of them than EPO."

In 2012 Armstrong was handed a life ban from all Olympic-sanctioned sports and stripped of his Tour de France titles.

All his results from August 1998 were declared void.

In 2015 the Union Cycliste International reported that doping in amateur cycling was becoming "endemic", raising particular concerns about abuse by over-40s weekend racers who are taking EPO.

Professor John Brewer, an expert in applied sports science at St Mary's University College, cautioned that the benefits of improved oxygen uptake might be more pronounced in professional cyclists than in amateurs and said EPO should remain banned.

The Daily Telegraph, 29 June 2017
© Telegraph Media Group Limited 2017

WHAT DO YOU THINK?

- Should the decision about Lance Armstrong be reversed?

- Is the answer to allow everyone to use the same drugs so that no one has an unfair advantage?

- Does this result call in to question all drug testing?

Drugs in sport

How doping stories are affecting public confidence in sport

When elite athletes take performance enhancing drugs in sport, this is often referred to as 'doping'.

2,027 British adults were interviewed ahead of the first National Clean Sport Week - a campaign by UK Anti-Doping (UKAD) to raise awareness amongst the public and ensure sport in the UK is clean.

Generally, which of the following statements comes closest to your view on doping in sport?

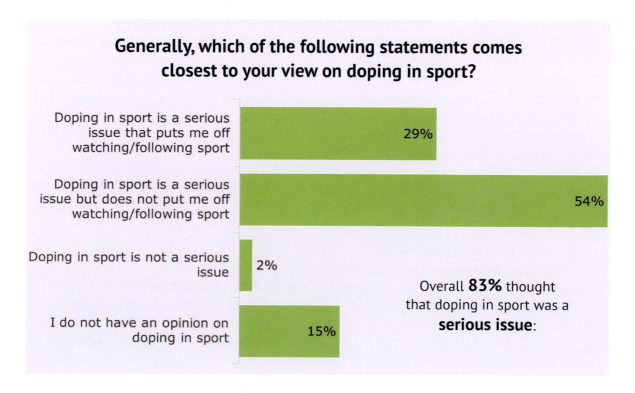

Doping in sport is a serious issue that puts me off watching/following sport — 29%

Doping in sport is a serious issue but does not put me off watching/following sport — 54%

Doping in sport is not a serious issue — 2%

I do not have an opinion on doping in sport — 15%

Overall **83%** thought that doping in sport was a **serious issue**:

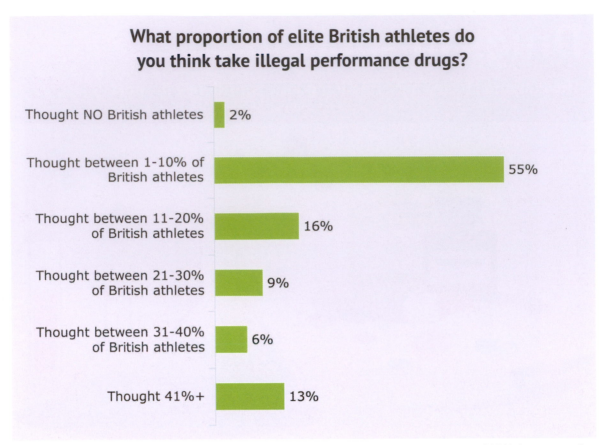

What proportion of elite British athletes do you think take illegal performance drugs?

- Thought NO British athletes — 2%
- Thought between 1-10% of British athletes — 55%
- Thought between 11-20% of British athletes — 16%
- Thought between 21-30% of British athletes — 9%
- Thought between 31-40% of British athletes — 6%
- Thought 41%+ — 13%

Figures do not add up to 100% due to rounding

They were asked whether stories they'd seen or heard about an elite athlete or athletes doping in sport, had an impact on their trust in the integrity of the sport - **66%** said it had a **negative impact**.

These stories include:

- **The Russian doping scandals:** The whole 2014 Russian World Cup squad is being investigated over possible drug offences. Russian athletes also face a complete ban from the 2018 Winter Paralympics for past manipulation of anti-doping tests.

- Russia has had **37 Olympic medals stripped** for doping violations.

- From 2011 to 2015, **more than 1,000** Russian competitors in various sports, including summer, winter, and Paralympic sports, benefited from a cover-up by the authorities.

- **Sir Bradley Wiggins and Team Sky:** Bradley Wiggins was allowed routine asthma drugs, but these were flown in on the eve of a big race rather than being sourced locally. The medical records relating to this don't exist.

- **Lizzie Deignan (Armitstead):** Missed three out-of-competition doping tests just before the Olympic road race in August. She has successfully appealed against a ban.

- **Sir Mo Farah:** His American coach, Alberto Salazar, may have broken anti-doping rules to boost the performance of some of his athletes.

In the World Anti-Doping Code there are 10 Anti-Doping Rule Violations (ADRV). They consist of the following:

1. The presence of a prohibited substance or its metabolites or markers in an athlete's sample.

2. Use or attempted use by an athlete of a prohibited substance or a prohibited method.

3. Evading, refusing, or failing to submit to sample collection.

4. Whereabouts failures: any combination of three missed tests and/or filing failures within a 12-month period by an athlete in a registered testing pool.

5. Tampering or attempted tampering with any part of doping control.

6. Possession of a prohibited substance or prohibited method.

7. Trafficking or attempted trafficking in any prohibited substance or prohibited method.

8. Administration or attempted administration to any athlete in-competition of any prohibited method or prohibited substance, or administration or attempted administration to any athlete out-of-competition of any prohibited method or any prohibited substance that is prohibited out-of-competition.

9. Complicity: assisting, encouraging, aiding, abetting, conspiring, covering up or any other type of intentional complicity involving an ADRV or any attempted ADRV.

10. Prohibited Association: associating with a person such as a coach, doctor or physio who has been found guilty of a criminal or disciplinary offence equivalent to a doping violation.

Since 2009, UK Anti-Doping (UKAD) has conducted over 58,000 tests in over 50 sports. It has prosecuted 194 ADRVs.

When asked about high-profile stories about doping in sport:

49% thought media outlets accurately report on doping in sport.

48% said that high-profile stories on doping in sport makes them think that the issue is widespread.

65% thought doping was more widespread amongst elite athletes in other countries than in Britain.

60% thought Britain had stricter rules, better education and testing for elite athletes to prevent doping in sport than other countries.

Source: UK Anti-Doping (UKAD) www.ukad.org.uk
www.ukad.org.uk/cleansportweek
ComRes survey on behalf of UKAD www.comresglobal.com

WHAT DO YOU THINK?

- **Think of your favourite sportsperson. Would you still watch and admire that athlete if you knew he/she was using a banned substance?**

- **What should happen to someone who is caught doping?**

- **What should be done in countries where doping is said to be widespread?**

THE PSYCHOLOGY OF

PERFECT PENALTIES

What strategies can players employ to give them the edge?

Nothing makes a sport psychologist cringe more than people saying that penalties are a lottery, that they are completely down to chance or that there is nothing you can do to prepare yourself for the unique pressure that comes from a penalty shoot-out. Chance certainly plays a part, but so does skill. So what strategies can players involved in penalty shoot outs employ that can give them the edge over their opponents? What does the research from sport psychology actually say about how to take the perfect penalty?

BEFORE

Before a penalty is even kicked, you can increase your chances of winning a penalty shoot-out if you win the coin toss and choose to shoot first. Professor Igacia Palacios-Huerta, of the London School of Economics, analysed 1,343 penalty kicks from 129 penalty shoot-outs and found that the team that started first won 60.5% of them.

This is most likely to be because of the increased pressure placed on the opposition penalty taker who is more likely to know the actual consequences of a miss. This overload of stress and split-focus hinders techniques by increasing tension in the player.

Which team won the penalty shoot out?

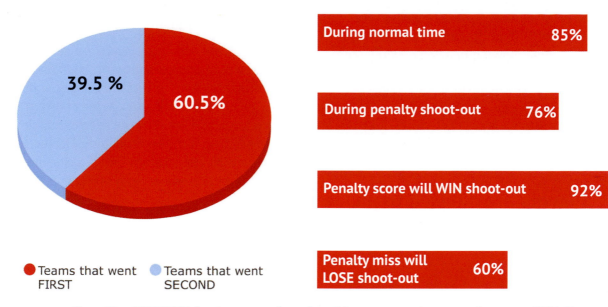

39.5 %

60.5%

● Teams that went FIRST ● Teams that went SECOND

Success rate depends on the type of penalty

| During normal time | 85% |

| During penalty shoot-out | 76% |

| Penalty score will WIN shoot-out | 92% |

| Penalty miss will LOSE shoot-out | 60% |

From May 2017 UEFA has been experimenting with a new penalty system, known as ABBA. Team A takes the first penalty, team B the second and third, team A the fourth and fifth and so on until each team has taken five. The sequence continues if the shootout then goes to sudden death.

Indeed, pressure seems to play a big role in penalty shoot-out success. Research shows that if a player takes a penalty during normal time, they score on average 85% of the time. However during a penalty shoot-out, players know that their penalty may decide the outcome of the match. This increased pressure and stress results in the conversion rate of penalties taken during a penalty shoot dropping to 76%.

Most interesting, though, is that if a player steps up to take a penalty that will win the penalty shoot-out, and so the match, the success rate rises dramatically to 92%, whereas if they have to score or else their team will lose, the likelihood of scoring drops to under 60%.

This reflects what Nobel Prize winner Daniel Kahneman calls 'loss aversion'. That is the stress and fear of losing something will dramatically influence someone's thoughts and behaviour. In essence, the pain of defeats weighs very heavily on our mind.

Clearly, those who have learnt to handle their nerves have an advantage. There are two tricks here, and both relate to the relationship between the penalty taker and the goalkeeper. The first trick is to realise

that after you have placed the ball down on the spot it is a mistake to turn your back on the goalkeeper as you walk back to the start of your run up. Psychologists have found that those who do are more likely to miss. This is because it interrupts their preparation, allows them to focus on things they cannot control, projects their nerves and provides the goalkeeper with subtle clues as to where the penalty is going to go.

The stress and fear of losing something will dramatically influence someone's thoughts and behaviour.

The second trick is not to spend too long looking at the goalkeeper before the kick. In a study of 167 penalties, researchers found that those who fixated on the goalkeeper were more anxious and missed more penalties. It is far better to focus on your target and your abilities, or something that calms you down, rather than the opposition goalkeeper.

DURING

Once the referee blows his whistle, don't rush to take your penalty. Take a bit of time to ready yourself. Footballers who take less than 200 milliseconds to respond to the referee blowing his whistle, only score around 57% of the time. To give this some context, that is half the time it takes to blink. Players who take a bit of time to ready themselves, be it only for one second, score on average over 80% of the time.

Players are advised to pick a spot and commit to it.

Historically, this has been a problem for players from England, who have a penalty shoot-out win record of only 17% and have been found to take their penalties quicker than any other nation. This is supported by quotes from Steven Gerrard who said in his autobiography, 'Why do I have to wait for the bloody whistle? Those extra couple of seconds seemed like an eternity and they definitely put me off'. Interestingly, this rushing used to be an issue for Spain as well (with a penalty win record of 33%), however their recent penalty wins at the last two European Championships suggest they have learnt from their previous mistakes (you can see their penalty wins in Euro 2008 against Italy and their Euro 2012 win against Portugal on YouTube).

As well as not rushing, players are advised to pick a spot and commit to it. Changing your mind leads to uncertainty, stress and poor technique. Some players leave it to the last minute and wait for the keeper to dive before hitting it to the other side. However, this is a high risk strategy and is associated with a greater number of missed penalties.

It is far better to pick a spot that you feel confident of hitting and commit to that. Penalties that are on target and high in the goal are rarely saved. This is because it is very hard for goalkeepers to reach these areas. However, it requires the penalty taker to trust their technique as there is a small margin for error as they may miss the target if they aim here. If they have the ability to execute this penalty (and trust in that ability), the payoff is worth it. A great example of this was when Germany beat England in a penalty shoot-out in Euro '96, with 9 out of the 11 penalties that were scored going in the top corner. By comparison, Gareth Southgate's saved penalty went low and to the left.

AFTER

Once you have scored your penalty, your job is not quite finished. It is important to celebrate. A study of 151 penalties from recent World Cups and Euro Championships found that if a player celebrated their successful penalty, their opponent was far more likely to miss their next penalty. Their analysis showed that when the score was equal, 82% of players who celebrated their successful penalties went on to be on the winning team. This is called 'emotional contagion', which describes how the emotions of one player can negatively affect the emotions of the next penalty taker. Every penalty taker for Italy celebrated their goal during their penalty shoot-out win against France in the 2006 World Cup.

WHAT ABOUT GOALKEEPERS?

A recent study has found that the colour of the goalkeeper's kit may impact the likelihood of their opponent scoring. The fewest goals was scored against goalkeepers who wore red (54%) or yellow (69%). The two worst colours? Blue (72%) and green (75%).

What is the best strategy for a goalkeeper to employ in order to save a key penalty? Research suggests it is for them to stand still. Analysis of 999 penalties from the Bundesliga found that 15% of players shoot down the middle. A separate study of 286 penalty kicks from the top leagues around the world found that only 2% of goalkeepers remain in the centre. It is calculated that goalkeepers are actually twice as likely to save a penalty if they stay in the middle of the goal rather than dive to one side or the other.

Researchers state that standing still is therefore the 'optimum strategy' for saving penalties. Goalkeepers can't do this for every penalty, as opponents will quickly work out that this is their strategy and hit it elsewhere (this is known as 'game theory'), so a degree of randomness is needed.

So why do goalkeepers rarely stand their ground? Psychologists refer to this behaviour as an "action bias", which is where the value of being seen to do something is higher than that of doing nothing. If they dive and the opponent scores, the goalkeeper doesn't attract blame, but if they stand still and the opponent scores then they do get blamed. It seems this fear of blame subconsciously overrules a perfectly good strategy.

SUMMARY: THE STRATEGIES TO 'BEAT THE ODDS'

Penalties are not a lottery. They are not completely random or down to chance. Often it is only the losing team who describe it as such. Players and teams can tip the balance in their favour by following some simple tricks and strategies:

- **Choose to shoot first**
- **Reduce your stress levels**
- **Don't dwell on the goalkeeper**
- **Don't turn your back on the goal before the run up**
- **Pause for a second after the ref's whistle before you take the penalty**
- **Pick a spot and don't change your mind**
- **Aim at one of the top corners of the goal**
- **Celebrate if you score**
- **For goalies - wear red**
- **For goalies - don't dive, stay in the centre**

Source: Inner Drive mental skills training company, www.innerdrive.co.uk

WHAT DO YOU THINK?

- **Which single piece of advice is most helpful?**
- **In what other situations could you use this advice about coping?**
- **Will this advice still work if it becomes well known?**

Sports salaries

The relationship between money and success in sport

The Global Sports Salaries Survey compares how much sportspeople earn at hundreds of different clubs and teams around the world in professional sports.

Football has dominated previous lists, but for the first time, the richest team is the National Basketball Association's Cleveland Cavaliers. Their players will earn, on average **each** this season, more than **£6.5m**, or more than **£125,000** per week.

Average WEEKLY salary per player of the first-team squads - Top 12 teams

NBA - National Basketball Association, MLB - Major League Baseball,
EPL - English Premier League, La Liga - Spanish football league

(Annual pay in brackets)

Team	Weekly salary
Cleveland Cavaliers - NBA (£6,545,934)	£125,883
New York Yankees - MLB (£5,817,167)	£111,869
LA Clippers - NBA (£5,789,976)	£111,346
Man Utd - EPL (£5,770,000)	£110,962
Barcelona - La Liga (£5,649,091)	£108,636
Portland Trail Blazers - NBA (£5,590,003)	£107,500
Memphis Grizzlies - NBA (£5,513,376)	£106,026
Dallas Mavericks - NBA (£5,500,474)	£105,778
Man City - EPL (£5,423,077)	£104,290
Orlando Magic - NBA (£5,385,535)	£103,568
Toronto Raptors - NBA (£5,372,233)	£103,312
San Antonio Spurs - NBA (£5,298,738)	£101,899

QUICK FACTS

- Average pay is important - as opposed to total wage outlay - because two teams spending the same totals on salaries will have very different averages if they are paying a significantly different number of players.

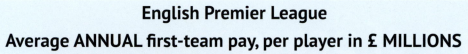

English Premier League
Average ANNUAL first-team pay, per player in £ MILLIONS

Club	Pay (£m)
Man Utd	£5.77
Man City	£5.42
Chelsea	£4.51
Arsenal	£3.71
Liverpool	£3.01
Tottenham	£2.68
West Ham	£2.26
Everton	£2.15
Leicester	£2.1
Southampton	£2.07
Crystal Palace	£1.97
Stoke	£1.9
Sunderland	£1.87
West Brom	£1.84
Watford	£1.55
Swansea	£1.41
Middlesbrough	£1.23
Hull	£1.23
Bournemouth	£1.11

QUICK FACTS: 2016-17 SEASON

- The EPL is the highest paying football league in the world, at an average of **£2.4m** per player, per season. That is about twice as much as the next highest paying football league - Spain's La Liga.

- Clubs can now afford to offer salaries that outdo nearly every non-English club in the world.

- The Premier League's **top 10%** of players earn 'only' **29%** of all the wages, a much lower and fairer figure than other football leagues.

- Premier League clubs benefitted from a new television deal worth **over £5bn**, meaning they had more spending power. Premier League spending on transfers reached over **£1bn** for the first time.

In most leagues, money matters when it comes to performance; the more you pay, the better you do, all other things being equal.

That is particularly true in elite football leagues but also true in the NBA and in MLB. The reason is that better players cost more, and if you're spending more it's generally because you have better players.

Sportingintelligence - Global sports salaries survey 2016 www.sportingintelligence.com

WHAT DO YOU THINK?

- **Should money have such a prominent place in sporting success?**

- **Are the huge wages of sporting stars justified?**

- **Where does the money to pay such wages come from?**

Cost of peace

United Nations peacekeeping helps countries torn by conflict create conditions for lasting peace

The United Nations was established on 24th October 1945 by 51 countries who were committed to preserving peace. Today, nearly every nation in the world belongs to the UN.

The UN has four purposes:

- to maintain international peace and security;
- to develop friendly relations among nations;
- to co-operate in solving international problems and in promoting respect for human rights; and
- to be a centre for harmonising the actions of nations.

UN workforce in the 16 current peacekeeping operations 31st January 2017

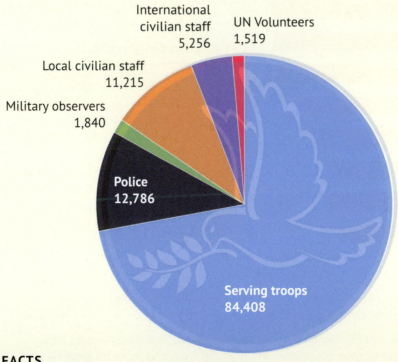

International civilian staff 5,256

UN Volunteers 1,519

Local civilian staff 11,215

Military observers 1,840

Police 12,786

Serving troops 84,408

QUICK FACTS

- Total number of personnel: **117,024**
- Number of uniformed personnel (troops, police and military observers) provided by 126 countries: **99,034**
- Other workforce: **17,990**
- Number of fatalities in current operations: **1,766**
- The UN has no military forces of its own. The military and police support needed for each peacekeeping operation is provided by Member States on a voluntary basis.

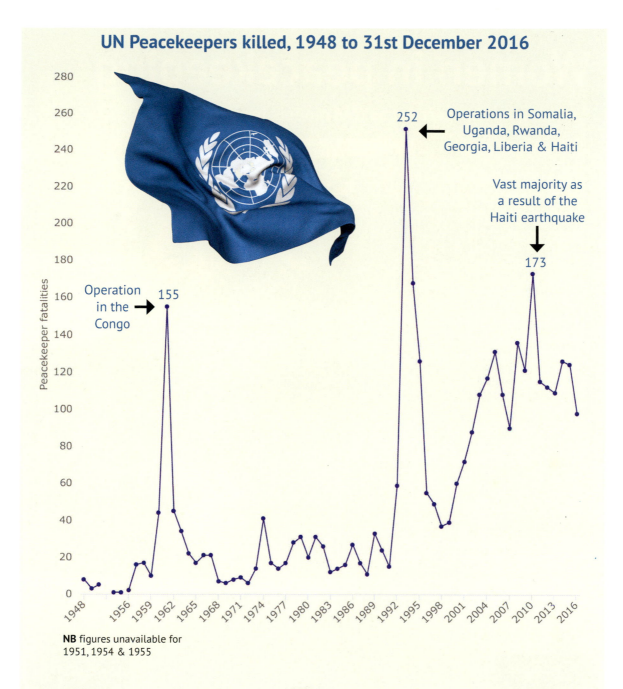

UN Peacekeepers killed, 1948 to 31st December 2016

Peacekeeper fatalities

Operation in the Congo → 155

252 ← Operations in Somalia, Uganda, Rwanda, Georgia, Liberia & Haiti

Vast majority as a result of the Haiti earthquake ↓

173

NB figures unavailable for 1951, 1954 & 1955

QUICK FACTS

Peacekeeping operations since 1948: **71**

Total fatalities in all peace operations since 1948: **3,545**

The budget for UN peacekeeping operations from 1 July 2016 to 30 June 2017: about **$7.87 billion**

WHAT DO YOU THINK?

- Is peacekeeping an important task?

- Is enough money being invested in peace as opposed to war?

- Should any organisation be trying to maintain peace in a foreign country?

Source: United Nations Peacekeeping
www.un.org/en/peacekeeping

Women in peacekeeping

Female peacekeepers act as role models inspiring women

Peacekeepers monitor and observe peace processes after conflicts and assist in keeping the peace agreements.

This assistance comes in many forms, including confidence-building measures, power-sharing arrangements, electoral support, strengthening the rule of law, and economic and social development.

UN peacekeepers can include soldiers, police officers, and civilian personnel.

Private Tara Yonjan is a vehicle mechanic and the only woman in her team in South Lebanon.
Photo: UN Photo/Pasqual Gorriz

Total female uniformed peacekeepers
31 January 2017

PAST

1957-1989
A total of only **20** uniformed women served as UN peacekeepers.

1993
Women made up **1%** of uniformed personnel.

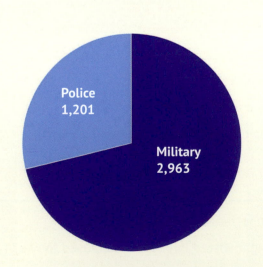

Police
1,201

Military
2,963

PRESENT

Women are increasing in all areas of peacekeeping

In 2017, out of a total of **100,231** peacekeepers, women made up **3.39%** of the military personnel and **9.38%** of the police personnel in UN peacekeeping missions

Total female peacekeepers 4,164

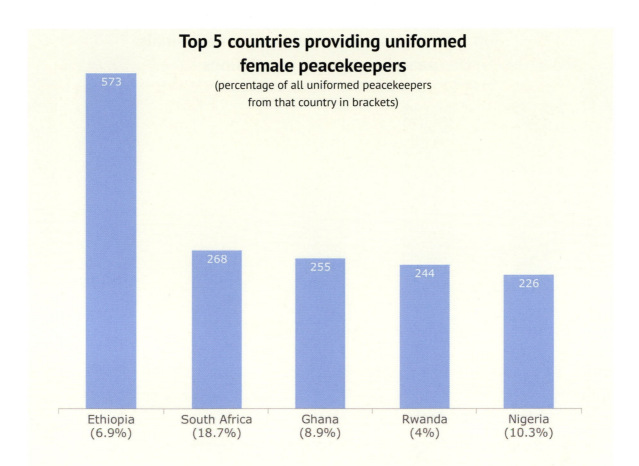

Top 5 countries providing uniformed female peacekeepers

(percentage of all uniformed peacekeepers
from that country in brackets)

573	268	255	244	226
Ethiopia (6.9%)	South Africa (18.7%)	Ghana (8.9%)	Rwanda (4%)	Nigeria (10.3%)

Corporal Norfazidatul Aina, Military Police is in charge of a UN Security Post in South Lebanon.
Photo: UN Photo/Pasqual Gorriz

Top 5 countries where most uniformed female peacekeepers are on missions

(percentage of all uniformed peacekeepers on that mission in brackets)

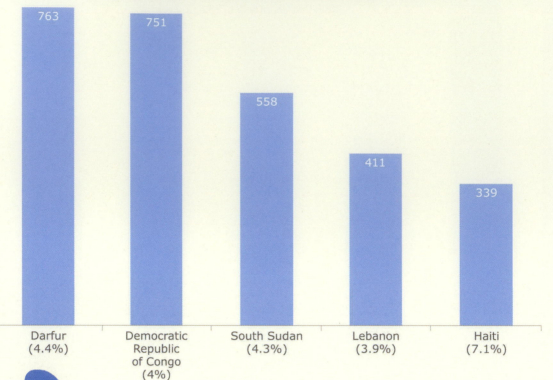

Darfur (4.4%)	Democratic Republic of Congo (4%)	South Sudan (4.3%)	Lebanon (3.9%)	Haiti (7.1%)
763	751	558	411	339

"By empowering women we build stronger societies. When a crowd needs to be controlled, a house searched or a suspect questioned, a policewoman's presence can defuse tension and guard against offence. When women and girls suffer sexual violence, they know they will find a sympathetic ear. And when they see female role models keeping the peace, we have seen women and girls become inspired to join the force and do the same."

Ban Ki-moon
UN Secretary-General (January 2007 to December 2016)

WHAT DO YOU THINK?

- Do you agree that female peacekeepers have a special role in defusing tension?

- How could the UN recruit more women?

- Should an organisation use 'positive discrimination' and deliberately favour people because of their gender or race in order to achieve something worthwhile?

Source: UN peacekeeping www.un.org/en/peacekeeping

Can we stop the killer robots?

Lethal Autonomous Weapons Systems - think about each of those words - are being developed and used now.

Imagine a machine designed and programmed to kill. A machine which can choose and fire on its targets without a human controlling it. This isn't science fiction, this is the natural progression of the use of artificial intelligence in weaponry. Killer robots - which would probably look less like Terminator and more like toy helicopters - could become a reality in the not too distant future.

We already have weapons that can kill at a distance such as Cruise missiles or remotely piloted drones, but humans make the decisions about the targets and the timing. Autonomous weapons, programmed to search for and eliminate people according to pre-set conditions, could select their targets and act without human intervention - or prevention. Who programmes them, and for what, will become one of the greatest challenges of our future.

New technology developed for other purposes has always been used to make combat more efficient. Warfare was radically changed by the invention of gunpowder, then by nuclear weapons. Artificial Intelligence (AI) could bring about a third revolution in methods of destruction.

Artificial Intelligence could bring about a third revolution in methods of destruction.

The arguments for such machines resemble those for any long range weapons. For the side possessing Lethal Autonomous Weapons Systems (LAWS) the advantages are obvious - the chief one being that they save the lives of combatants on one side and at the same time increase the range, size, power and capability of forces. They expand the reach of a fighting force, taking it into areas that would be difficult with only manpower. They offer the critical ability to have a faster response. Since they keep a constant watch (a machine doesn't blink or turn away) this results in greater precision in targetting.

For those outside the military, this precision is the strongest (perhaps the only) argument in favour of Artificial Intelligence being used for this purpose. Their supporters argue that LAWS would actually reduce incidents of 'friendly fire', when troops are fired upon by their own side or their

Intelligent Surveillance & Security Guard Robot (SGR-A1)

Tracking Device
2km range (1km at night)

Weapon
Machine gun or grenade launcher

Surveillance Device
4km range (2km at night)

allies. Greater precision could also reduce civilian casualties and damage to property.

Those advocating the development of these weapons point to war crimes as evidence of human frailty. When you have been losing comrades, you have an enemy who has been presented as less than human, your commanders are weak or absent, you are young or inexperienced, your orders are unclear, you are under extreme stress, you are unlikely to be much troubled by ethical considerations. Human combatants make mistakes and can be led by emotion into acts of revenge or into atrocities. Robots, they say, could address some of these issues, because, ultimately, AI will allow these machines to make better decisions than us, taking into account more factors, having a longer view and thinking more quickly.

But their opponents say that these qualities are exactly what makes them so dangerous. Machines lack empathy - the ability to imagine themselves in the situation of others and to imaginatively share their emotions. Precisely because human beings are emotional they are able to see the harm that they might do, they are able to feel compassion for someone's suffering and, crucially, they are able to feel guilt. Humans can benefit from past experience, can make individual

decisions and can change their response in proportion to the situation.

Could a robot be pre-programmed to handle every different scenario? When an autonomous machine makes a decision that is wrong in human terms - who is to blame?

But this is science fiction or the distant future, isn't it? How long will it be before such weapons are a reality? "20 or 30 years" according to some very eminent scientists or "probably feasible now" according to our own Ministry of Defence.

The Artificial Intelligence required is already in place - think about self driving cars or computers that can beat the best at chess. The hardware components are readily available and relatively cheap - drones were a favourite Christmas present in 2016. All that is needed is research investment to bring it to completion.

So can the advance of the killer robots be stopped? Perhaps, but part of the problem is that they are already here and there is an incentive to use them. Drones were originally surveillance machines but are now weapons, though controlled by a distant

If a machine makes a wrong decision - who is to blame?

human. Nations are already defended by automated systems designed to destroy incoming missiles without the need for some lumbering human to notice and act in time - but that human can override the system if need be.

There are already completely autonomous systems available such as the SGR-A1 rumoured to be in operation on the border between North and South Korea. Israel uses the 'Harpy' system to take out enemy radar. Its promotional description says: "Harpy is a 'Fire and Forget' autonomous weapon, launched from a ground vehicle behind the battle zone. The Harpy weapon detects, attacks and destroys enemy radar emitters, hitting them with high hit accuracy." Of course what the Harpy doesn't know - and cannot care - is whether that radar system is located in an area with a civilian population.

Among the countries currently developing autonomous weapons are Israel, Russia, China the US and the UK. The developments are not just for external use. Controlling a crowd would be much easier if the police had access to the right technology - and police in the US state of Dakota are allowed to use drones equipped with tasers, pepper spray and rubber bullets. In the UK drones have been used to photograph protestors - itself possibly a breach of privacy.

Stuart Russell, professor of computer science and engineering at the University of California, Berkeley gives us an insight into the nightmare that might come: "A very, very, small quadcopter, one inch in diameter can carry a one- or two-gram shaped charge … A one-gram shaped charge can punch a hole in nine millimetres of steel, so presumably you can also punch a hole in someone's head … You need only three guys to write the program and launch them. So you can just imagine that in many parts of the world humans will be hunted. They will be cowering underground in shelters and devising techniques so that they don't get detected. This is the ever-present cloud of lethal autonomous weapons."

The fact that these weapons are, in part, already here makes a ban particularly difficult, though campaigners are trying. There is an open letter to the UN (https://futureoflife.org/open-letter-autonomous-weapons/) signed by a host of eminent scientists and technologists, including Stephen Hawking and Elon Musk, calling for a ban.

They are already here

In December 2016, 123 nations agreed to 'formalise their efforts' to deal with the development of Lethal Autonomous Weapons Systems. They would bring together a group of experts during 2017 as a step towards negotiating a ban. But while international agencies move forward with glacial slowness, individual nations are pressing ahead with their development.

And once nations have the weapons, will others, criminals, tyrants or terrorists, be far behind?

Sources: Various, including
www.buzzfeed.com/sarahatopol/how-to-save-mankind-from-the-new-breed-of-killer-robots?
http://theconversation.com/losing-control-the-dangers-of-killer-robots-58262
www.livescience.com/57306-un-addresses-killer-robots-in-2017.html

WHAT DO YOU THINK?

- **What should be done in the face of this threat?**
- **Do you agree that machines will eventually be better decision-makers than humans?**
- **Do you know of any rules or agreements about the way warfare should be conducted?**

Killer robots

Public opinion on developments in weapons of war

What are killer robots?

Killer robots are lethal autonomous weapons systems (LAWS) that would be capable of selecting targets and using force without any human input or interaction.

Low-cost sensors and advances in artificial intelligence are making it more practical to design weapons systems that would target and attack without human intervention.

Armed drones currently in operation over Afghanistan, Iraq, Yemen and other countries depend on a person to make the final decision whether to fire on a target.

Newer military drones can already can take off, land and fly to designated points without human commands.

In February 2017, Ipsos surveyed a global sample of 11,500 adults aged 18-64 in the US, Israel and Canada, and aged 16-64 in all other countries.

They were asked:

How do you feel about the use of autonomous weapons in war?

25% strongly or somewhat **SUPPORTED** their use;

56% strongly or somewhat **OPPOSED** their use;

19% were **not sure**.

QUICK FACTS

Differences of opinion by country:

- **55%** of people in **Great Britain opposed** the use of LAWS.

- **Russia 69%** and **Peru 67%** topped the list of **most opposed** countries, closely followed by **Spain** and **Argentina** both at **66%**.

- The **most supportive** countries include **India 60%, China 47%** and the **US 34%.**

Gender:

- **29%** of **men supported** the use of these weapons compared to **women - 20%**.

Age:

- **29%** of those **under 35** were **supportive** of using these weapons, while only **18%** of respondents **aged 50-64 supported** their use.

A YouGov survey of 1,765 GB Adults asked the following questions:

Would you support or oppose Britain signing an international agreement to ban the use of fully autonomous weapons from use in battle?

(Figures do not add up to 100% due to rounding)

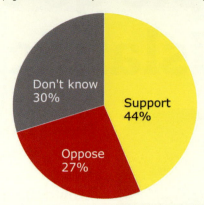

Don't know 30%

Support 44%

Oppose 27%

How likely or unlikely do you think it is that the following will be true by 2033?

(The remaining percentages were made up of those who didn't know)

● Likely ● Unlikely

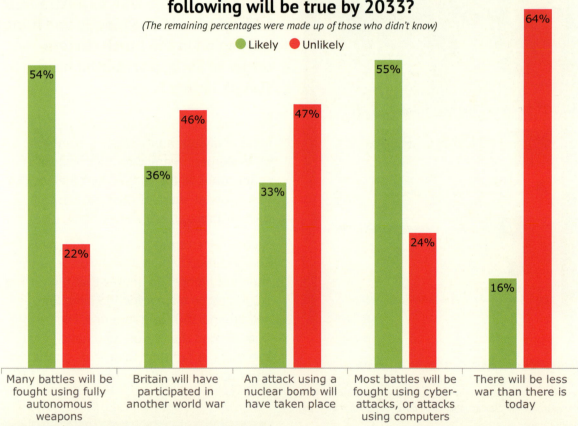

	Likely	Unlikely
Many battles will be fought using fully autonomous weapons	54%	22%
Britain will have participated in another world war	36%	46%
An attack using a nuclear bomb will have taken place	33%	47%
Most battles will be fought using cyber-attacks, or attacks using computers	55%	24%
There will be less war than there is today	16%	64%

Ipsos MORI © 2016 Ipsos www.ipsos-mori.com
YouGov www.yougov.co.uk

WHAT DO YOU THINK?

- Is this a good use of technology?

- Are there any reasons for the way different groups of people feel about these weapons?

- Most people in Britain seem to think that there will be more war and autonomous weapons will be in use. Do you share that opinion?

Why do 'ordinary' people go to fight Islamic State?

Kurds - Between 25 and 35 million Kurds live in a mountainous region on the borders of Turkey, Iraq, Syria, Iran and Armenia. Although they are the fourth-largest ethnic group in the Middle East, they have never obtained their own nation state.

YPG - these initials translate to "People's Protection Units". They are defence forces formed when the war in Syria started to spill over into Syrian Kurdistan, now known as Rojava.

IS -This jihadist group has been referred to by different names such as ISIS and ISIL. The term "Daesh" (or Da'ish) is also used precisely because it has negative connotations.

Jihad -this is often translated as "holy war," but actually means struggling or surviving. Islamic scholars say the misuse of the word by extremist groups contradicts Islam. However the term jihadi is often used as a description of someone who believes in using violence to achieve political or religious aims.

There's nothing ordinary about the men and women who go to fight Islamic State in Syria or Iraq. Why would there be? Why leave the stability and security of an 'ordinary' life in the UK, the USA or Australia, to take up arms in the bloody and brutal war raging in the north eastern corner of Syria, just south of the Turkish border?

For many of us, Kurdistan could be a million miles away, but an increasing number of Westerners, many with no obvious connections to the region, feel the need to 'get involved', most of them on the side of the self-proclaimed Islamic State, IS.

No one is certain how many have gone. The Soufan Group (which advises on security and intelligence) estimates that more than 3,000 people have joined IS from Europe and around 150 from America. The people from beyond the region who have joined the Kurds in fighting against IS, on the other hand, probably number at most 1,000.

> ## "There's a lot of crazy people who come out here"

One of these not so ordinary individuals was Tim Locks. He is typical of the (mainly) men and women who made a spontaneous decision and travelled to Iraq. His background of a tough childhood, a long-standing regret about not joining the army and a spell as a night-club bouncer does not suggest someone easily moved. Yet news of an atrocity sent him half way across the world.

"Unless I'm there I can't do anything"

In August 2014 the Yazidi population in northern Iraq were massacred by ISIS because of their religious beliefs. The west seemed unable to prevent this or help the survivors. Locks had never heard of the Yazidi people before this, yet he explained: "I just thought 'right', that's enough. I don't know what I can do, but unless I'm there I can't do anything".

Another volunteer, Dean Parker, 49, from Florida, USA, says he felt God's call as he watched a news clip of the IS attack on the Yazidi. An Iraqi helicopter with a western cameraman on board went to help the besieged women and children. A woman with her son caught Parker's eye.

"She was crying, holding him. He was looking at the camera and that look of sheer terror in his eyes overwhelmed me with emotions I have never felt before...that was it. I knew I had to come, and never in the month before coming did I have any doubt."

However, not everyone went on the basis of a knee jerk reaction. Jac Holmes, 22, from Bournemouth, was shot and injured by IS while fighting in northern Syria with a group called the Lions of Rojava.

"I was studying the whole Syrian civil war on the internet for six months or more. I thought I want to get over there and get involved."

He reflected that some of the Westerners he was fighting alongside had their own issues: "It was a wide spectrum of people. Some of them were really professional ex-military guys. Then there's other people who, like me, had no military experience beforehand. But unlike me they're not mentally sane. There's a lot of crazy people who come out here, basically."

Once they made a decision to go, reaching Kurdistan was, for most of them, surprisingly straightforward; flights went from London, visas were obtainable on arrival and, at the airport, people they had contacted online were happy to pick up and deliver them to a military unit.

In the conflict zone most foreign fighters join the Lions of Rojava (LoR) - a part of the Kurdish People's Protection Unit (YPG). Since the setting up of their Facebook page in 2014 the LoR has proved to be something of a magnet for Westerners. The LoR has become almost famous in some circles, spoken about with a certain reverence and, occasionally, jealousy.

These are the guys who are engaging in offensive operations against IS whilst other foreign fighters are essentially used for defensive duties away from the front lines. Kurdish forces are keen to avoid the public relations nightmare of western volunteers being killed on a regular basis. However, according to the LoR Facebook page, individuals have died fighting for the YPG.

I thought "I want to get over there and get involved."

Jac Holmes was shot fighting to retake control of a village, and says he is lucky it was only a flesh wound. He retains a positive view of his time with the LoR: "It was a pleasure and a honour to fight and be integrated in their way of life. It was great to go to Rojava."

Sadly, not all volunteers return. In early January 2017 the YPG announced that Englishman Ryan Lock, 20, had died in action with the LoR, while attempting to retake the city of Raqqa from IS.

Some of the Western fighters explain their motivation on their Twitter accounts

Lock is the third British national to be killed in action against IS since the first foreign fighters arrived in the Kurdistan region in 2014. Konstandinos Erik Scurfield, 25, from Barnsley, an ex Royal Marine, was killed in 2015 in heavy fighting. Dean Carl Evans, a 22 year old dairy farmer from Wiltshire, died in July 2016 as he tried to help an injured comrade during a street battle.

Kimberley Taylor, aged 27, from Blackburn is believed to be the first British woman to take part in the active fight against Islamic State when she joined the Woman's Protection Units (YPJ) an all female force attached to the YPG.

A maths graduate from Liverpool University, she spent 11 months learning Kurdish as well as weaponry and tactics at a military school run by the YPJ. In phone interviews in February 2017, she said, "I'm willing to give my life for this. It's for the whole world, for humanity and all oppressed people, everywhere."

"Torn apart"by seeing the living conditions of refugees, she was also inspired by the politics of the Kurdish people she is fighting alongside - feminist and anti-capitalist.

Ryan Lock's body was returned to the UK on 18th February 2017. Ozkam Ozolil, a north Londoner who arrived in Syria only in September, said of him: "He said he came to make a difference where many wouldn't dare to step up."

Kimberley's father worries about her safety but says, "She is truly one in a million and we are very proud of who she is and what she stands for."

There is nothing 'ordinary' about these people. 'Extraordinary' would be, perhaps, more apt. It seems that to follow the urge to make a difference in Kurdistan you need, indeed, to be quite different from the rest of us.

Sources: Various

In July 2017, 22 year old Luke Rutter from Merseyside became the fourth Briton to die fighting IS

WHAT DO YOU THINK?

- **Can you understand the reasons people went to join the fight? Do you agree with their reasons?**

- **Is a war in a far off country any of our business?**

- **People returning from fighting (on either side) can be arrested as potential terrorists. Is this the right thing to do?**

World Population

Will the world's population continue to grow?

The UN's population predictions show that population growth may slow down significantly over the next 80 years.

World population from 1950 to 2010 and predicted population from 2020 to 2100

(Billions)

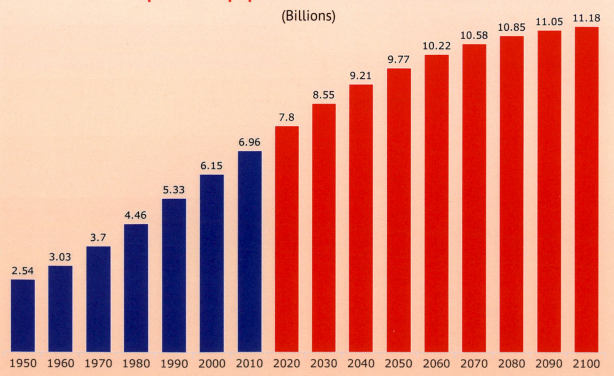

1950	1960	1970	1980	1990	2000	2010	2020	2030	2040	2050	2060	2070	2080	2090	2100
2.54	3.03	3.7	4.46	5.33	6.15	6.96	7.8	8.55	9.21	9.77	10.22	10.58	10.85	11.05	11.18

Where will most people live?

More than half of the anticipated growth in global population between now and 2050 is expected to occur in Africa. Of the additional **2.2 billion** people who may be added, **1.3 billion** will be added in Africa. Asia is expected to be the second largest contributor, adding just over **750 million** people.

World population predictions by region (millions)

Regions not included: North America, Latin America, the Caribbean, and Oceania

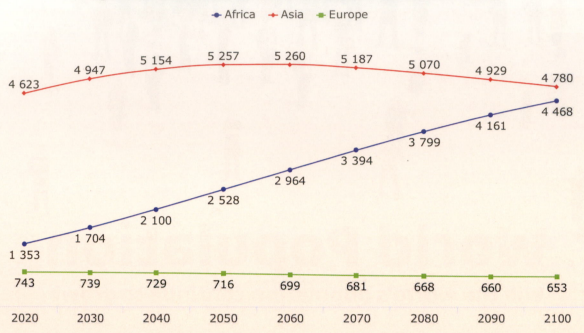

- By 2060 the only region to have a fast growing population will be Africa, all other regions will have a more stable, or even falling population.

- Asia's population has boomed in recent years from just **1.4 million in 1950** to **4.4 million in 2015**, but the rate of growth is slowing and by 2060 it is expected to start falling. In Europe we are already seeing the population fall.

- In Africa the population is expected to continue to rise, but the rate of growth is slowing down.

- One of the main contributors to population growth is that people are living longer.

Life expectancy at birth, by region

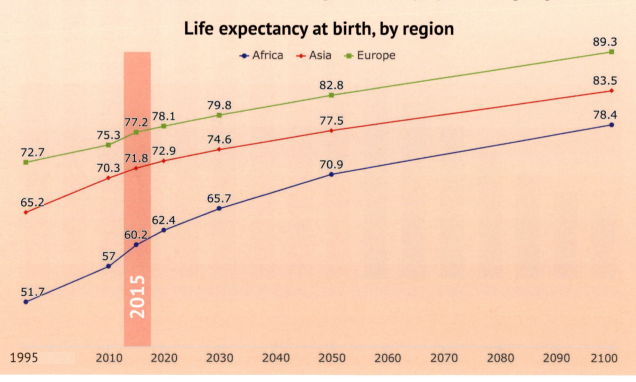

- Globally, life expectancy at birth rose by **3.6 years** between 2005 and 2015. But the greatest gains were in Africa, where life expectancy rose by **6.6 years** in the same period.

- The **under-five mortality rate**, which is the probability of a child dying between birth and its fifth birthday, has also reduced globally **from 70 to 48 per 1,000 children**. Sub-Saharan Africa saw the greatest fall of **from 141 to 95 per 1,000.**

- Globally, life expectancy at birth is projected to rise **from 71 years in 2015 to 77 years in 2050** and Africa is projected to gain nearly **11 years** of life expectancy by mid-century, reaching **71 years**. Such increases are reliant on further reductions in HIV/AIDS, and other diseases.

- Another major contributor to population growth is **birth rate.**

- Global fertility is expected to fall from just over **2.5 births per woman in 2015 to around 2 in 2100**. In Africa the fall in birth rate will be higher, falling from **4.7 births per woman in 2015 to 2.1 in 2100.**

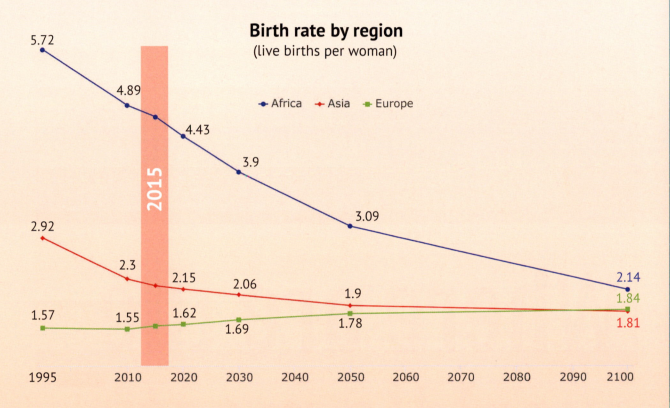

Birth rate by region
(live births per woman)

● Africa ◆ Asia ■ Europe

In many regions the population is still quite young:

- In Africa, **children under age 15 accounted for 41% of the population** in 2017 and young persons aged 15 to 24 accounted for an additional 19%. **Just 5% were over age 60.**

- In Europe, only **16% of the population was under age 15**, and **25% were over age 60.**

- As **birth rate decreases** the proportion of the population that is **under age 16 will decrease** and as **life expectancy increases** the proportion of the population **over age 60 will increase.**

- This phenomenon, known as **population ageing**, is occurring throughout the world.

São Paulo, Brazil: The main reservoir supplying São Paulo dropped to just 6% of its capacity and residents were hit with regular water rationing.

Where are the world's most water-stressed cities?

More than 2.5 billion people don't have access to basic levels of fresh water for at least one month each year – a situation growing ever more critical as urban populations expand rapidly

Katherine Purvis

In the southern reaches of Egypt, the city of Aswan is one of the hottest and sunniest in the world. Temperatures reach 41C in the summer and less than a millimetre of rain falls each year. Some years it doesn't rain at all.

Aswan may be one of the world's least rainy places, but it's not even close to being the most water-stressed city. It nestles on the east bank of the Nile, close to the Aswan High Dam and the vast Lake Nasser, one of the largest manmade lakes in the world. With a capacity of 132 cubic km, the dam serves the irrigations needs not just of Aswan, but Egypt and neighbouring Sudan as well.

Water stress – where the human or ecological demand for water is not met – is caused by a variety of factors. There's the physical scarcity of water due to lack of rainfall, the natural aridity of the area and, increasingly, changes in climate; but poor management and investment in water infrastructure, and pollution, also play their parts.

The problem affects an estimated 2.7 billion people for at least one month of every year, across every continent – and is particularly pressing in cities as the global urban population grows. At present, almost four billion people live in cities, with a further 2.5 billion expected to join them by 2050.

860 million people live in slums around the world; their lack of access to clean water carries enormous health consequences

As the urban population grows, so too does the number of people living in settlements that are not connected to a formal piped water supply. Currently, some 860 million people live in slums around the world; their lack of access to clean water carries enormous health consequences.

As freshwater supplies dry up, many cities are engaged in a race to the bottom as they turn to groundwater – with some underground aquifers now so overexploited that water is extracted much faster than it is recharged. During the height of the recent drought in California, farms and cities were apparently drilling so deeply for groundwater that they tapped into reserves that had fallen to earth as rain 20,000 years ago.

Over the past few years, both Los Angeles and São Paulo have been hit by major droughts affecting their surrounding states. For California, 2014 and 2015 were the two hottest years in its history; in April last year, the state's Department of Water Resources found "no snow whatsoever" during its survey in the Sierra Nevada mountains.

"We get all of our water for the year through the winter months, and we hope that accumulates in reservoirs and as snowpack to draw on as a resource over the summer," says Paul Ullrich, assistant professor of regional and global climate modelling at UC Davis. "In the absence of snow pack or precipitation in winter, we turn to pumping groundwater – but it's our insurance policy, our emergency fund."

In response to the absence of snow, the governor of California, Jerry Brown, announced mandatory regulations that prohibited the watering of ornamental grass, required new homes to use drip irrigation, and directed water agencies to set up new pricing structures to maximise conservation.

In Brazil meanwhile, the main reservoir supplying São Paulo dropped to just 6% of its capacity and residents were hit with regular water rationing. Some were forced to move away to more water-reliable areas.

Droughts can last for decades, but they are temporary. "Droughts creep up and develop over a period of time, through an uncertain space – and get worse," says Carolyn Roberts of the Knowledge Transfer Network. "But very often they end suddenly, with a crash, bang and wallop of flooding."

While the droughts affecting Los Angeles and São Paulo – both of which are now said to be over – had a severe impact on these cities, neither can be placed among the world's most water-stressed. In Los Angeles, "after per capita use, there is twice as much water as there is in the UK even now," says Roberts.

And São Paulo? "It's not in a structurally water-scarce environment. But as the city has grown, the ability of the water management infrastructure to withstand a multi-year drought was clearly overwhelmed," says Steven Schonberger, water global practice manager at the World Bank. "It may have been one of the top water-scarce cities last year – but two or three years from now, with some significant rain, that could all turn around."

There are many cities, like Aswan, that never receive any significant rainfall. Lima is a particular concern, built on the Peruvian coast: one of the driest desert regions in the world. The city, with a population of around 8.5 million, depends mainly on the Rímac river, plus the Chillón and the Lurín. But due to such an arid climate – just one centimetre of rain falls on average each year – water supply is irregular, and a fifth of the population is cut off from the drinking-water network.

But what Lima lacks in rain, it makes up for in humidity – reaching 98% at times – and Limans are making good use of this. The Peruvians Without Water movement has built vast nets to trap the thick sea fog and mist that surrounds the coastal city for more than half the year. To date, the local grassroots organisation has erected more than 1,000 nets

Built on the Peruvian coast, Lima is one of the driest desert regions in the world. One centimetre of rain falls on average each year, its water supply is irregular, and a fifth of the population is cut off from the drinking-water network.

Singapore has limited access to freshwater relative to its population, but has found a way to create water security - 100% of residents have access to fresh water 100% of the time.

around Lima, gleaning between 200 and 400 litres of water a day from each net– depending on the amount of fog. The nets won't solve Lima's water woes on their own, of course, and the city is also planning to restore a pre-Inca network of channels to make the water supply more reliable.

It doesn't rain much in the Middle East either, and nor are there many freshwater sources. Indeed, the top five countries with the lowest renewable freshwater resources per person are all in that region: Kuwait, Bahrain, the United Arab Emirates, Egypt and Qatar.

Major cities in these countries – such as Kuwait City, Abu Dhabi and Doha – could certainly be considered among the world's driest. But while the Middle East doesn't have much water, it does have a great deal of wealth-generating oil – ensuring that 70% of the world's water desalination plants are found there (the majority in Saudi Arabia, the UAE, Kuwait and Bahrain). So while parts of the Middle East might not have much natural freshwater, it is certainly investing in creating it.

Singapore, too, has limited access to freshwater relative to its population, but has found a way to create water security. Despite getting rain for an average of 178 days each year, this densely-populated island city still has only 110 cubic metres of freshwater per capita, per day.

Surrounded by sea water, Singapore does not have a hinterland from which to draw water, and instead relies on its "four national taps": rain, imported water from Malaysia, recycled wastewater and desalinated sea water. These measures come at a huge cost, but mean that 100% of residents have access to fresh water 100% of the time.

But many less well-resourced cities struggle to manage their water supply in such a holistic way. The aquifer used by Gaza City, for example, has become partly contaminated by saltwater: when freshwater is extracted in a coastal area, seawater rushes in. Meanwhile, reservoirs and pipelines have been intermittently damaged by bombings over the decades.

Amman is also struggling to cope with changes beyond its control. Between 630,000 and 1.27 million Syrian refugees now live in the already parched nation of Jordan (it had just 92 cubic metres of freshwater per capita in 2014). While not all refugees live in Amman, a 20%-to-40% increase in the number of people drawing on water resources will add a significant strain on the system. It is hoped that the $900m water sharing agreement between Israel

and Jordan, agreed in February 2015, will go some way to alleviating this added pressure.

So is the world's most water-stressed city one where all these contributing factors – natural aridity and low rainfall, poor management, increasing population and exploitation of the aquifer – converge? Sana'a, the capital of Yemen, might just be that city.

Water was scarce even before the current conflict began, made worse by an increasing population and poor water management.

Just 48% of the Yemeni capital's 2.2 million inhabitants receive piped water and the rest get water through tankers, which is five-to-10 times more expensive. Around 60% of water is lost through leaks, while the cultivation of khat – a popular mild narcotic – accounts for 40% of the water drawn from the Sana'a Basin.

What's more, Sana'a draws water from the world's most over-stressed aquifer, the Arabian Aquifer System, which 60 million people in Saudi Arabia and Yemen rely on. But Yemen doesn't really have a backup plan: despite having more than 1,000 miles of coastline, the country hasn't been able to invest in desalination in the same way as its more wealthy neighbours. The conflict has only exacerbated this existing water stress, and there is evidence to show the country's water infrastructure has been targeted deliberately.

But the experts are still divided on Sana'a. While a common saying there says it will run dry in just 10 more years, Schonberger reckons people have been saying that for decades now. Only time will tell if it becomes the first capital city to run out of water.

The Guardian, 26 July 2016 © Guardian News & Media 2016

To see the water nets in action go to:
http://www.bbc.co.uk/news/av/magazine-38175202/the-fog-catcher-who-brings-water-to-the-poor

WHAT DO YOU THINK?

- Have you ever experienced a shortage of water or had to think about water running out?
- How could poorer countries be helped to overcome their problems?
- Could water become a source of conflict?

Access to safe water

Climate change is contributing to a growing water crisis and putting the lives of millions of children at risk.

Fresh water makes up a very small fraction of all water on the planet. While nearly 70% of the world is covered by water, only 2.5% of it is fresh. Even then, just 1% of our freshwater is easily accessible, with much of it trapped in glaciers and snowfields - this means that only 0.007% of the planet's water is available to fuel and feed the world's 7.4 billion people.

Without access to safe water, children are more likely to die in infancy - and throughout childhood - because they are most vulnerable to diseases caused by water-borne bacteria.

When these diseases don't kill children outright, they can contribute to their impaired growth and development - known as stunting.

Thirst itself kills children and a lack of safe water and sanitation exposes children to other threats.

200 million hours are lost every day by women and girls gathering water in drought-affected areas. Children miss out on a chance to go to school and girls are especially vulnerable to attack during these times.

Children suffer most from a change in climate. In times of drought or flood, in areas where the sea level has risen or ice and snow have unseasonably melted, children are at risk, as the quality and quantity of water available to them is under threat.

In the coming years, demand for water will increase as populations grow and move, industries develop and consumption increases. This can lead to water stress, where demand outweighs the actual supply of water available.

Rising temperatures, greater frequency and severity of droughts and floods, melting snow and ice, and rising sea levels, all threaten the water supplies that children rely on:

- **530 million** children live in areas highly prone to flooding. Floods can destroy toilet facilities which leads to contamination of water supplies, making water deadly to drink.

- Cholera can spread through contaminated water and can kill children within hours if left untreated.

- A lack of water can lead to unsafe sanitation and hygiene practices - as supplies of water are rationed, practices such as hand washing and toilet cleaning are often carried out less frequently in order to save water.

Drought conditions and conflict in **Nigeria**, **Somalia**, **South Sudan** and **Yemen** mean that nearly **1.4 million** children face imminent risk of death from severe acute malnutrition as famine grows in these areas.

In **Ethiopia** alone, it is thought that **more than 9 million** people will be without safe drinking water in 2017.

By 2040, **1 in 4 children** - **600 million** - will live in areas of extremely high water stress.

Every day, **more than 800** children under 5 die from diarrhoea linked to inadequate water, sanitation and hygiene.

Unsafe water and sanitation are also linked to stunted growth - around **156 million** children worldwide suffer from stunting.

Hand washing facility at Bondo township primary school, Kenya © Julius Mwelu/ UN-HABITAT

Global use of types of drinking water service, 2015

Key:

Type of service	Definition
Surface water	Directly from a river, dam, lake, pond, stream, canal or irrigation canal
Unimproved	From an unprotected dug well or unprotected spring
Limited	From an improved* source for which collection time exceeds 30 minutes for a round trip, including queuing
Basic	From an improved source, provided that collection time is not more than 30 minutes for a round trip, including queuing
Safely managed	From an improved water source, that is located on premises, available when needed and free from contamination.

*An improved water source includes piped water, boreholes or tubewells, protected dug wells, protected springs, and packaged or delivered water.

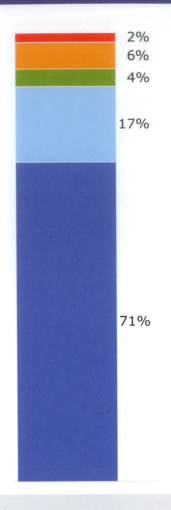

2%
6%
4%
17%
71%

QUICK FACTS

In 2015:

- **5.8 billion** people used improved sources with water available when needed.

- **159 million** people still collected drinking water directly from surface water sources - **58%** lived in sub-Saharan Africa.

- **263 million** had a **limited** service.

- **844 million** people still lacked even a **basic** drinking water service.

- **1 out of 3** people - **1.9 billion** - using a **safely managed** water service lived in rural areas.

Thirsting for a future – Water and children in a changing climate
© United Nations Children's Fund (UNICEF) March 2017   www.unicef.org
Progress on Drinking Water, Sanitation and Hygiene 2017
© World Health Organization (WHO) and UNICEF, 2017   www.who.int
National Geographic   www.nationalgeographic.com/freshwater/freshwater-crisis.html

WHAT DO YOU THINK?

- Which category of water service do you use?

- If access to safe water is a basic human right, why are so many people left without it?

- What can be done about limited supplies and increased demand?

Which is the world's favourite city?

New York ranks top overall in the Ipsos City index

18,557 adults aged 16-64 were surveyed in 26 countries - Argentina, Australia, Belgium, Brazil, Canada, China, France, Britain, Germany, Hungary, India, Italy, Japan, Mexico, New Zealand, Peru, Poland, Russia, Saudi Arabia, Serbia, South Africa, South Korea, Spain, Sweden, Turkey and the United States.

They were shown a list of 60 global cities and asked:

Based on what you have seen yourself, or heard about from others, which three cities in the world do you think are the best to...

1. Live in?
2. Visit?
3. Do business in?

The scores from the three questions were then added together to create the Ipsos Cities Index.

New York

23% chose it as the best city **to do business in**;

16% chose it as a great place **to visit**;

11% chose it as the best city **to live in**.

Top 10 cities OVERALL

City	Score
New York	50%
Abu Dhabi	46%
London	41%
Paris	39%
Sydney	36%
Zurich	36%
Tokyo	36%
Rome	34%
Los Angeles	28%
Amsterdam	27%

The bottom cities were **Nairobi** and **Tehran** – both scoring 1.

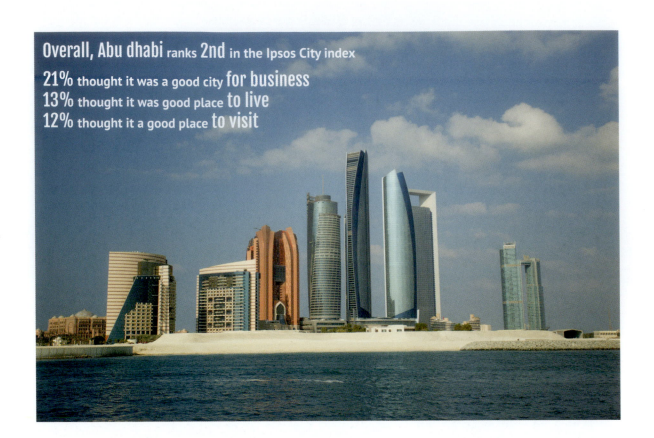

Overall, **Abu dhabi** ranks **2nd** in the Ipsos City index

21% thought it was a good city **for business**

13% thought it was good place **to live**

12% thought it a good place **to visit**

Different generations have different views of what makes a top city

Zurich is the favourite city for Baby Boomers (those born 1945-65), whilst the younger generations all ranked **New York** and **Abu Dhabi** as their top two overall.

Favourite cities chosen by the younger generations to live in

Millennials (1980-95)

City	Score
Abu Dhabi	14%
Zurich	14%
New York	13%
Sydney	13%
London	13%
Paris	12%
Amsterdam	12%
Toronto	12%
Vancouver	11%
Stockholm	11%

Gen Z (1996-)

City	Score
Los Angeles	16%
Abu Dhabi	15%
New York	15%
London	14%
Amsterdam	13%
Paris	12%
Zurich	11%
Rome	11%
Sydney	11%
Tokyo/Vancouver/Toronto	10%

Favourite cities chosen by the younger generations to visit

Millennials (1980-95)

City	Score
Paris	21%
Rome	19%
New York	16%
London	13%
Abu Dhabi	13%
Tokyo	13%
Sydney	10%
Amsterdam	10%
Los Angeles	10%
Madrid	8%

Gen Z (1996–)

City	Score
Paris	23%
Rome	20%
Tokyo	17%
New York	17%
London	15%
Abu Dhabi	15%
Los Angeles	14%
Sydney	10%
Amsterdam	9%
Rio de Janeiro/Madrid/Cairo/Osaka	7%

Overall, 21% chose Paris as the best city to visit

Source: Ipsos Mori Top Cities © Ipsos 2017 www.ipsos.com

WHAT DO YOU THINK?

- What makes a city a great place to live?
- Why are some cities better places to visit than to live in?
- Which city would you like to live in, and why?

On 12 May 2017 at the Sab'een Hospital in Sana'a, Yemen, a child with severe diarrhoea or cholera receives treatment.
© UNICEF/UN065873/AlzekriYemen, 2017

A Liverpool lifeline for a Yemeni hospital at the front line of the cholera epidemic

By Raf Sanchez,
Middle East correspondent

It wasn't the airstrikes that was bringing the intensive care unit at Sabeen hospital to the brink of collapse, nor was it the wave of children beginning to show up with signs of cholera or the shortages of medicine to treat them. It was the bus fare.

Staff at the hospital in the Yemeni capital Sana'a had not been paid salaries in months and though they were eager to come to work, many did not have even the 100 riyal (30p) for the bus each day. Some nurses were walking two hours to reach the hospital.

Dr Najla al-Sonboli, the hospital's head of pediatrics, knew the situation was not sustainable. The intensive care unit and the A&E could not keep running with ragged staff who often did not have food for themselves or their families.

Essential Articles & Facts

So Dr al-Sonboli did as she often did when she needed advice and turned to old friends at Liverpool School of Tropical Medicine, where she obtained her masters and PhD before the outbreak of war in Yemen in 2015.

Her former colleagues in Liverpool moved quickly to start raising funds in £5 and £10 increments from a global network of epidemiologists and public health experts. Soon a lifeline was opened from Merseyside to distant Sana'a.

Each month the group sends £500 to £1000 to help make sure staff can get to work and afford a meal during long shifts. "The amount of money is small but it's made a great difference," Dr al-Sonboli told The Telegraph. "The emergency room didn't collapse and we can cope with patients."

The doctor and her team at Sabeen hospital are on the frontline of Yemen's cholera epidemic, which has killed more than 1,800 people this year and spread to 21 of the country's 23 provinces. More than 400,000 people have had the disease.

Each day Sabeen hospital, which is being supported by Unicef, takes in around 200 cholera patients. Often they are young children whose malnourished bodies shudder with constant vomiting and diarrhoea as their helpless parents look on.

"I wish we could do more," said Dr Luis Ceuvas, one of the Liverpool physicians who helped organise the funds and supervised Dr al-Sonboli's PhD. "This war has taken Yemen back 20 years but people like Najla are still there working and showing a lot of courage."

Abdul Hamed al-Zalab, a 42-year-old school administrator, was one of the desperate parents in Dr al-Sonboli's ward. His two

> **Cholera is a potentially fatal bacterial infection caused by consuming contaminated food or water**
>
> **Yemen is in the grip of a cholera outbreak:**
>
> - **There have been more than 30,000 suspected cases of cholera and 300 associated deaths from acute watery diarrhoea**
>
> - **4 children die every day**
>
> - **578 people died of cholera in May 2017.**
>
> - **25% were children**

daughters Alanoud, 8, and Azahraa, 14, both came down with cholera after the holy month of Ramadan and both survived after treatment at Sabeen.

The family sold their furniture to raise money for rehydration tablets and other medicines to keep the girls alive. Their brother Ali had been killed a few months before in an airstrike conducted by the Saudi-led coalition, which is armed and supported by the UK and US. More than 10,000 civilians have been killed, according to the UN.

Doctors recommended that the older girl be kept in hospital for treatment but she refused to stay among the screaming women and sobbing children who crowd the hospital's halls. Each day her family would navigate through streets where uncollected rubbish is piled like small mountains to get her to treatment.

"In Yemen, we are killed by the bombing or the cholera or the starvation." said Mr al-Zalab wearily.

Although Sabeen's bare wards are overstretched and they are badly short of basic medicines, the patients who arrive there are the lucky ones. Half of Yemen's hospitals have been destroyed in the fighting and in rural areas there are often no medical facilities left.

> **The patients who arrive there are the lucky ones. Half of Yemen's hospitals have been destroyed**

"Many people die silent and unrecorded deaths, they die at home, they are buried before they are ever recorded," said Jamie McGoldrick, the UN humanitarian coordinator for Yemen.

Humanitarian agencies say the cholera outbreak is "a man-made crisis" that has exploded out of an almost perfect storm of misery in Yemen.

The country was already the poorest in the Middle East before the war began and fighting has systematically toppled the pillars of a healthy society - the economy, the healthcare system, electricity infrastructure, clean water provision, and food supply have all collapsed.

Out of the country's 28 million people around more than half are food insecure and around 7 million are severely food insecure. "In layman's terms it means those 7 million don't know where their next meal will come from," said Dr Sherin Varkey, the deputy Unicef chief in Yemen.

> ## "7 million don't know where their next meal will come from"

Facing a crippling shortage of healthcare facilities, Unicef has tried to mobilise a volunteer army to go house to house to counter the spread of cholera. The goal is to have people telling their neighbours about best practices to avoid the disease and carrying simple treatments to help those who already have it.

Fathyah Ahmed Faraj, a stout 45-year-old woman and a mother of nine, walks through her neighbourhood of Raisin Hill in a full niqab knocking on doors and issuing brisk advice to frightened residents.

In one home she finds a 35-year-old man with cholera and his family are afraid to go near him. Make him bath with soap and don't eat near him, she tells them, but don't isolate him all the time. "He will become melancholy otherwise," she says. Two of her own children had cholera and she knows how crushing it can be for a sick person to be alone.

Mrs Faraj goes wherever there are people, including to weddings and engagement parties that still take place amid the bombed out rubble of many areas of Sana'a. She urges people to use boiled water to wash their food and their khat, a plant that Yemenis like to chew to provide a mild stimulant.

Back at the Sabeen hospital, Dr al-Sonboli arrives for another day of work and walks through a lobby that has been hit countless time by bombs dropped from Saudi or UAE aircraft. She has moved house three times because her own home has been continually hit.

"Nowhere is really safe," she mused. "Whenever we move from one place to another the danger is never far away."

She thinks about Liverpool sometimes and how homesick she was during her first three months in the city. Over time she made friends with both locals and internationals and she remembers long nights at Kimos, a restaurant that serves Middle Eastern fare alongside British staples.

"I think of Liverpool now as a second home," she said. "Maybe one day, if the good times come back, I can go back to Liverpool."

Daily Telegraph, 28th July 2017
© Telegraph Media Group Limited 2017

WHAT DO YOU THINK?

- What is the saddest part of this article?
- How could the people of Yemen be helped?
- Should Britain stop selling weapons for this war?

#AskEddie: Meet the work experience boy who saved Southern Rail

Radhika Sanghani

When 15-year-old Eddie Smith came in for his fortnight of work experience at Southern Rail, his main goal was to do more than make tea. He never expected that just ten days into his placement, he would end up a viral Twitter sensation, labelled a national treasure and hailed as Southern Rail's 'saviour'.

The Croydon schoolboy became a social media star when he was given a chance to take over the railway company's Twitter account. After a few days of answering sensible train-related questions, on Tuesday, eager Eddie was granted permission to post: "Hi, Eddie here! Here on work experience and ready to answer your questions!" Smiley face.

Within hours, the GCSE student had more than 6,000 likes and questions had flooded in. From the banal, "Shall I have chicken fajitas or chicken Thai green curry?" ("It has to be the fajitas" replied Eddie); to the practical, "Can you drive a train?" ("No, not yet. I am 15"). Eddie, it seemed, had an answer for everything.

There were the diplomatic ones - "I like both trains and Twitter, so I couldn't possibly say which I like better" - and the feminist - "I don't think [there will ever be a boy born who can swim faster than a shark] but you never know, there could be a girl that can."

His responses won over thousands of disgruntled commuters, and soon #AskEddie was trending across Twitter.

"It's been absolutely crazy," says the teenager, who finished his work experience last Friday. "At first I was excited because I didn't know what would come my way. Nervous wouldn't be the word, but I was intrigued. I had a feeling they wouldn't all be serious, but I didn't know it would be quite like that. "But it was amazing looking at all the Tweets and thinking if I hadn't put out that first message, nothing would have happened. It has taught me that if you can just be yourself, everything will sort itself out."

His Twitter takeover has granted Southern Rail - the train line labelled Britain's worst and whose poor performance saw its parent company Govia Thameslink Railway, fined £13.4million this week - positive publicity, and many have speculated as to whether it was all a stunt, or if Eddie even existed. But the football-loving boy, who got his placement through a family friend who works at the company and with a little help from his older brother who works for Network Rail, dismisses the notion that it was staged.

Jules Graham @_julesgraha... · 11/07/2017 ⌄
Why do English men always wear socks and sandals on holiday? #AskEddie

💬 7   ↻ 2   ♡ 58   ✉

Southern ✓
@SouthernRailUK

Replying to @_julesgraham_

Personally, i prefer flip-flops so i couldn't answer! ^Eddie

11/07/2017, 15:25

4 Retweets 113 Likes

Ads @Adam_W48 · 11/07/2017 ⌄
Eddie, question...

Shall I have chicken fajitas tonight or chicken thai green curry? #AskEddie

💬 3   ↻ 37   ♡ 264   ✉

Southern ✓
@SouthernRailUK

Replying to @Adam_W48

It has to be the chicken fajitas 😉 ^Eddie

11/07/2017, 15:19

23 Retweets 365 Likes

"We even got a tweet saying that I was a Russian hackbot, which I thought was a bit excessive," he says. "I don't even know any Russians. I'm a person, I'm 15-years-old, I'm here, and I don't think a Russian hackbot would like Doritos."

The Wallington County Grammar School pupil couldn't help but tackle every question that comes his way with humour. "I just answered like my friends would. I have a lot of banter at school. It's definitely excited me for adult life because it shows I don't have to change that much."

Right now, Eddie doesn't have a girlfriend - "I'm focusing on my GCSEs, but you know, if there's anyone out there..." - but he did receive several marriage proposals during his Twitter takeover.

"People were trusting me with their lives," he says. "I got one question that I didn't answer because it stumped me. It said 'my wife's just left me - how long do I have to wait before I join Match.com?'

"I was worried if I said something too soon, his wife might be concerned. But if it was too late, he might be."

As a Southern Rail passenger himself, Eddie has direct experience of their late-running services, but is diplomatic: "If people don't like them, that's fine. But it's a train service, there are going to be delays, so deal with it. I understand that people on their morning commute can get frustrated, but I can now say for a fact that everyone in that office works their absolute hardest."

Photo: Southern Rail

With his natural gift at handling tough questions, it's no surprise that Eddie now wants to pursue a career in PR. "The past two weeks have been a real eye-opener and I've had a lot of fun. I even stayed two hours late - until 5.30pm on Tuesday. I missed my train."

The company have already told him that he is welcome to return, but for now, Eddie is mourning the end of his "crazy" placement.

"It's going to be weird going into school," he sigh. "People will be like, 'aren't you that guy who was on the news?' I'm going to miss it."

Daily Telegraph, 15 July 2017 © Telegraph Media Group Ltd 2017

 John Bickerton
@johnbickerton

When problems are unprecedented, so are the only successful solutions. #askEddie is an unpaid 15yo and he's fixing a PR disaster on his own.

Eddie's top tips for work experience students

1. Be helpful
Always make sure you ask people if they want a drink, or if you can help. Put yourself out there.

2. Be yourself
You're the person lucky enough to have this work experience, so fight off any nerves and make the most of it.

3. Be nice
Don't become an annoyance or think you're above any small jobs. This will be reflected on your reference

4. Be persistent
Ask to come back if you enjoy it. It will look good on your CV.

What do employers want from young people?

The Education and Skills survey 2017 had responses from more than 340 organisations, ranging in size from firms with fewer than 50 employees to those with more than 5,000.

The survey results show the importance of young people's **attitude to work** in determining their job prospects and future success. **86%** of employers rate this as one of their **three most important considerations**. In fact it ranks as the single most important factor for **51%** of businesses when recruiting school and college leavers.

Most important factors in recruiting school/college leavers

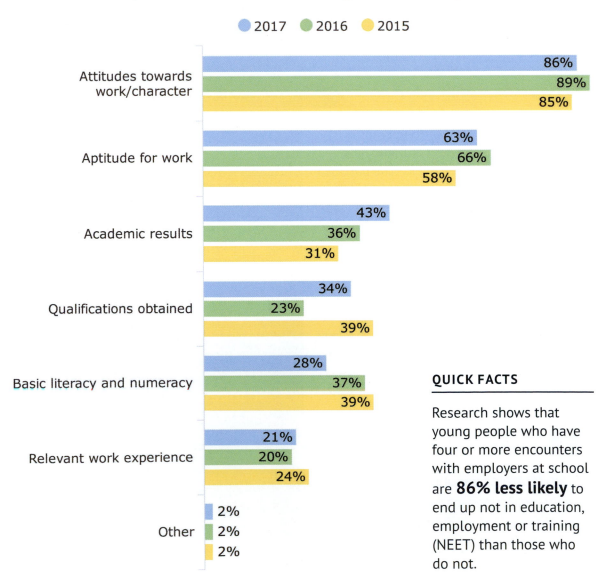

● 2017　● 2016　● 2015

Attitudes towards work/character
- 2017: 86%
- 2016: 89%
- 2015: 85%

Aptitude for work
- 2017: 63%
- 2016: 66%
- 2015: 58%

Academic results
- 2017: 43%
- 2016: 36%
- 2015: 31%

Qualifications obtained
- 2017: 34%
- 2016: 23%
- 2015: 39%

Basic literacy and numeracy
- 2017: 28%
- 2016: 37%
- 2015: 39%

Relevant work experience
- 2017: 21%
- 2016: 20%
- 2015: 24%

Other
- 2017: 2%
- 2016: 2%
- 2015: 2%

QUICK FACTS

Research shows that young people who have four or more encounters with employers at school are **86% less likely** to end up not in education, employment or training (NEET) than those who do not.

Many young people are leaving school and college equipped with most of the skills and attributes essential for their success, but there are others with some serious weaknesses.

Employer satisfaction with school/college leavers' skills

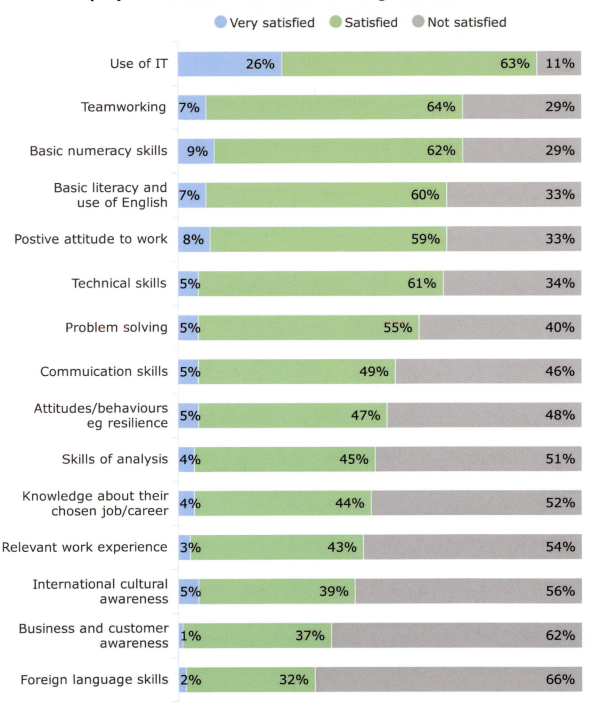

- Very satisfied ● Satisfied ● Not satisfied

	Very satisfied	Satisfied	Not satisfied
Use of IT	26%	63%	11%
Teamworking	7%	64%	29%
Basic numeracy skills	9%	62%	29%
Basic literacy and use of English	7%	60%	33%
Postive attitude to work	8%	59%	33%
Technical skills	5%	61%	34%
Problem solving	5%	55%	40%
Commuication skills	5%	49%	46%
Attitudes/behaviours eg resilience	5%	47%	48%
Skills of analysis	4%	45%	51%
Knowledge about their chosen job/career	4%	44%	52%
Relevant work experience	3%	43%	54%
International cultural awareness	5%	39%	56%
Business and customer awareness	1%	37%	62%
Foreign language skills	2%	32%	66%

Source: Helping the UK Thrive - CBI/Pearson Education and Skills Survey July 2017
www.cbi.org.uk   www.pearson.com

WHAT DO YOU THINK?

- **What are your views on the value of work experience?**

- **What could schools do to prepare you for the world of work?**

- **Employers seem to value attitude and aptitude over academic results. How can you be helped to develop the right attitude?**

The future of work

Projections for jobs in the future

Working Futures projects the future size and shape of the labour market.
Overall, the number of jobs in the UK is projected to rise by around
1.8 million between 2014 and 2024.

The prediction is that there will be more jobs in management and professional areas and in caring and leisure roles. At the other end of the scale - in unskilled jobs - there will some losses but also some growth because there are jobs which cannot be automated. Most job losses will be in the middle of the skill range.

Projected share of occupations in 2024

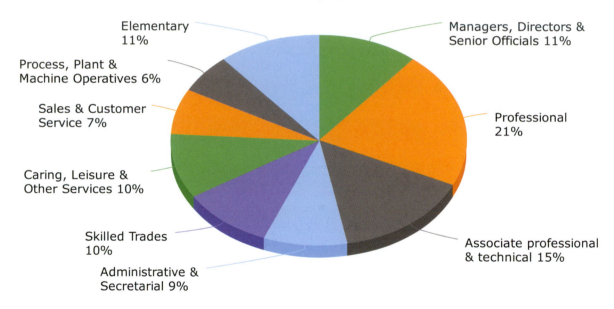

Elementary 11%
Process, Plant & Machine Operatives 6%
Sales & Customer Service 7%
Caring, Leisure & Other Services 10%
Skilled Trades 10%
Administrative & Secretarial 9%
Managers, Directors & Senior Officials 11%
Professional 21%
Associate professional & technical 15%

Employment growth rates, 2024 projections

● Men   ● Women

Managers, Directors & Senior Officials
2014-2024 overall change +15%

% change
occupations

Corporate managers & directors
- Chief executives and senior officials
- Senior police officers

11%   31%

Other managers & proprietors
- Leisure and sports managers
- Healthcare practice managers

7%   16%

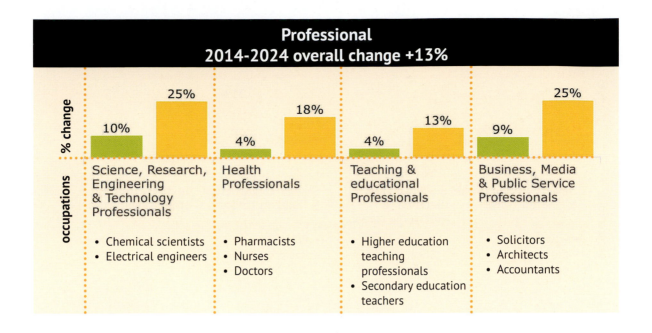

Professional
2014-2024 overall change +13%

% change

10%	25%	4%	18%	4%	13%	9%	25%

occupations

Science, Research, Engineering & Technology Professionals
- Chemical scientists
- Electrical engineers

Health Professionals
- Pharmacists
- Nurses
- Doctors

Teaching & educational Professionals
- Higher education teaching professionals
- Secondary education teachers

Business, Media & Public Service Professionals
- Solicitors
- Architects
- Accountants

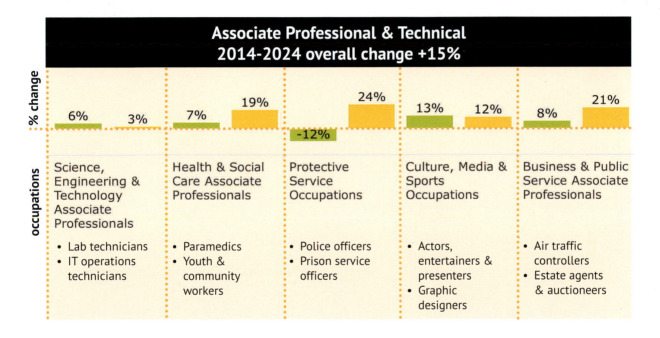

Associate Professional & Technical
2014-2024 overall change +15%

% change

6%	3%	7%	19%	-12%	24%	13%	12%	8%	21%

occupations

Science, Engineering & Technology Associate Professionals
- Lab technicians
- IT operations technicians

Health & Social Care Associate Professionals
- Paramedics
- Youth & community workers

Protective Service Occupations
- Police officers
- Prison service officers

Culture, Media & Sports Occupations
- Actors, entertainers & presenters
- Graphic designers

Business & Public Service Associate Professionals
- Air traffic controllers
- Estate agents & auctioneers

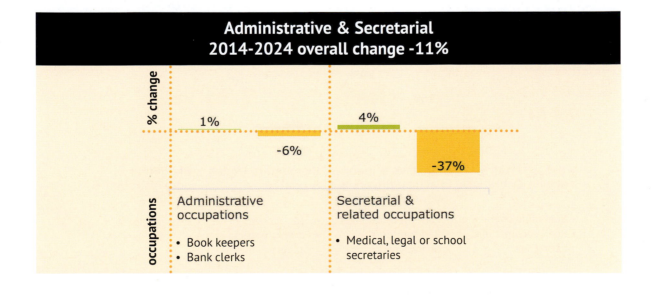

Administrative & Secretarial
2014-2024 overall change -11%

% change

1%	-6%	4%	-37%

occupations

Administrative occupations
- Book keepers
- Bank clerks

Secretarial & related occupations
- Medical, legal or school secretaries

Skilled Trades
2014-2024 overall change -3%

% change

3%   5%   -9%   -20%   6%   31%   -15%   0%

occupations

Skilled agricultural & related trades	Skilled metal, electrical & electronic trades	Skilled construction & building trades	Textiles, printing & other skilled trades
• Farmers • Groundsmen & greenkeepers	• Welding trades • Sheet metal workers	• Plasterers • Roofers, roof tilers & slaters	• Tailors & dressmakers • Printers

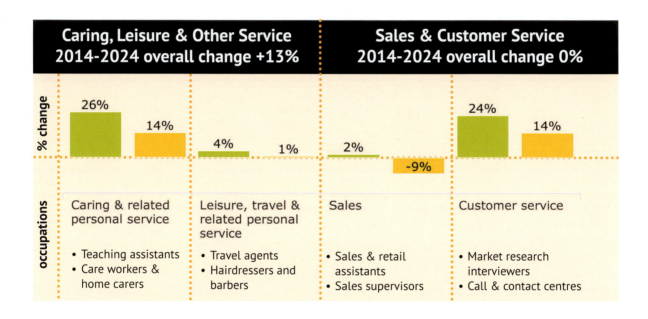

Caring, Leisure & Other Service
2014-2024 overall change +13%

Sales & Customer Service
2014-2024 overall change 0%

% change

26%   14%   4%   1%   2%   -9%   24%   14%

occupations

Caring & related personal service	Leisure, travel & related personal service	Sales	Customer service
• Teaching assistants • Care workers & home carers	• Travel agents • Hairdressers and barbers	• Sales & retail assistants • Sales supervisors	• Market research interviewers • Call & contact centres

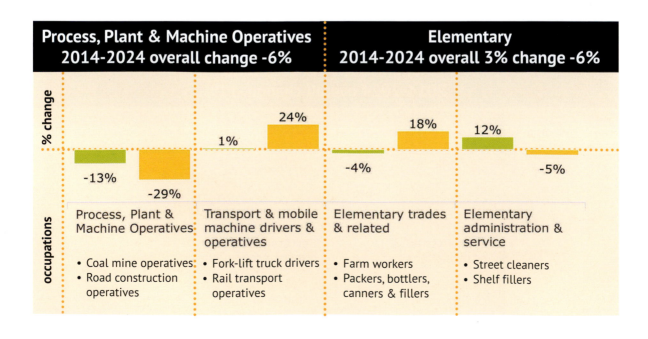

Process, Plant & Machine Operatives
2014-2024 overall change -6%

Elementary
2014-2024 overall 3% change -6%

% change

-13%   -29%   1%   24%   -4%   18%   12%   -5%

occupations

Process, Plant & Machine Operatives	Transport & mobile machine drivers & operatives	Elementary trades & related	Elementary administration & service
• Coal mine operatives • Road construction operatives	• Fork-lift truck drivers • Rail transport operatives	• Farm workers • Packers, bottlers, canners & fillers	• Street cleaners • Shelf fillers

Qualifications

By 2024, around **55%** of people in employment are expected to be qualified at level 4 and above, whilst the proportion of people with no formal qualifications is expected to fall to **11%**.

In future there should be more skilled people in the labour market as people continue in education and more people (especially young people) gain higher level qualifications.

At the same time, older people who are less well-qualified on average, will retire from the labour force.

Number of people at different skill levels 2014 and 2024

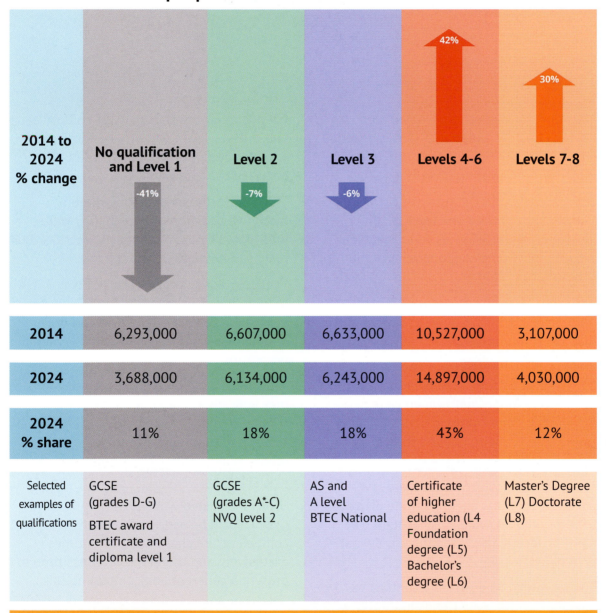

2014 to 2024 % change	No qualification and Level 1	Level 2	Level 3	Levels 4-6	Levels 7-8
	-41%	-7%	-6%	42%	30%
2014	6,293,000	6,607,000	6,633,000	10,527,000	3,107,000
2024	3,688,000	6,134,000	6,243,000	14,897,000	4,030,000
2024 % share	11%	18%	18%	43%	12%
Selected examples of qualifications	GCSE (grades D-G) BTEC award certificate and diploma level 1	GCSE (grades A*-C) NVQ level 2	AS and A level BTEC National	Certificate of higher education (L4 Foundation degree (L5) Bachelor's degree (L6)	Master's Degree (L7) Doctorate (L8)

WHAT DO YOU THINK?

- **What sort of job do you imagine yourself doing?**
- **Do you expect to have one type of job throughout your working life?**
- **How do you think these changes in employment patterns will affect society as a whole?**

Women are given a tougher time in interviews than men, scientists find

Harry Yorke,
online education editor

According to researchers, women are more likely to be interrupted mid-sentence and face more follow-up questions in academic interviews, suggesting there is a gender imbalance in top jobs.

The study, published last week in the journal of Social Sciences, found that men are also twice as likely to interject while speaking to a woman.

And when they do cut-in during a man-on-man discussion, it is "generally more positive and affirming".

Analysing job interviews at two leading US universities over a two-year period, researchers found that women were questioned more by hiring panels, making them more prone to rushing through a presentation.

The findings also show that there is a pervasive "prove it again" attitude displayed towards women, which may explain why many academic fields continue to be male-dominated.

The research comes in stark contrast to recent undergraduate trends in the UK, with female students now outnumbering men in two-thirds of undergraduate courses.

It suggests that, despite greater access to higher education, there are still sizeable gender barriers for women hoping to progress in academia.

Conducted by the University of California and University of Southern California, 119 job interviews were video recorded and analysed by researchers.

They found that on average, women faced five questions in which they were interrupted by the interviewer, whereas their male counterparts only faced four.

Female academics also received two more follow-up questions, and 17 in total - at least three more than a typical male interviewee - meaning they spent a "higher proportion" of their time fielding queries.

"Questions piled on to previous questions... may indicate a challenge to the presenter's competence – not only in their prepared talk but also in their response to questions," the report found, adding that women are caught in a "catch-22".

"Even shortlisted women with impressive CVs may still be assumed to be less competent, are challenged, sometimes excessively, and therefore have less time to present a coherent and compelling talk.

> **"Even shortlisted women with impressive CVs may still be assumed to be less competent"**
>
> *University of California and University of Southern California report*

"[These] subtle conversational patterns... form an almost invisible bias, which allows a climate of challenging women's competence to persist."

In engineering departments, where female staff quotas varied between four and 18 per cent, it claims that the frequent disruption caused during their talks resulted in women "often" having less time to deliver a "compelling conclusion".

While the study did not collect data on whether more questions helped or hindered candidates, video recordings revealed that "verbal cues...clearly indicate that they [women] are rushing to get through their carefully prepared slide decks and reach the punchline of their talk".

As a result, many female interviewees responded by saying "for the sake of time, I'm going to skip this part", "there's not much time left; I will rush through this" and "I'm going really quick here because I want to get to the second part of the talk".

This, the researchers concluded, revealed a clear correlation between the number of questions faced by women and their tendency to rush more.

They add that in a "masculine-typed job" there are "stricter standards of competence demanded by evaluators" when women are shortlisted.

The study came on the same week that PwC, the international financial services consultancy, disclosed that women employed in its UK operations earn on average 14 per cent less than their male counterparts, and receive smaller bonuses.

Nationwide, the difference between men and women's salaries stood at 18 per cent in 2016, according to the Office for National Statistics.

Daily Telegraph, 3 July 2017
© Telegraph Media Group Limited 2017

Gender and pay

Basic hours worked and gender pay comparison

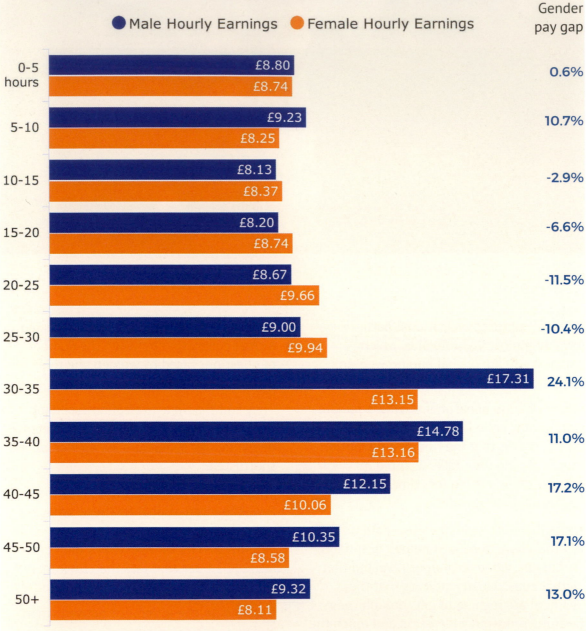

● Male Hourly Earnings ● Female Hourly Earnings

Gender pay gap

Hours	Male	Female	Gender pay gap
0-5 hours	£8.80	£8.74	0.6%
5-10	£9.23	£8.25	10.7%
10-15	£8.13	£8.37	-2.9%
15-20	£8.20	£8.74	-6.6%
20-25	£8.67	£9.66	-11.5%
25-30	£9.00	£9.94	-10.4%
30-35	£17.31	£13.15	24.1%
35-40	£14.78	£13.16	11.0%
40-45	£12.15	£10.06	17.2%
45-50	£10.35	£8.58	17.1%
50+	£9.32	£8.11	13.0%

QUICK FACTS

- Typically, more men are employed in jobs that involve working a higher number of hours, and for these jobs, it can be seen that the gender pay gap is in favour of men.

- For jobs where the number of paid hours worked by an employee is between 10 and 30, more women work in these jobs and the gender pay gap is in favour of women.

Occupations with the biggest gender pay gap

Construction & building trades supervisors	45.4%	Shopkeepers & proprietors - wholesale & retail	33.1%
Financial managers & directors	36.5%	Medical practitioners	29.8%
Printers	35.1%	Chief executives & senior officials	28.7%
Financial institution managers & directors	34.1%	Officers of non-governmental organisations	26.8%
Assemblers (vehicles & metal goods)	33.5%	Town planning officers	26.3%

BBC pay: male stars earn more than female talent

In July 2017 the BBC Annual Report and Accounts made public, for the first time, revealed that two-thirds of its stars earning **more than £150,000** were male, with **Chris Evans** the top-paid star on between **£2.2m and £2.25m**.

Claudia Winkleman was the highest-paid female celebrity, earning between **£450,000 and £500,000** last year.

The top seven earners, in the list of the BBC's 96 best-paid stars, were all male and the total bill for them all was **£28.7m** but the figures show a large difference between what men and women are paid.

Source: Annual Survey of Hours and Earnings (ASHE), Office for National Statistics © Crown copyright 2016 www.ons.gov.uk
BBC Annual report and accounts 2016/17 www.bbc.co.uk

WHAT DO YOU THINK?

- **What reasons would you give for this pay gap?**
- **What should be done about it?**
- **Which occupations were you surprised to find in the list of biggest pay gaps?**

A young entrepreneur's route to success

Scottish entrepreneur Fraser Doherty built his business out of a passion for making jam and years of hard work.

It's a recipe others should look to follow.

For me, the definition of success is getting up every morning and doing what you believe you were born to do. Life is too short to devote yourself to anything less. In my case, I enjoy being an entrepreneur so much that there's nothing I'd rather do.

I sometimes imagine what I might say if I were to meet the 14-year-old me. If I were to tell him that the tiny jam-making enterprise he had just started would grow into what it has since become, he simply wouldn't believe me.

There's no way he'd imagine that what started with a few jars of homemade jam sold to neighbours would grow into a company that has since sold millions of jars through thousands of stores around the world. He'd have no idea that SuperJam would end up winning more than 20 innovation awards and be on display in the National Museum of Scotland, or that his story would be made into a television drama in Japan.

This adventure that I have been on has been all about doing what I love – making jam. Its success hasn't been down to experience or planning, but rather to years of continuous improvement: tweaking of recipes, improving of packaging and crafting of brand stories. I was happy to put years of work into this project only because I thought it was fun. If it hadn't been, I'd have done something else.

Starting a business is hard work. You will have to make sacrifices in your family life, your social life and, most likely, your health. You're going to make these sacrifices only if you feel this idea is what you should be devoting your life to. Otherwise, it's likely you will quit at the first hurdle.

So, if I have any advice for someone starting out on the entrepreneurial journey it is this: start small. So many people imagine that to start their business, they'll need to jump in at the deep end – quit school or their job, remortgage their house or sell their car. In fact, you can test your idea on a tiny scale with very little money to prove to yourself that there's a market for it.

I'd also recommend finding a mentor, someone who has been there and done it before, who can maybe give you some advice. By sharing some of the lessons that they have learnt and mistakes they have made in their own careers, you can avoid making the same mistakes yourself.

Sometimes people wonder how they can come up with a business idea when many have been done before. Most things have been done, but done badly. My story shows that it is possible to make something extraordinary out of something as 'ordinary' as jam.

The one thing that you can have is a unique story. If you can figure out what your story is and tell it in a compelling way, it can be the most powerful form of advertising. Your story can help you build a brand that competitors can't beat.

But, above all, find the thing that you feel you were born to do. Because if you work on something you love, you won't mind putting in the pain and years of hard work. And, if you do that, your idea might just succeed.

> **For me, the definition of success is getting up every morning and doing what you believe you were born to do.**

Fraser Doherty MBE is the founder of SuperJam, a 100 per cent fruit jam company he started in Scotland at the age of 14, using his grandmother's recipes. fraserdoherty.com

Source: This article first appeared on the Federation of Small Businesses website 13th May 2016: www.fsb.org.uk

WHAT DO YOU THINK?

- **What is your definition of success?**
- **Is this route to business success open to everyone?**
- **Do you think that the sacrifices he made will have been worth it?**

Work and relationships

Our working life and home life are linked, and it is important to get the balance right

Our relationships at home and at work impact upon each other.

Being able to achieve an effective balance between work and family life is essential to our wellbeing, as well as being important to how we perform at work and our productivity.

Over 5,000 UK adults were surveyed by Relate about their relationships in the workplace and how their home life was affected.

Relationships with colleagues

75% of employees said they had good quality relationships with their colleagues.

Despite how well we might get on with colleagues, **30%** of employees said they did not feel able to discuss personal problems going on at home during work.

Gender:

78% of **women** said they had good relationships with colleagues compared to **72%** of **men**.

Age:

69% of employees aged **16-30** said they had a good relationships with colleagues compared to **74%** of those aged **31-50** and **80%** of those **over 50**.

Working arrangements:

Some employees have flexible working arrangements such as job share (two people do one job and split the hours), working from home, working part-time, compressed hours (working full-time hours but over fewer day), and flexi-time (where the employee chooses when to start and end work within the main working day). People who had these flexible working arrangements were more likely to say they had good relationships with **colleagues**:

- **80%** said their relationships with colleagues were good, compared to **70%** of those without the flexibility.

- Those who worked **part-time** were more likely to say they had good relationships with colleagues - **89%** compared to **74%** who did not work part-time.

- **Working from home** seemed to be particularly associated with better relationships: **82%** of employees who worked from home said they had good relationships with colleagues compared to **74%** of those who did not work from home.

Relationships with bosses

63% said their relationship with their boss was good.

However, **12%** said their boss behaved in an intimidating/bullying way towards them.

Overall, **30%** of employees agreed that they felt pressured to work by their manager even if they are ill.

Women were slightly more likely than men to feel this pressure from a manager to work even when ill: **33%** of women compared to **27%** of men.

Gender:

As with their colleagues, women were more likely to report good relationships with their boss – **67%** of **women** compared to **59%** of **men**.

Working arrangements:

Just as with relationships with colleagues, employees with flexible work arrangements were more likely to say they had good relationships with their boss:

- **70%** said their relationships with their boss was good compared to **58%** of those without the flexibility.

People who had **flexi-time** working arrangements in particular were more likely to say they had good relationships with their boss:

- **71%** said they had good relationships, compared to **62%** of those without the flexibility.

Similarly, **71%** of employees who worked **compressed hours** said they had good relationships with their boss compared to **64%** of those without the flexibility.

"Today's workplace is a highly pressurised place, with more demanding workloads, uncertain hours and higher levels of stress and burnout."

Sarah Jackson OBE, Chief Executive, Working Families

Work/family balance

- **33%** of employees agreed that their employer assumed the most productive employees put their work before their family life.

- **33%** of employees also agreed that their employer thought the ideal employee would be available 24 hours a day.

- **31%** of employees said that their work interferes with their home and personal life and caring responsibilities. Younger people were more likely to struggle with this work/home life balance than older people - **36%** of those aged **16-30** compared to **29%** of those aged **over 50**.

- Not only did **more than a third** of employees feel required to prioritise work over family, **21%** agreed that attending to caring responsibilities for children or partners was frowned upon at work.

Long working hours

A recent TUC survey reported that there had been a **15% increase** since 2010 in people **working more than 48 hours** a week.

Regularly working more than 48 hours per week is linked to a significantly increased risk of developing heart disease, stress, mental illness, strokes and diabetes.

- **27%** agreed that they worked longer hours than they would have chosen and this had damaged their physical and mental wellbeing.
  Younger employees were more likely than older employees to say this - **31%** of those aged **16-30** compared to **26%** of those **over 50**.

- **29%** of employees said that they felt pressured by their employer to work long hours to advance their career. Younger employees were more likely to feel this pressure - **32%** of people aged **16-30** compared to **25%** of employees **over 50**.

Source: YouGov survey for Relate. The Way We Are Now - The state of the UK's relationships www.relate.org.uk

WHAT DO YOU THINK?

- **What would your ideal job involve?**

- **Why do people work long hours at the expense of family life?**

- **How can people generate a good working atmosphere?**

What's the problem with millennials in the workplace?

TANITH CAREY

Have you ever laughed at your parents for not being able to change their social media settings - and then had to Google how long it takes to boil an egg?

Or rung your boss on Monday because you felt ill on Sunday, and therefore felt deserving of another day off - in order to enjoy "a proper weekend"?

If so, don't say another word.

You are already pegged as a **'millennial'** – born roughly in the decade after 1983 - and a member of the generation branded the most **entitled** and **self-absorbed** in human history.

Yesterday the CBI, representing the heavyweights of British industry, issued yet another exasperated harrumph on the fecklessness of young people entering the workplace; its latest study of business leaders reporting that a third of companies are dissatisfied with graduates' attitude to work and ability to "self-manage".

Text-speak and Twitter reductionism is also letting our young hopefuls down, a similar number complained, with literacy and numeracy skills so poor among university leavers, that they have to be topped up in the workplace.

If there was ever a moment which laid to rest the image of the eager be-suited graduate, plucked fresh from a university milk-round for a job-for-life, and confirmed its replacement with a casually-dressed slacker, strolling into work late on his phone, only to complain there's no room on the office bean bag, this must surely be it.

Indeed, when British marketing guru Simon Sinek gave his blistering analysis of everything that's wrong with Generation Y

> **"They're thrust in the real world and in an instant they find out they're not special, their mums can't get them a promotion, that you get nothing for coming in last"**
>
> Simon Sinek

last year, it hit such a nerve that it went viral within a day and has now racked up over a million hits on You Tube.

With devastating clarity, he painted a picture of how a generation given everything for nothing has created a crisis of unmet expectations in the workplace: "They're thrust in the real world and in an instant they find out they're not special, their mums can't get them a promotion, that you get nothing for coming in last - and by the way, you can't just have it because you want it."

Chief Operating Officer of Be Wiser Insurance group, Crescens George is one of the business leaders bemoaning the cost of "graduate ego massaging time".

George recalls one young man he recruited a few years ago straight from university onto an accelerated future talent programme on a good wage. Far from being keen to learn the job from the bottom up, George said the young man let it be known that dealing with customers in the call centre was too far beneath him to contemplate.

"We were almost on the verge of terminating his employment contract. But he had good analytical skills, so we saw the future potential, supported him in learning the basics and today he is in a relatively successful and relevant role."

George adds: "You would expect that university education would teach some basic business etiquette, and certainly communication skills. He did not

Employer satisfaction with graduate applicants' work-relevant skills (%)

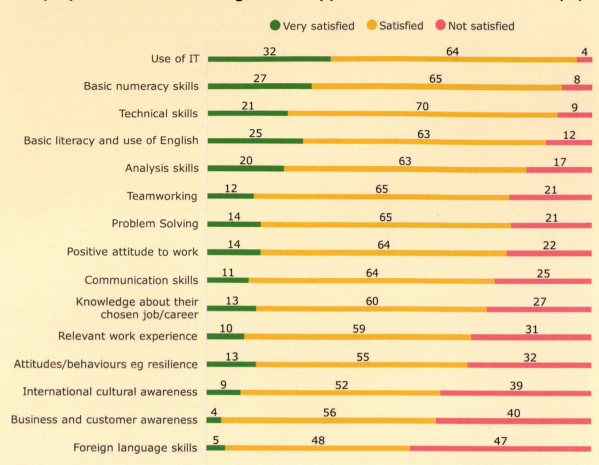

● Very satisfied   ● Satisfied   ● Not satisfied

Skill	Very satisfied	Satisfied	Not satisfied
Use of IT	32	64	4
Basic numeracy skills	27	65	8
Technical skills	21	70	9
Basic literacy and use of English	25	63	12
Analysis skills	20	63	17
Teamworking	12	65	21
Problem Solving	14	65	21
Positive attitude to work	14	64	22
Communication skills	11	64	25
Knowledge about their chosen job/career	13	60	27
Relevant work experience	10	59	31
Attitudes/behaviours eg resilience	13	55	32
International cultural awareness	9	52	39
Business and customer awareness	4	56	40
Foreign language skills	5	48	47

Source: CBI 'Helping the UK Thrive' July 2017

communicate, besides showing a sheer lack of interest in the job. He was not willing to make the sacrifice of learning through the ranks.

"I can only attribute this to the stress of £50k debt (from student loans) hanging over his head and finding out the real world of work is different to how it's painted in the lecture rooms. Had we not had to waste 12-14 months on unnecessary graduate ego massaging time, I am sure this employee would have tasted his success a little sooner, and opened doors to leadership opportunities by now."

Professor Cary Cooper of the Manchester Business School agrees with the CBI that some young graduates do seem to be lacking in social skills: "They have been raised on Facebook and texting. The way you develop your social skills is by face to face interaction and this generation has had the least of that."

But he maintains young graduates are every bit as enthusiastic and eager to learn as previous generations. They just have little interest in kowtowing to traditional management structures and are viewed with suspicion by bosses because they don't expect to stay at the same company for long.

"The new graduates have seen older employees, who have been at their companies for many years, dismissed and treated like disposable assets. They are trying to protect themselves. So in other words, that traditional contract of employment has been broken for that generation. They don't have the same company loyalties that were expected in the past.

"Senior managers are hanging on to the old ways and expect these young people to act and behave in the way they did when they were picked up at their university milk rounds in the Eighties. As a result, I don't

> ## "They have often seen one or both of their parents working flat out and not coming home till late, knackered after the commute - they want a more balanced life"
>
> Averil Leimon

think employers know how to use them. But if you push them to the best of their capabilities, they will still come up with the goodies."

Averil Leimon, leadership psychologist with the White Water Group, agrees that millennials "certainly want different things" – and it could be this which is making us uncomfortable.

"They want a more balanced life. They have often seen one or both of their parents working flat out and not coming home till late, knackered after the commute. They want to find ways to incorporate real relationships, be hands on in bringing up their kids, keep up external interests and be fit and healthy.

"They grew up with technology so they know how to work remotely and cannot see why sitting in a building is required. They don't 'go to work', they just work. Technology is integral to their lives so they do not split home and work as rigorously as previous generations. They seek close and rewarding relationships at work, not just in their personal lives."

Indeed, some business leaders are already proclaiming we need to be more like millennials, instead of trying to making them more like us.

Retail guru Mary Portas now describes herself as a "fiftysomething millennial, or what you might call a slashy," and sees nothing wrong with Generation Y demanding the work-life balance their parents never had.

"I'm a businesswoman/TV presenter/ author/ charity retailer/mother/wife/ DJ/anything that comes along that inspires me," she recently told the Telegraph; as a result, she has now reshaped her company in line with that thinking. Her management and board "now have the right to take as much holiday as they like, when they like, set their own hours and take open-ended maternity leave."

So why are we condemning young people for wanting the balanced lifestyle we never achieved?

Psychologist Averil Leimon says: "I was recently working with an investment banker. He told me: 'Millennials have no values'. "I said: 'Gosh, really? Don't you mean they have different values?'

"He then inveighed about his son, who has rejected his father's absent, workaholic, money-focused way of life for something different and more personally rewarding.

"Indeed, if we were to design a business all over again to suit human nature, allowing people the chance to use their strengths for fair reward and have a satisfying home life, wouldn't we want this, too?"

Daily Telegraph, 10 July 2017
© Telegraph Media Group Limited 2017

WHAT DO YOU THINK?

- **In what ways is your generation different from those labelled as 'millennials'?**

- **Why do people attach a label and a set of characteristics to a whole generation?**

- **How do you see your future working life?**

Call centre staffed by 'resting' actors

Billing itself as the only firm that wants its staff to quit to pursue their dreams, RSVP has 600 wannabe performers on its books

Josh Halliday

Olivia Colman cleaned houses, George Clooney was an insurance salesman and Angelina Jolie wanted to be a funeral director. But the stars of tomorrow may come from another run-of-the-mill occupation: the call centre.

A call centre staffed entirely by "resting" actors is to open its doors in MediaCityUK, Salford, next week, employing up to 150 wannabe stars to answer the phones between auditions.

Billing itself as the only company that wants its staff to leave and pursue their dreams, the sales firm RSVP has more than 600 actors on its books in London but wants to tap into the north's rising reputation as a media hotspot.

Based near the Coronation Street set and BBC studios, the actors can leave at short notice for an audition and return when an acting job has finished. When they are not selling boutique wines, they are busy planning for their next big break.

"They drill it into you to never think that working in a call centre is your career because it's not," said Lee Worswick, a 24-year-old actor who appeared in the BBC's Our Girl this year. "You are an actor and you will make it as an actor. This is just a stepping stone."

Worswick, who has had roles in Casualty, Shameless and Waterloo Road, previously worked at a clothing store to make ends meet but says some of the staff turned on him because he was allowed months off at a time for filming.

Working in a shop "wasn't a nice environment to work in but I went for an audition two weeks ago and everyone here shouted good luck to me. I've never found a job like this", he said.

The office looks just like any other call centre in the UK. The "agents" type away as they talk into headsets on a cluster of desks around the office, whose walls are decorated with portraits of the London office's standout performers. Those who have a knack for selling often end up rising to a managerial role, though they never truly leave their dream behind.

Even the boss wants to leave. "I love RSVP and I love my job, but I'm always going to want to be a successful actor," said Hiten Patel, 33, the head of the new office who had bit parts in EastEnders and The Bill. "Coming here, where there's more casting available, has made me more determined to make it as an actor. I've still got an agent."

The 36-member team, which is set to grow to 150 over the next year, are given scripts as a guide but are encouraged to go off-piste. "If you can learn Hamlet, you can learn 46 different cases of wine from different regions," said Patel. Handily, he added, they are also used to rejection.

Unlike some call centres, which pester people with automated calls and unsolicited text messages, Patel said RSVP only contacts customers who have previously subscribed to that company and opted in to take calls.

The pay is not great – the national living wage of £7.20 an hour plus a performance-based commission – nor would most imagine the work to be particularly stimulating. But it has tapped into an enthusiastic workforce, lured by the security of a full-time wage and the ability to hang up their headset at a moment's notice.

The artists' union, Equity, estimates that about one third of its 41,000 members are working at any given time. Up to 70% of them earn £10,000 a year or less from the entertainment industry, according to the union; hence the need for them to have other, more stable, work.

"It's a welcome break from what is a brutal world," said Andrew Sutton, 30, who has had small roles in Coronation Street and Waterloo Road and previously appeared in ITV's Houdini and Doyle, playing the son of Arthur Conan Doyle (Stephen Mangan). "My mum thinks acting is a bit silly, that I'm joking about, and now she thinks it's great I'm doing something that resembles normal.

"What we're wanting to do is the furthest from nine-to-five. We're wanting to get on stage, tread the boards, and be a different person. When I say that out loud it sounds absolutely nuts. You've got to be crazy to not also want to do something that has a bit of normality to it."

> **"If you can learn Hamlet, you can learn 46 different cases of wine from different regions"**

Its staff are employed on zero-hours contacts, but those on shift said they welcomed the ability to fit their 12pm-8.30pm call centre job around TV, stage or film commitments. Many young actors previously survived on tips from bar or restaurant work, while others struggled to fit in part-time work for high-street retailers.

Lucy Mason, 22, who graduated from drama school at the University of Central Lancashire in July, is yet to land an on-screen role – but said her full-time call centre job will help her do just that. She said the retailer she was working for "wasn't good with letting me go for anything. I basically would have had to fake an illness if I wanted to leave. I could end up paying off some of my student loan here."

Now, Mason said, she can walk past the Rovers Return on her way to work in the hope she will one day be a regular on the cobbles. "It's really nice walking past Corrie. It's got a real buzz about it," she said, before sloping back to work the phones.

The Guardian, 27 October 2016
© Guardian News and Media 2016

WHAT DO YOU THINK?

- Are the young people right to believe that they will make it in their chosen career?
- Do people have to be more adaptable and flexible in the way they work than in previous generations?
- Should all employers be as supportive as this one?

Jobseekers

Your social media habits could harm your job prospects

2,058 employers were asked what they looked for in potential candidates for jobs.

QUICK FACTS

75% of employers said existing skills and knowledge were the characteristics they thought were important for an interviewee to have.

68% thought the way candidates behaved during the interview was important so face-to-face interviews were a good way of choosing.

51% thought a candidate's overall appearance was important.

Employers were far less worried about gaps in a potential candidate's work history - **21%**.

When you look to take on new employees, which of the following types of social media would you search for the candidates on?

48%
Linkedin

46%
Facebook

28%
Twitter

15%
Instagram

31%
I would not/ did not search for candidates on social media.

5%
Myspace

5%
Tumblr

5%
Flickr

4%
Other

3% said they don't know

Icons made by Freepik; Madebyoliver & Pixel Buddha from www.flaticon.com

19% of employers had turned down a potential candidate based on their online activity ie comments/posts made on social media.

Which, if any, of the following types of activity on social media would put you off taking on a new employee?

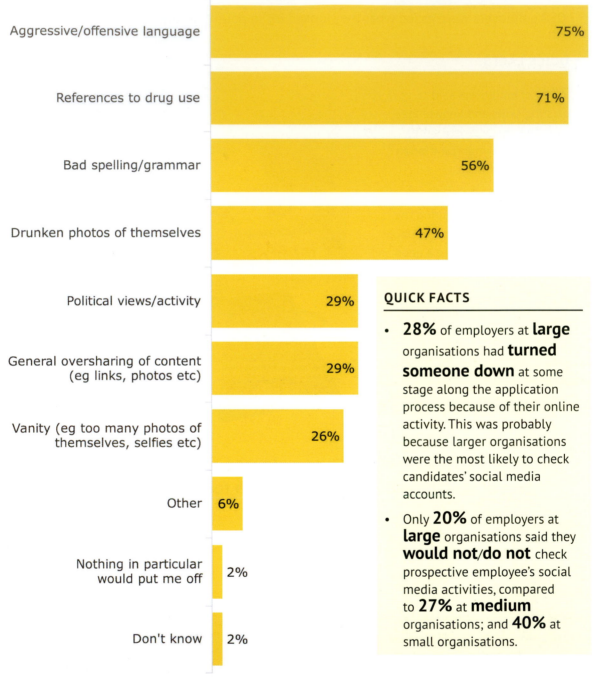

Aggressive/offensive language	75%
References to drug use	71%
Bad spelling/grammar	56%
Drunken photos of themselves	47%
Political views/activity	29%
General oversharing of content (eg links, photos etc)	29%
Vanity (eg too many photos of themselves, selfies etc)	26%
Other	6%
Nothing in particular would put me off	2%
Don't know	2%

QUICK FACTS

- **28%** of employers at **large** organisations had **turned someone down** at some stage along the application process because of their online activity. This was probably because larger organisations were the most likely to check candidates' social media accounts.

- Only **20%** of employers at **large** organisations said they **would not/do not** check prospective employee's social media activities, compared to **27%** at **medium** organisations; and **40%** at small organisations.

Source: YouGov   www.yougov.co.uk

WHAT DO YOU THINK?

- Is your life on social media any of an employer's business?

- If an employer looked at **your** online profile, what do you think the reaction would be?

- What do you think an employer would be impressed to see on social media?

Essential Articles & Facts

Index

Section names a
Page numbers refer you to the loc
the article rather than the specifi

Essential Articles & Facts

Published by Carel Press Ltd

4 Hewson St, Carlisle CA2 5AU
+44 (0)1228 538928

office@carelpress.co.uk
www.carelpress.uk

This collection © 2017
Christine A Shepherd & Chas White

ACKNOWLEDGEMENTS

Editors: ...... Christine A Shepherd
.... Chas White

Editorial team: .... Debbie Fuller
.... Jack Gregory
.... Robbie White
.... Rachel Carr
.... Pip Brown

Cover design: .... Jack Gregory
Cover photos:
Refugees in Calais (top left) ....
.... Malachy Browne (CC-BY2.0)
Corporal Norfazidatul Aina (bottom
centre) .... UN Photo/Pasqual Gorriz
Syrian man and child (bottom right) ....
.... © UNHCR/Ivor Prickett

Subscriptions: Ann Batey (Manager)
.... Brenda Hughes

Printed by: .... Interpress, Budapest

We wish to thank all those writers,
editors, photographers, press
agencies and wire services who
have given permission to reproduce
copyright material. Every effort
has been made to trace copyright
holders of material but in a few
cases this has not been possible.
The publishers would be glad to
hear from anyone who has not been
consulted.

**BRITISH LIBRARY CATALOGUING
IN PUBLICATION DATA**

A catalogue record for this book is
available from the British Library

ISBN 978-1-905600-52-6